Peevees
On Parade

Private John Albert Nelson Galipeau, South Alberta Regiment, Nanaimo, B.C., 1940. I had this picture taken as a Christmas gift to my mother.

Peewees On Parade

WARTIME MEMORIES OF A YOUNG

(AND SMALL) SOLDIER

John A. Galipeau

as told to Pattie Whitehouse

Foreword by Donald E. Graves

J. A. Galipeau

ROBIN BRASS STUDIO
Toronto

Published 2002 by
Robin Brass Studio Inc.,
10 Blantyre Avenue, Toronto, Ontario M1N 2R4, Canada
Fax: 416-698-2120 • www.rbstudiobooks.com

Printed and bound in Canada by AGMV-Marquis, Cap-Saint-Ignace, Quebec

National Library of Canada Cataloguing in Publication

Galipeau, John A., 1921–
      Peewees on parade : wartime memories of a young (and small) soldier /
John A. Galipeau as told to Pattie Whitehouse.

Includes index.
ISBN 1-896941-30-3

1. Galipeau, John A., 1921– 2. World War, 1939-1945 – Personal narratives,
Canadian. 3. Canada. Canadian Army. South Alberta Regiment – Biography.
4. Soldiers – Canada – Biography. I. Whitehouse, Pattie, 1950– II. Title.

D811.G336 2002   940.54'8171   C2002-903955-X

*I am dedicating this book to Ivy, my wife, who kept
me well supplied with the cigarettes and parcels
containing luxuries from home that made life more
bearable in war-torn Britain, and with regular
letters that I failed to answer;*

*And to all the mothers and fathers, wives and family
members who waited at home in Canada, praying
for the safe return of their loved ones from that man-
made hell; who, all the while, did their part to
provide their men and women overseas with the
materials needed to bring peace back to the world.*

*It has been said, although not often enough:
They who waited at home also served!*

The South Alberta Regiment marches through Nanaimo in April 1941 after being granted the freedom of the city. (Courtesy Jack Porter)

Contents

List of Maps

Foreword

It gives me great pleasure to contribute a few words to introduce *Peewees on Parade*, John Galipeau's memoir of his service during the Second World War. I first encountered this work in manuscript form some six years ago while researching the history of the South Alberta Regiment, John's wartime unit. At that time, I had appealed to the South Alberta veterans for copies of any diaries or correspondence they might still possess, or any postwar recollections they may have written. At best, I hoped to get two or three contributions and I was therefore pleasantly surprised, if not amazed, to become the beneficiary of a half dozen diaries, three collections of wartime correspondence as well as many individual letters, and about two dozen memoirs ranging from three pages in length to more than a thousand. Why such a practical, down-to-earth, western Canadian unit (once described by their own adjutant as "a rather plebeian bunch") should produce such a literary bonanza has always been a mystery to me but I took due advantage of this windfall.[*]

Of the South Alberta memoirs that I received, *Peewees on Parade* became one of my favourites. It was not that *Peewees* was crammed full of military *minutiae* that brought back many memories of my own brief and inglorious career in a reserve unit in the mid-1960s, a time when the army had not changed all that much from the war – memories of battle dress, bell tents, Blanco, right markers, defaulters' parades (many memories of those), button hooks, puttees, lanyards, and lectures on sexual hygiene intended solely to put you off the business forever. Nor was it that John,

---

[*] The wartime history of John Galipeau's unit can be found in my book, *South Albertas: A Canadian Regiment at War*, published by Robin Brass Studio of Toronto in 1998.

working with Pattie Whitehouse, a professional author, had produced a polished effort (with the success of the collaboration evident in the fact that anyone who knows the man can hear him speaking in the pages that follow). Nor was it the author's interesting account of his experiences in combat in 1944-1945 because most of *Peewees* is concerned with John's army life before he saw action.

What I found fascinating about *Peewees on Parade* was that, in telling his own story during the Second World War, John Galipeau has managed to encapsulate the story of a generation of young Canadians who, in his phrase, were put to the supreme test when most were but "one step beyond boyhood." And what an interesting story it is. We first meet John Galipeau in 1939 as a teenage farm boy and we follow him through basic training, stand beside him at the altar when he marries at the age of twenty, sail overseas with him and ride in his tank through France and the Low Countries and, finally, across the German border. After accompanying the author on a personal journey through six long and eventful years, we say goodbye to John in 1945 as a veteran sergeant about to be demobilized in Calgary.

John Galipeau's experiences were mirrored by the thousands of other Canadians who were his contemporaries in this nation's wartime army. The modern reader, living in an era when large-scale international conflict has supposedly been brought under control, may be tempted to ask why men like John did what they did and how they endured it – two important questions that the author answers in the pages that follow.

Regarding their motivation, it is best summed up in the expression that many of John's regimental comrades used when I interviewed them about the war – there was "a job to be done in Europe," and they did it. It is a somewhat trite phrase but one that rings more true than all the long words and fancy phrases in the speeches and other utterances of politicians and diplomats. As for enduring the war, what the author makes clear is that he survived it because he functioned as the member of a team at various levels. He fought first and foremost for his tank crew, secondly for his troop (the infamous Peewees and I, for one, am very happy they were on our side), and finally for his regiment, the South Albertas, one of the best armoured units in the Canadian army. Such high flown concepts as King and Country (let alone Prime Minister William Lyon MacKenzie King of Canada) receive scant mention below – nor should they.

The generation that fought the Second World War is leaving now because time, as the old hymn reminds us, does bear all its sons away. It is not enough that we remember and honour their courage, we must also try to understand it. Thanks to John Galipeau, his experiences as a member of a generation that was "touched by fire," in the words of a veteran of an earlier conflict, are now available to younger readers who will, hopefully, never forget the price that was paid for freedom between 1939 and 1945.

DONALD E. GRAVES
Dominion Day, 2002
Wolf Grove, Upper Canada

Cubs

The wolves closed in about the chalky cliffs,
    Where lightly slept the lioness at rest,
Because they thought her toothless, old and spent,
    Useless and battle-scarred, alone, hard-press'd.

She called across the world, and answer came,
    Loud and full-throated from the cubs she bore,
And each in quiet purpose came to aid,
    Lithe bodies tensed to fight in Britain's war.

From camp and mine, by portage, lake and trail,
    From prairie, wood and island gave they heed:
The chalk-white cliffs shall yet in victory rise –
    The lioness hath whelped a mighty breed.

ISABEL STAPELY FRASER
Commanding Officer
Women's Auxiliary Service Patrol
Niagara Falls, Ontario, 1941

Preface

There were many hundreds of infantry platoons in the Canadian army during the Second World War, each with its complement of high spirited young men ready for fun and frolic. I have always thought that my platoon, Number 12 of "B" Company, South Alberta Regiment, was slightly different. Slightly demented might be a more appropriate description, as there were two or three of the members whose personalities acted as catalysts for the dedicated pursuit of practical jokes, harassment, devilry, or anything else that would cause a disturbance.

When an organizational decision left Number 12 Platoon with the shortest men in the company, we were promptly dubbed the Peewees. The possession of a distinctive name, combined with the endless succession of antics and practical jokes, seemed to create a closeness and esprit-de-corps among the Peewees not evident in other platoons in our regiment.

I had always wanted to write a history of my platoon. I did not want, nor did I attempt, to record in detail the course of the battles or historic events in which the Peewee Platoon took part. Historians have already done that. I did hope to provide the reader with a sense of what it was like to live with the boys and men of the Peewees and to endure or enjoy their daily acts of mischief. It was a hopeless task. I had not kept a journal, and over half a century has passed since my time among those wild and wonderful war buddies who stood by each other through thick and thin. The incidents recalled and laughed about at regimental reunions, when committed to paper, seemed not much different from the antics indulged in by young men everywhere.

Sadly, I came to the conclusion that the soul and spirit of the platoon could only be understood and appreciated by those who were part of it.

Instead, my intended history of the Peewees has become my personal story of the two thousand and seven days I spent in the service of King and Country, during those dreadful times when young men dealt with situations created by old men and politicians. It was a very important period in my life; a time when my friends and I were tested to the extreme and survived, a time when many of us, only one step beyond boyhood, became men.

As any veteran will agree, I am proud to have had that experience, but I have absolutely no desire to repeat it.

Acknowledgements
My thanks and appreciation are extended to Pattie Whitehouse; for the experience and expertise she brought to our collaboration, for the patience and understanding she conveyed while I struggled for words when putting my memories on tape, and for the skill with which she brought my words to life to tell the Peewees' story.

My thanks and appreciation also to Donald E. Graves, author of *South Albertas*. It was his encouraging comments that persuaded me to pursue publication of *Peewees on Parade*, and his suggestions for revision and professional advice and guidance have contributed much to the successful completion of this project.

In addition to my own recollections and those of fellow members of the South Alberta Regiment, the following written sources have provided information and in some cases are quoted: Major G.L. MacDougall, *A Short History of the 29 Cdn Armd Recce Regt*, Spin's Publishing Co., Amsterdam; Major R.A. Paterson, *A Short History of the Tenth Canadian Infantry Brigade*, 1945; various newsletters of the South Alberta Regiment; Donald E. Graves, *South Albertas: A Canadian Regiment at War*, Robin Brass Studio, Toronto, 1998.

Pictures are from my personal collection except where otherwise noted in the captions. I am grateful to Chris Johnson for allowing use of his sectional drawings of a Sherman tank.

JOHN A. GALIPEAU
Brentwood Bay, B.C.
July 2002

Boy of the Backwoods

In the summer of 1939, I was living with my mother on a homestead at Corbett Creek, about forty miles west of Fort Assiniboine, Alberta, which is 200 miles west of Edmonton. My father, Nelson Edward Galipeau, had gone to work as a cook on the river boats in the Northwest Territories, leaving Mother and me with half a dozen chickens, two cows, a team of horses with a colt, and a quarter section of practically untouched wilderness. I was doing the best I could, at eighteen, to clear the land with an axe and a one-man crosscut saw ready for the time when we would have four horses to pull the plough and break the land for planting a crop.

Corbett Creek was coal oil lamp and wood stove country. There was no power. We didn't have a radio, and neither did most of our neighbours except for a few who had battery-operated sets, but we knew about the hostilities in Europe and the buildup to war. Mail came by team and wagon once or twice a week to the little local post office, and that was when we would get the supply of newspapers and magazines that kept us up to date with what was going on in the world. Everybody followed the stories of Hitler's rise, though people like me really didn't have much understanding. I read in *Life* magazine about Hitler's Brownshirts burning books, for example, and had no idea why in the world they were burning books. I did understand that Hitler had taken power in Germany and was building an army and threatening nearby countries, and I read about the mighty Maginot Line that the French had built after the Great War that was supposed to be impenetrable and protect France from German invasion. I was quite interested to hear about the Hitler Youth. We read that Hitler was giving boys wooden guns and putting them in special battalions where they were trained to be soldiers, and that girls were being put in camps to cohabit with Aryan soldiers on leave and produce Aryan children. As young fellows will, we followed the developments in Europe with great interest and were excited by all that was happening. Occasionally, we talked among ourselves about what we would do if Britain did go to war.

I was out fighting a forest fire about two miles from the homestead when war was declared. All us young fellows rushed out when there was a chance to go fire fighting because it meant we could make a couple of dollars, and we were well fed while we were there. Sometimes we got two or three extra days' work patrolling after the fire was out. This time my friends and I were let go once the fire was under control, and we dropped by one of the homesteads as we were walking home. That was when we learned that Britain had declared war on Germany. Canada followed suit a week later, and immediately we began talking about who was going to join up and which service they would go to. My best friend went into Edmonton the following week and enlisted, but I stayed on the homestead with Mother.

In November we got a letter from my father saying that he was leaving the north and going to Wetaskiwin, Alberta, forty miles south of Edmonton, to open a café. He told us to close everything up on the homestead. He sent a ticket for Mother, so I hitched up the team and drove her into the town of Blue Ridge, fifteen miles from Corbett Creek, and put her on the train. I stayed behind to dispose of what we owned. Finding buyers for the farm equipment was a pretty big job for a boy of eighteen. There wasn't much money around; I got five dollars for something here, ten dollars for something else there. I sold a bit of the furniture. The remaining furniture, most of it home made, was in poor condition and was abandoned in the cabin. There was some fairly nice lumber on the roof of the log house we lived in, and I found a buyer for it. We still owed money on the team, so I gave the mare and colt back to the rancher we had bought them from and left the other horse with a friend of mine until I could come back and claim him. That horse got old and died before I returned from military service years later.

After a couple of weeks I had the grand sum of about fifty dollars, more than a month's wages in those days, and I walked out to Blue Ridge with a friend and caught a train into Edmonton. We spent the night in Edmonton, then I went on to Wetaskiwin the next day. My so-called friend helped me spend some of my fifty dollars on meals and rooms in Blue Ridge and Edmonton. This was normal for that time and place. If you were "flush," you willingly shared your funds with someone who was broke.

I joined my parents at the Wales Hotel in Wetaskiwin, where my father was trying to make a go of the restaurant. Except for his unsuccessful attempt to develop the homestead, Dad had been working – whenever he could find work, which wasn't too often – as a cook, most often at logging camps or on fishboats, since he'd got back from England after serving in the First World War. It was while he was in England that he had met and married my mother, Florence Bulmer Neesom, an English widow with two daughters. My half-sisters, Ethel and Crissie, were several years older than I was, and both were married long before Dad had taken Mother and me up to the homestead at Corbett Creek in 1933.

The restaurant in Wetaskiwin wasn't working out any better than the homestead. it had been closed for so long that people had got out of the habit of going to it, and it was in an out-of-the-way location. It was a good thing that there wasn't enough business that my father needed me, because I had no intention of being anywhere near that café. I'd had my fill of peeling potatoes and washing dishes when I worked, not for very long, as a flunky at a lumber camp. I found a group of young people my age and spent my winter looking for work and hanging around town with my friends.

Jobs were not plentiful. I used to help a friend deliver telegrams, just for something to do; I didn't get paid for it. I recall being offered a job feeding cattle for a rancher who said he would pay me fifteen dollars a month. Smart young fellow that I was, I told him I would take it if he made it twenty dollars. I knew that I would be alone on his remote farm seven days a week, shovelling manure, feeding and watering the cattle twice a day, and feeding myself as best I could while the rancher showed up occasionally to see what was going on, and I knew that an older man doing the same work would have been paid the twenty dollars I'd asked for. Besides, life on the homestead had left me with no desire to feed cattle or do any farm work. The rancher called me an ungrateful young pup and went looking for somebody else to do the job.

Two or three of us decided we would join the militia to get ready for the day when we would enlist in active service. I wasn't too sure when or where, but I knew that eventually I would be joining up. At that time the country wasn't in a financial position to raise a large army quickly, so there wasn't much active recruiting going on. Once a week we went to the armories for two hours and trained with the Edmonton Fusiliers militia regiment, for which we were paid fifty cents a night. At that time the Fusiliers were a machine gun unit, so as well as learning how to march in step and left and right turn, we trained on Vickers .303 machine guns. Of course, it appealed to me to learn how to operate this marvellous piece of machinery. However, it was a terrible disappointment that I never was issued a uniform and couldn't walk through town looking heroic and important, a trained soldier preparing to go off to war.

In January 1940, an older fellow who sold lightning rods asked me if I would work for him. He would go around to the farms and line up sales, then take me out with him to do the installations. The lightning rods were fastened on top of a building, usually a barn, and then a cable was run from the rods to the ground. The idea was that the lightning rods and cable would lead any charge off to ground before it built up to the point that lightning would strike. I was paid five dollars a week when we had installations to do, and I enjoyed it. Sometimes climbing to the top of a hip roof barn tested my nerve.

We used to chug down the road in my boss's old car. As I recall, it was a 1928 or '29 soft-top Chevrolet. The top folded down to convert it to an open four-seater. With the top up, it had leatherette curtains with isinglass windows fitted on the sides. About the only way to heat the car was to warm some large rocks in a wood stove oven and place them on the car floor, where you put your feet on them and spread a blanket over your knees. My employer, it seems, did not believe in these luxuries, as we never had them. Only the small amount of heat that managed to seep from the engine through the holes in the fire wall moderated the frigid air.

I recall that, coming back one night from an installation, it got so foggy we couldn't see where we were going. My boss said to me, "You'd better drive," and I was embarrassed to have to tell him I couldn't drive. I'd been around vehicles and had been shown how to put the clutch in and shift the gears, but I was far from ready to take over driving at night in such conditions. Give me a team of horses to drive and I was fine, but anything powered by gasoline was another matter. What made it so embarrassing was that most young fellows my age lived in areas where there were automobiles and learned how to drive as a matter of course, and so my boss had just assumed I could, like any other young fellow he knew. I made some lame excuse about having no licence. Oh, the pride of youth. Looking back, I realize that, had I admitted I did not know how to drive, he would have taken the trouble to teach me.

The winter went by, and in the early spring my father closed the restaurant, as there was not enough business to pay the bills. We were off again to Edmonton, where we settled in a rented apartment above a store. I had the Winnipeg couch. You don't see them any more. The Winnipeg couch consisted of a metal frame with a pad filled with cotton waste for a mattress, laid on a spring made of clothes line cable hooked to coil springs spaced around the frame. During the day it folded up to make a settee, and at night you unfolded it to make a bed. It wasn't the most comfortable thing to sleep on, but for me, in those days, it was fine. The Winnipeg couch was Depression-era furniture. When the economy improved after the war, Winnipeg couches were relegated to rumpus rooms and lakeside cabins. There was one in a lakeside cabin my wife and I purchased in 1956. You can be sure I never slept on it.

I still wanted to get a job, so I travelled all over the city looking for work. The Edmonton airfield was just being built out by the Municipal Airport. That was a large construction project, putting up barracks and hangars for the Royal Canadian Air Force station at Edmonton. I had no trade, but I hung around out there occasionally trying to get hired for work of any kind. It was such a huge project that it seemed to me that they must need lots of people, though when I think about it now, I realize that I wasn't going about it the right way. I was using the same method I'd used when I worked at logging camps. You walked into the camp, way out in the bush, went to the camp office and asked the foreman if they were hiring. In Edmonton, same thing; I went on site and asked for the foreman, who didn't need to be bothered by young fellows looking for jobs. Or, because there were a lot of people looking for work, it's possible that they really didn't need anybody. Then, too, it might have been that they had a policy not to hire eighteen-year-olds, and instead took on older, married men who would not be going off to war. At the time, I couldn't understand why I just kept getting the brushoff. No one told me to go to the company personnel office.

I ended up spending a lot of time with a group of young people I'd become acquainted with, including a couple I had known when we lived in Edmonton when I was a little guy. There were two or three girls in the group, but nobody was especially dating. None of us had any money. We spent our days down in the North Saskatchewan River valley and at the municipal public park, just living the good life. We couldn't go swimming at the park pool because it cost money, but we could sit in the stands and watch the girls swimming. One of the fellows had a canoe, and we'd all pile in until the water was within an inch of the gunwales and paddle out to the middle of the North Saskatchewan River, which luckily is not deep. Another fellow had a brother who was a doorman at the theatre downtown and would turn his back while we sneaked in through the fire door. We did whatever we could think of just to kill time. It didn't satisfy us at all. We all wanted to be doing something worthwhile, but your options were limited when you couldn't get a job and didn't have any money.

I used to read the paper and follow the course of the war. In those days newspapers would post the front page in the office window, and I always read the headlines when I went downtown. It was in a newspaper office window on Jasper Avenue one day in late May 1940 that I read about the British forces being evacuated from Dunkirk. It struck me that if I was going to enlist, now was the time to do it, so I began the rounds of the recruiting offices.

My first choice was the Royal Canadian Air Force, of course. The air force is the junior service, having come into being after World War I.* The navy, which was the first to be established, is the senior service, followed by the army. However, the air force was considered the most glamorous.

---

* Over 20,000 Canadians served in the British Royal Flying Corps (later the Royal Air Force) during World War I, but the Canadian Air Force was not established until November 1918. It was disbanded in February, 1920, but reformed by the army as a reserve force. The Royal Canadian Air Force was formed April 1, 1924.

King George had promoted that image when he referred in a speech to "sailors of my Navy, soldiers of my Army, gentlemen of my Air Force."

I knew that I could never be a pilot. In the RCAF pilots were officers and had to have at least a Grade 12 education. I only had Grade 8. Still, I hoped to fly, and thought I could be an air gunner or wireless operator. I imagined myself a dashing hero in an air force blue uniform with wings on my chest and the girls falling at my feet. The truth is that not everybody could do the glamour jobs, and even if I had made it into the air force, I probably would have ended up on general duties: in stores or in the kitchen, on patrol or guard duty. But as long as I had a blue uniform, I figured I could make out pretty well. With glowing visions of the illustrious career ahead of me, I made my way to the recruiting office. It was closed, and there was a big sign on the door saying that they weren't recruiting until further notice.

The next choice was the Royal Canadian Navy. The army didn't appeal to me because I didn't want to walk. I'd spent my life getting wherever I wanted to go by walking, and I wanted to ride for a change. If I couldn't fly the wild blue yonder, sailing the ocean wide seemed pretty attractive. But it was not to be. I went down to the Naval Reserve office, HMCS *Nonsuch*, and there was not a soul in sight. Everything was shut tight.

Finally in the last week of May there was a notice in the paper that an infantry regiment was being formed in Edmonton. "This is my chance," I thought, and I went down to the Prince of Wales Armoury, where they were recruiting, and spent a week trying to enlist.

Recruiting began on Tuesday, June 4, 1940. The new regiment was being formed from five Alberta militia units that were being activated, each of which would contribute a company. They were the South Alberta Regiment, the Edmonton Fusiliers, the 19th Alberta Dragoons, the 15th Alberta Light Horse, and the Calgary Regiment (Tank). People who were in the Non-Permanent Active Militia at the time, including the officers and NCOs, changed status from reserve to active service. If I'd had the sense to transfer to the local unit of the Edmonton Fusiliers when I moved to Edmonton, I would have been activated along with the rest of them, but for some reason I hadn't – I'm not sure why. It would have been a good move, but it never crossed my mind. I'd only been with the militia in

Wetaskiwin a couple of months and never did get a uniform, so it might be that I never really felt part of the unit, and I think I was more interested in finding full-time work.

Whatever the reason, since I was no longer with a militia unit, I found myself sitting with a thousand other fellows outside the Prince of Wales Armoury waiting to be called in. So began a very discouraging week. Every so often, out of the building would come a sergeant major. He would go down the row saying, "You, you, you," and the fellows he chose would go in to be processed. Each militia unit was recruiting for its own company, and each wanted the finest looking soldiers, the best looking men, so they were choosing the tallest, strongest, handsomest fellows first. I learned later that this competition among the companies resulted in our being an excellent regiment. Not only did the sergeants major and company commanders want the best looking troops they could get; they were determined that their men were going to form the best qualified, best trained company in the regiment, and so they made sure that we were as well prepared as we could be. What it meant, though, was that the little five-foot-six-inch guys like me were passed over. I arrived at the armouries every morning at eight o'clock and sat there all day on a bench with a bunch of other fellows, watching all the big guys being chosen, until I walked home across the city in the late afternoon to get something to eat. As the days went by, the number of hopeful recruits dwindled until there were only fifty or sixty of us left. I finally decided that I would give it one more day. If they didn't choose me, I was going to let the big guys go and fight the war. If the army wanted me, they were going to have to come and get me.

Back I went the next morning, and the routine started all over again. By three in the afternoon there were only a couple of dozen of us left, and a dejected looking bunch we were. Finally, out came a sergeant major who said, "All right, you lot, come on in, all of you."

We straggled into the building and signed all the papers attesting that we would serve King and Country. Then we were marched off in groups to downtown Edmonton for our medicals. With my extensive militia experience – all of eight two-hour lessons in how to right and left turn – I expected, fully and surely, that I would be given responsibility for one of these groups. I was terribly disappointed when some fellow, wearing civvies just like me, was put in charge. What I didn't know at the time was that, despite their lack of military dress, these men were members of the militia units that were forming the regiment.

I almost didn't pass my physical. You had to be at least 5′3″, which was OK because I stood 5′6″, and you had to weigh at least 135 pounds. I hadn't eaten much during the week I sat outside the armoury and meals were pretty skimpy at home anyway, and I was a few pounds underweight. The medical officer looked at the scale and said, "Well, you're kinda scrawny; get a couple of good army meals in you and you'll put the weight on. You're in."

There I was, by the skin of my teeth. I was no longer Mr. Galipeau, I was Private Galipeau of the South Alberta Regiment, Infantry.

CHAPTER 1

A Warrior I

I was happy to be a soldier at last. I had a place to sleep, regular meals, and, right from the first pay, $1.10 a day. This was undreamed-of wealth! Thirty-five dollars a month plus room and board! I had never felt so secure. For this rate of pay I could cheerfully follow orders and carry out any sort of duty they gave me.

The barracks full of young men with money brought out a platoon of insurance salesmen. They approached us all to buy life insurance. This I could not understand. *Why* sell life insurance to men who were going off, possibly to be shot? They sold a large number of policies. Why not? The odds were in our favour. I still have mine. It becomes an endowment when I'm ninety. When you are nineteen and buying your first insurance, who looks at the details?

It has been said that a lot of guys joined up just to get a place to sleep, enough to eat and a paycheque, and I won't refute that. The Depression had been pretty tough, and there were a lot of young fellows like me who hadn't had much luck at finding work. Still, I think that the majority of us would have gone to war anyway. We had to. We knew what was happening in Europe, we'd heard about the army Hitler was building, the alliances he was forming with Italy and Japan, and we didn't know how strong Britain was going to be. In our hearts, every one of us felt that if we didn't go and do what had to be done, one day we were going to be standing on Canada's shores watching as German invaders attacked us. I think that everyone believed that, regardless of any responsibility we might feel we had towards Britain, to save Canada, the time was going to come, one way or the other, when we were going to have to do our part. Underlying it all was the normal Canadian response to a neighbour in trouble. In peacetime, the community responds when a house burns or some other catastrophe takes place. In this case, the people of Europe were being enslaved and so, as Canadians, we responded to the need to free them.

What also appealed to us young men was the adventure that going to war promised. We were going to have a chance to travel, to go overseas and see danger, and it was very exciting. Buried deep was the knowledge that someday we might get shot, but we accepted that. There used to be great arguments about whether it was better not to get married because your wife might be left a widow, or to get married and then at least you would have had that time together. We knew what we were getting into, we didn't go into the army with our eyes closed, but that thirty-five dollars a month spending money – raised some time later to the magnificent sum of forty dollars a month to enjoy life with – went a long way to offset any worries we had about what might happen to us.

Not that everybody could stand army life. Two of the people who joined up with me went to the Company Orderly Room (the Orderly Room was part of Headquarters and served as the administration office of a company or regiment) on the third day and asked to get out; they "washed out," as we called it. There were others as time went on, and some who didn't want to leave but were washed out because they just couldn't become soldiers. They fought the system, resented the orders, couldn't handle the living conditions or the routine.

The routine and living conditions were no problem for me because of my experience working in logging camps, but they were quite a shock for some people. We were quartered at the Prince of Wales Armoury. The offices were in the armoury itself, and beside and behind the armoury were wooden huts that had been built when the Edmonton Regiment went active in September 1939. They were our barracks. They were built in an H configuration, with thirty double bunks, sleeping sixty men, in a long row on each side of the barracks at either end and a communal ablutions room running between. Reveille blown on the bugle at six o'clock in the morning got us up. We folded our bedding up neatly and went to the ablutions room to wash and shave. After a logging camp and the homestead, the facilities seemed palatial. There was running water, hot and cold, and rows of wash basins and showers. There were flush toilets; in fact, there were ten of them in a row with no partitions in between. For some of the fellows who had lived in homes with doors on the bathrooms, it was quite unsettling to have to do in public what they had always done in private. Once you got used to it, it could be quite sociable; you would have a chat and a smoke with your buddies while you sat on the toilet. You didn't have time to shower every morning, but you had a good wash, and then you were off to breakfast.

The mess halls, again, were a familiar environment for me. They were just like back in the bush camps where you sat down and grabbed what you could, except the food wasn't as plentiful and the cooks were not as well selected. As soon as you had eaten, you were back on parade. We assembled and were marched out to the parade ground, where all thousand men would be put through physical fitness training. This was good, old fashioned PT (Physical Training); arms up, arms down, arms to the side; jumping jacks; pushups; on your back with your feet pumping the air like bicycle pedals. The PT was led by the most magnificent man, a fellow by the name of Sergeant Major Pearkes. He was the Garrison Sergeant Major* and had come from the Permanent Forces to garrison duty at the Prince of Wales Armoury. Nothing much got by him. When we did pushups, everybody had to do them in unison. We all went down together and we all came up together, and no such thing as having your rear end in the air; your back had to be perfectly straight. If you thought you could get away with letting yourself sag or with only going down part way, you were sadly mistaken, because out of that mass of a thousand men, he would see you and single you out. It was strange, though; none of us resented him. We admired Sergeant Major Pearkes, who was a physical fitness specialist, and his regimental counterpart, Regimental Sergeant Major Chris Seal, a military drill specialist who was just as tough with us on parade. It shows how young men will appreciate proficiency.

---

* The Garrison Sergeant Major is the senior noncommissioned officer of a fortification or military camp and is responsible for the order and discipline of the camp. The Regimental Sergeant Major is concerned only with his own regiment. Since the Prince of Wales Armoury was occupied by components of the militia as well as containing offices for the medical corps and recruiting officer, quartermaster stores, and the orderly room of the South Alberta Regiment, it was considered a garrison.

Dad and me at Edmonton in the summer of 1940, on my first leave home after enlisting. My father, Nelson Edward Galipeau, was a veteran of the 1914-18 war.

Some mornings we were woken up with a nice little routine they called "gunshot." Reveille was at 5 a.m., and when we were dressed we went to the mess hall and had a mug of hot tea and a piece of dry toast. You'd better have shown up in running shoes, because as soon as the tea and toast were gone you were marshalled for a physical fitness ordeal, most often a half hour run. We came back to a proper breakfast and then went on parade for our usual training.

After PT we returned to the barracks to change into our issue boots, if we had them, our own shoes if we didn't, and were marched out onto Kingsway Avenue for parade drill. The only parade square was the ground floor of the armoury, which could accommodate a large number of troops. However, a thousand men in groups of ten or twenty, each receiving instructions and orders, would create bedlam in the building. Kingsway was a four lane street leading out of the city centre. It stretched for two miles beyond the Prince of Wales Armoury with no buildings along it, only open fields. Squads of men drilling in the outside lanes caused no disruption to the occasional vehicle that went by. It made an excellent training area. On Kingsway Avenue we learned to right turn, to left turn, to march in step. We had no uniforms at first, so we probably looked a pretty motley bunch. I was more fortunate than a lot of the new recruits because I had my logging boots, which had thick soles and stood up to the rigours of parade drill. We were issued running shoes for PT when we joined up and army boots before we got uniforms, but many men developed blisters and calluses and wore out their shoes before the boots arrived.

There was one very special group that everybody tried to stay away from. It was called the Awkward Squad. These were fellows who could not remember to turn right when they were told to turn right, could never coordinate the pivot on one toe and the opposite heel that you used to make a turn, couldn't get in step when they marched, couldn't manage to swing their arms in military fashion. They were all put into a group on their own and drilled until they worked out their problems and could march with the rest.

Quite early in our training we were introduced to the *King's Rules and Regulations*, which laid out the conduct expected of the soldiers of the Canadian army and the penalties you were subject to if you violated the rules. We had to obey civil law, same as anyone else, but we were also subject to military law. The *Rules and Regulations* covered every type of offence you could think of, from purely military transgressions such as disobeying an order, disorderly conduct, being absent without leave and insubordination, to major crimes such as theft, rape and murder, and set out the kinds of penalties associated with each. For minor infractions, such as coming in late in the evening, for example, you would be brought before the Commanding Officer who might give you some CB, or Confined to Barracks, for a week, which meant you wouldn't be allowed to go out during the free time in the evenings or on the weekends. If you were very bad – for example, took off for a month without leave so they had to come and get you – you might find yourself spending thirty days in the military jail. If you didn't respond to training, they could discharge you under Section 40, which was "unlikely to become an efficient soldier."

We were encouraged to study the *King's Rules and Regulations* so we knew what was acceptable behaviour and what was not, because ignorance of the regulations was not considered a valid excuse. Some did study them. There were people who used to be called "barrack room

lawyers" who knew the book from one end to the other. I thought I was
going to be one of these. We used to have to do duty in the Orderly Room.
There was never much going on, but somebody had to be there to answer
the phone. I can remember snooping around in the desk and digging out
the *Rules and Regulations.* I started to read them, and soon became utterly
bored. So much for my career as a barrack room lawyer. I didn't have any
problem with the discipline. I even got a Good Conduct stripe once,
which was one stripe worn upside down on the lower sleeve. Most of the
fellows who got them didn't wear them, because anyone who did was
branded a bit of a wimp. The truth is that all a Good Conduct stripe
meant was that you'd never been caught doing something you shouldn't.

As part of the training in discipline, we had to learn how to salute.
Saluting had to be done properly. You swung your right hand in a wide
circle out from your side, ending with your palm forward and your first
finger in line with your eyebrow. You held that pose for a count of three,
then brought your hand smartly down to the side. You took the longest
way up, held it for a count of three, then took the shortest way down. We
spent hours out on the parade square under the supervision of an NCO,
who repeated the order "Salute! One, two, three, down!" until we could
do it in our sleep. Not only did we have to learn how to salute, we had to
learn *who* to salute. That meant that we had to learn the insignia of the
different ranks. A second lieutenant wore one button, or pip, on his
shoulder. A first lieutenant had two, a captain had three. A major had a
crown, a colonel had a crown and two pips, and so on up to brigadiers
and generals. As if it weren't enough to learn the Army insignia, we also
had to learn to recognize navy and air force officers, nursing sisters, anybody who had the royal commission. We were told that we were saluting
the uniform, not the person, honouring the authority of the King. You
could get yourself in deep and dire doo-doo if you failed to salute when
you were supposed to, and there are plenty of stories of fellows going
downtown and saluting bus drivers, doormen, Salvation Army captains,
anybody with buttons on their shoulder. To be safe, the saying went, "If it
moves, salute it."

It was even trickier for the sentries on guard duty. Many a soldier got
his tail chewed by the sergeant of the guard because he gave the wrong

salute. As a rule, the sentry stood easy, with the rifle butt on the ground, holding the barrel. When an officer went by, the sentry would come to attention and slope his rifle, and then give a salute appropriate to the rank of the officer. Sloping the rifle was a drill procedure in which the rifle was placed on the left shoulder. Any officer below the rank of major received a butt salute; the sentry placed his right hand on the butt of the rifle for the count of three, then moved his arm to hold it down his right side at attention. For officers with the rank of major and above, you had to present arms, which meant taking the rifle off the shoulder and through the proper drill, ending with right foot behind the left foot at a 45° angle and the rifle held perpendicular, directly in front of your body, until the officer passed. Then the rifle was sloped back on the shoulder, then to the order position with the butt on the ground, and you returned to standing easy.

More than once a sentry would be daydreaming about the hot date he had lined up for tomorrow night when suddenly an officer appeared. The sentry, in a bit of a panic, would put his rifle to the slope position and give a butt salute, and next thing he knew, somebody had turned loose a raging bull behind him, only this bull stood on two feet and wore three stripes. The sergeant of the guard had been notified by the offended officer that the sentry had butt-saluted a major, or worse yet, a colonel. After the sentry was berated at length about what kind of imbecile he was, with a few choice remarks about his ancestry thrown in, ending with the dire warning that if he ever did that again he would be forever consigned to kitchen fatigue, a good many captains and lieutenants got a Present Arms when they went through the gate. It was a strange and confusing world at times.

Of course, like everything else in the army, there was a purpose in this insistence on procedure. It wasn't just a matter of showing the proper respect for rank. If you were chewed out by the sergeant of the guard for not giving the right salute, you made doubly sure that you paid attention from then on, and that was what you were there for. It was the sentry's responsibility to know who was coming through the gate, and to challenge anybody he wasn't sure was authorized to be there.

Not only did we have no uniforms when I joined up, we had no rifles. When we finally did get some they were old equipment. We had Ross rifles and a Lewis machine gun, weapons from the Great War that I had heard my father talk about. We did a little bit of field craft with the Lewis, learning how to set up a defensive position with a machine gun. We eventually got the .22 calibre Lee Enfield rifle, another First War weapon, and did some shooting on the indoor range in the armoury, but there weren't enough rifles to go around. One group would work on rifle drill, then pass them on to the next. We had to learn how to take a rifle apart and put it back together until we were so proficient we could do it without thinking. We learned how to clean it and the accepted way to fire it. Even though I'd lived with rifles all my life, there were things that were different from what I was used to. I had my own technique for firing a rifle, for example, but had to learn a whole new way based on technical details I had never heard of before. When we went to the ranges to fire at targets I found that my accuracy suffered with the army system, so went back to my own.

We had to achieve the same proficiency with every weapon we were issued. We learned to strip and reassemble machine guns blindfolded to prepare for the time we might need to do so in the dark. Periodically we underwent TOETs (Tests of Elementary Training) that evaluated our skills and ability to meet time requirements.

We got our first taste of bayonet drill, which was really the first time we learned something that had to do with actually killing the enemy. Bayonet drill began with the procedure for "on the gun the knife put," as somebody used to say; for taking the bayonet out of the scabbard on your belt and fixing it on your rifle. The next step was learning the proper stance, and then the proper handling. You would stand with your rifle in position like a fencer with his foil, and the instructor would go by and make sure you had a firm grip. Then you would practise thrust and parry. Occasionally we would practise our bayonet attack and defence against an opponent armed with a four foot long pole with a device like a boxing glove fastened on the end so that nobody was hurt.

Of course, we had all the usual extra duties that soldiers have: kitchen fatigues, cleanup, sentry duty. The barracks floors had to be swept daily. Each day one man would be detailed as "hut orderly." He would sweep and clean his part of the quarters and clean the latrines (washroom and toilets) and keep unauthorized people out of the barracks. Most often, this duty fell to someone who, not feeling well due to a cold or other minor illness, was relegated to "light duty" by the medical officer. In the Canadian army of those days, you *might* be "excused duty" if you were carried, suffering from broken bones, into the MIR (Medical Inspection Room) on a stretcher, or possibly if you crawled in with a collapsed lung, but this would be a rare occurrence. Malingerers were not tolerated. I might be a bit extreme in my characterization of the medical care we received, but my description is close to the mark.

Sometimes we would be assigned to sweep out the armoury, which was almost half a block square. A group of us would be lined up and given push brooms, two and a half to three feet long, and we worked as a team to sweep that vast space. You soon learned the technique. Saturday morning was a major cleanup in the barracks. The wooden floors had to be scrubbed with a scrub brush, the windows cleaned, everything had to be polished. The company commander didn't check the ledges for dust with white gloves as they did with the Permanent Force in peacetime, but they always found some fault. I hated that inspection, but there was no way to avoid it. It was part of the routine.

We did our own laundry. Our heavy serge uniforms, when we finally got them, were sent to the cleaner's, but our shirts and socks and underwear and our denim fatigue uniforms we washed by hand, with a scrub board in the big laundry tubs in the ablutions room. When the weather was good enough, we hung the laundry on a clothes line outside to dry during off-duty hours on Saturday and Sunday. We were not permitted to hang clothes outside on weekdays. As I recall, there was an area where we could hang laundry inside during bad weather. You could send your washing out. Trucks from one of the commercial dry cleaners in Edmonton would come into the barracks area at noon and return with the cleaning the next day. Unless you sent them to the laundry, you ironed your own uniforms, you darned your own socks – and polished your own boots, of course. There were two large commercial hand irons in the laundry area. Ironing was done on a table covered with a wool blanket. Boots always had to be spotless for morning parade, and polished so bright the sergeant major could see his face in them. Your appearance had to be presentable at all times. When you appeared on parade you had to be clean

shaven and your hair had to be neat. You were told to get a haircut if it
wasn't acceptable. Mind you, there wasn't much hair to cut after the military barbers got through with you.

Our packs and the web straps that held them had to be scrubbed clean
using soap and water and a brush. The webbing was all treated with a liq-
uid solution called Blanco so that all the equipment would appear a uniform colour. Blanco was a solution coloured somewhat like a piece of pale
brown paper. Most often, it was applied before an important inspection
by a senior officer or dignitary. The rest of the time, scrubbing with soap
and water was all that was required.

I must mention army-issue general-purpose soap. It came in blocks a
foot long by three inches square, from which you would cut off a piece of
the size you needed. It was very potent, with a strong carbolic smell, and
would take the hands off a brass mannequin. If you spent a half hour
doing laundry on a scrub board with army-issue general-purpose soap,
you could be sure there would be no dirt under your fingernails when you
were finished.

The first issue we received in the way of clothing was the fatigue uniform we wore for daily drill and work around the barracks. Whoever arranged for that fatigue uniform had a diabolical mind. It consisted of
khaki work pants, a khaki shirt and a dark khaki cardigan sweater. The
sweaters were good. The pants were all a size 46 waist with a 40-inch leg.
To fit out everybody smaller than size 46, they whittled the waist down
and chopped off the legs. The appearance was hilarious. The crotch hung
somewhere between where it should be and your knees, and the seat resembled the front end of a Corvette. We were a fine looking bunch of fellows, marching around in our fatigues.

Eventually we were issued a uniform, a very distinctive one. It was
made out of a mustard-coloured denim and worn with a regulation
wedge cap. The people of the city called us "The Mustard Battalion." The
fatigues were our everyday working wear, and we wore the mustard uniforms when we went on parade or to town on our time off. It was our
dress uniform until we were issued the proper serge uniform. The Orders
of the Day posted on the barrack bulletin board detailed the duties for the
day and the type of dress to be worn.

The quartermaster stores issued a lot of strange things to help us adapt to army life. We had three wool blankets. Should you be killed in action, one blanket would be used as a shroud to wrap your body for burial, at which time $2.50 would be deducted from your pay. Then we were introduced to Brasso, boot polishing brushes (two), a brass polishing brush, a button stick, a housewife, a holdall and a 4 x 2.

Brasso was for polishing buttons. A button stick went along with it. It was a piece of brass, 1/16 " thick, with a lengthwise slot that went three quarters of the way down. You slid it under a button when you were polishing it so you would not get Brasso on your clothing or cap.

A housewife was not the kind we would have liked to have had for cleaning the barracks, but it was still a handy little item. It was a little, rolled-up piece of cotton cloth with a number of pockets containing needles and thread for darning and sewing. We all had to learn to darn socks, sew on buttons and do minor repairs.

The holdall was what you would now call a shaving kit. It was a cotton cloth holder that rolled out flat and had pockets for shaving cream, toothpaste, toothbrushes, razor and razor blades.

A 4 x 2 was a piece of flannelette cloth, four inches long and two inches wide, which was used for cleaning a rifle. It was slipped into the pull-through, the cord that you pulled through the barrel of the rifle to clean out deposits left after firing. It was also used for daily cleaning of the rifle. Each time you went on parade with the rifle the sergeant would inspect it for cleanliness, and the bore had better shine … or else.

We were learning, whether we liked it or not, to take care of ourselves. That's one element of military life that I think is really beneficial to young men. When I see all the problems we're having with our young people today, I can't help but think that a couple of years of military service, being subject to military discipline and learning how to take care of themselves as I did, would do them a world of good. It didn't hurt anybody.

I never did get used to that bugle at six o'clock in the morning, and I wasn't too crazy about kitchen fatigue, but all the training interested me. I was learning to be a soldier, and I was happy in what I was doing. For the first time in my life, I guess, I had security. As long as the war lasted, I had a place to be and a part to play.

CHAPTER 2

Peewee Platoon

It wasn't long after we were recruited that an event took place that would
determine what kind of experience I was going to have as a soldier of the
Canadian army. It began with our learning to fall in on parade. An infantry regiment consists of about a thousand personnel. The commanding
officer is a lieutenant colonel; he has overall responsibility for the regiment. The rest of the personnel are assigned to one of five companies – a
headquarters company and four rifle companies. The rifle companies are
identified by letters, "A" Company through "D" Company. Each is commanded by a major, with a captain as second in command, and is further
divided into four platoons, identified by numbers. Headquarters Company has 1 through 4 Platoon, "A" Company has 5 through 8 Platoon, and
so on. A lieutenant has charge of each platoon, with a sergeant as his second in command. Each platoon consists of three sections of nine men
with a corporal, or occasionally a lance corporal, in charge, answering to
the platoon sergeant. One corporal is senior to the other two. In general,
the officers are responsible for the administration, while the non-com-
missioned officers, or NCOs, take care of the training and discipline of
the men. There is also a company sergeant major, who is the senior NCO
in the company. The senior NCO in the regiment is the regimental sergeant major.

There has always been some discussion about whether it's the colonel
or the regimental sergeant major who really commands a regiment. The
general opinion of the enlisted men is that the RSM is the top man, and
I've talked to commanding officers who agree. As far as we were concerned, our regimental sergeant major was the most powerful man in the
world. He could put the fear of whatever there was to fear into anybody at

any time. He walked on water. The colonel might talk to generals and other big brass, but the Regimental Sergeant Major talked to God.

Ours was a magnificent man, Regimental Sergeant Major Christopher Seal. He had been a Permanent Force soldier with the Princess Patricia's Canadian Light Infantry, but spoke with a British accent and had the bearing of a sergeant major of the British Guards. He had been well trained, and he knew how to drill and handle a regiment. Whatever the South Alberta Regiment demonstrated in the way of proficiency, precision in drill, and deportment on parade and in dress was due to the efforts of Sergeant Major Seal. To my mind, he was the image of how young men want a leader to be. He knew what he was doing, he was competent, he was decisive. He had a voice that you could hear for four miles, and eyes like a hawk. He could have the whole regiment lined up in front of him, and he would spot somebody way in the back ranks whose dress was not acceptably precise. "Fourth man, centre rank, 16 Platoon!" he would bellow. "You're not a bunch of bloody cowboys. Straighten that bloody belt!"

He drove us until we reached a level of proficiency that was recognized as excellent. Any man that served in our regiment at that time will say Sergeant Major Seal made us what we were.

Headquarters Company mostly handled administration, but also contained all the ancillary units that provided special services. They included the transport drivers, the Pioneer Platoon* that did repairs and was made up of tradesmen such as carpenters and blacksmiths, the signallers who ran the telephone lines, the regimental clothing and equipment stores, the shoemakers, a mortar platoon, a machine gun platoon. Each company also had a headquarters platoon that handled the administrative duties for that company, while the three rifle platoons were the fellows that were going to do the fighting. The company clerk, who was in the headquarters platoon, had to type out daily orders, handle all the correspondence for the major, run a business office for the company and manage the orderly room where the company records were kept. Headquarters Platoon

---

* Pioneer Platoon was a name borrowed from the British army. They were responsible for repairs and construction of anything that was needed, such as bridging or road work. The men in the Pioneer Platoon had a mixture of trades and abilities and were trained to construct what the army needed using materials at hand.

got the same training as the rest of us for the most part, but, except on formal or special occasions, seldom went on parade. Later on, when we got into battle, they sometimes had to fight when the line of defence was infiltrated and their position was attacked.

The rest of us went on parade daily, and, as you would expect in the army, there was quite a procedure that was followed when you were fallen in. We had been assigned to particular companies when we joined up; I was in "B" Company, which had been formed from the 19th Alberta Dragoons. When it came time to assign us to platoons, the company was formed up in three ranks with the tallest on the right, shortest on the left. The sergeant major had the front rank number off, from tallest to shortest. The usual procedure was to divide the company into platoons alphabetically, so that the men in any given platoon were a mixture of different heights. On this day, though, the sergeant major told us off into four permanent platoons by height, assigning the men in files numbered 1-10 to Headquarters Platoon, 11-20 to Number 10 Platoon, and so on, until we were segregated by numbers into four groups of thirty men. All the tallest men were in "B" Company's Headquarters Platoon, all the shortest in Number 12 Platoon. The sergeant for each platoon was introduced, and then we were given the order "Break off," which meant that we were to move away and could relax and chat for a bit, but we were still on parade and couldn't leave. The next order was: "Sergeants, fall in your platoons."

The first step in falling in a platoon is calling out the marker. The marker is one of the tallest men in the platoon, or one of the corporals, and is the person everybody else uses as a reference point when forming up. When the platoon is marching in ranks of three, the marker's position is at the left end of the front rank, and everybody dresses, or lines up, to his right and rear. When the platoon stops and executes a left turn forming three lines facing front, his position is the right front rank; everybody dresses to his left and rear. On this particular afternoon, the sergeants were told to fall in their platoons for the first time. It began with the sergeant for "B" Company's Headquarters Platoon calling his marker, then giving the order, "Headquarters Platoon, on parade," and all the members of Headquarters Platoon formed up on the marker. In turn, the sergeant for Number 10 Platoon called his marker and ordered his platoon on parade, then the sergeant for Number 11 Platoon did the same. Finally, it was the turn of Number 12 Platoon, which consisted of all the little fellows, including me, who stood between 5'3" and 5'6". Sergeant MacAskill was our designated sergeant. He called his marker, and then changed the course of Canada's military history for all time by calling out, not "Number 12 Platoon on parade," but, loud and clear, "Peewees on parade!"

We formed up, pleased as a bunch of children. No longer were we just the short guys in Number 12 Platoon; we were somebody special. Other than in formal parades, we were known as the Peewee Platoon from then on, and it gave us a sense of identity and a cohesiveness that no other platoon had.

We got together in the barracks after we were dismissed and discussed our new identity. The Peewees on Parade. We liked that. In fact, we decided, that was going to be our war cry. If any of us, at any time, was in trouble, all he had to do was shout out, "Peewees on parade!" and any other Peewee in hearing distance was obligated to rush to his aid. We put our war cry to the test many times over the coming many months. The Peewees were in the same barracks as 11 Platoon, with Headquarters and 10 Platoon in the opposite end of the hut. Every so often after we were off duty for the day, one of the fellows would slip over into the other section and start up a ruckus of some kind, bug some big fellow, until his victim gave chase. Then he would call, "Peewees on parade!" and immediately about ten Peewees would leap on the poor man. We never beat anybody up, that wasn't the intent. We were just harassing, making sure that the whole world knew we were the Peewees.

We soon adopted one very, very vile practice. It became an initiation rite with the Peewees, and there was none other like it. The new Peewee would be held securely by several of his fellows, his pants forcibly removed, and his testicles covered with black shoe polish. We called it being "blackballed," and made out that we were doing it to protect the fellow's virtue. If the guy got lucky when he went out on his weekend pass and met an accommodating young woman, he would have to behave himself, or face having to explain the condition of his private parts when he undressed.

Eventually we extended the practice to unsuspecting innocents who wandered, or were chased, into the Peewees' area of the barracks. The poor guy would be leapt upon by about ten Peewees. Off would come the pants, out would come the shoe polish, and he would be sent back to his platoon with an unforgettable souvenir of his foray into Peewee territory. I don't know why they didn't kill us! Mind you, we stayed away from our victims in the barracks for quite a while after the ambush, but over time we managed to work our way through quite a few fellows who sauntered in. You would think they would have known better.

On one occasion we got the message that maybe we were carrying things a little bit too far. Some of the Peewees tried to blackball a big Native fellow. He fought like a wild man, and kicked a couple of fellows in the face when he was down. I think that was just about the only time any of us got hurt by somebody outside the platoon.

The Peewees were quite a mix. There were a few older fellows who just went on their way; growled a bit if anyone gave them grief, so nobody bothered them too much. There were serious-minded young fellows like me who enjoyed a bit of horsing around, but were never the leaders when it came to practical joking or other devilment. Sammy Marshall was another, and Sammy, who was from Edmonton, and I immediately became close friends. I suppose we were compatible. We had the same temperament and thought the same way, and we chummed around together.

And then there were quite a number who were real characters in one way or another.

Joe Spence was a full blood Indian, a chief's son from the Hobbema Reserve, just south of Edmonton. He fitted in well and everybody liked him, but he told me later that he had a terrible time when he first joined up. He was right off the reserve, far away from the people and the kind of life he'd known, and mixing with white people for the first time. He felt so insecure and unsure of himself that he was afraid to ask for or reach for anything at meals, with the result that the white boys grabbed all the food and Joe ended up being the last to get anything until he got up the courage to fend for himself. He was worried he was going to bother somebody.

Abie Polsky was a glamour boy and a ladies' man. His family had a dry cleaning establishment and were quite well off, so Polsky had money before he joined the army. When we finally got our proper serge uniforms, they followed the hallowed army tradition of being either too large or too small. Polsky was one of those who took his uniform downtown and got it tailored, so he always looked smart. I didn't bother. I was proud as heck to be able to walk the streets and show everybody that I was there to fight for my country, even if my uniform didn't fit that well.

Frenchy Marcotte stood only five foot three, but he was a miniature Charles Atlas, solid muscle. I think he was a coal miner from Cape Breton originally. Mickey McDonald was a Métis. He had been a game guide and done quite a bit of hunting. He was a good-looking young fellow, and it seemed he was always being picked up in bars and dance halls by older women, of the advanced age of thirty-five or so. He would tell us about them when he got back to barracks.

Hugh McCleary was a First World War veteran, and an excellent piano player. I think he had played professionally at one time. He would play at night in the wet canteen, which was what we called the regimental bar, and never have to buy his own drinks. He was our company commander's batman, making his bed, keeping his room clean, shining his shoes, so Hugh never went on parade; but he used to berate us younger fellows and tell us we would soon be smartened up. Hugh was a typical drinker. His cure for a hangover was to bring home a bottle of beer, pull the cap off, and leave it sit all night so it became flat and stale. In the morning he would get out of bed, down the bottle of stale beer, and he'd be ready for the day.

Herb Roulston was another older fellow, though not as old as Hugh; Herb was close to thirty at the time, married with two little boys. He was an Irishman from the country east of Edmonton. Herb had the greatest contempt for authority. He carried out his duties, but so far as he was concerned, everything about the military was "chickenshit." Herb could be very belligerent, and after a few drinks, the first thing he'd look for was a fight, whether or not he was in any condition for one. Later on, when we got into action, there was not a better soldier in the squadron.

The youngest Peewee was C.J. Smith, who had sneaked into the army when he was only sixteen, though he looked older. He turned seventeen a month later. Unless his parents complained, no one would check his birthdate as long as the regiment was in Canada. C.J. was a clown. Herb gave him quite a hard time, with the result that the day C.J. turned twenty-one shortly before we left England in July of 1944, he invited Herb outside, threatening to punch him out.

As well as C.J. Smith, we had J.C. Smith. He came out of the woods around Edson, and, as I too had spent my formative years in the backwoods, I often wonder if I was like him. He was a friendly fellow and a nice lad, fairly sensible and intelligent, but not sophisticated at all. The niceties of life seemed to elude J.C. His girlfriend sent him a homemade cake when the regiment was at training camp in Dundurn. He showed it around, then, half an hour later, he went to the canteen and came back with a cake he'd bought there. He asked me, "Do you think this is a suitable gift for my girlfriend?" I had quite a time trying to explain to him why I didn't think it was appropriate, and in fact I didn't succeed; he sent the cake off to her.

Another pair of backwoods boys were Rocky and Jim Bennett. They were just like the hillbillies of Tennessee, except that they came out of the hills of Rocky Mountain House, Alberta, where the family had some sort of a woodland farm. They were good soldiers, but they were quiet and didn't say much. Sometimes their brothers from another regiment came to visit them. The four of them would gather on a bottom bunk. One would say, "Have you heard from Ma?" There would be silence for as long as three minutes, then another would say, "Yeah, she wrote me last month." Another pause of a couple of minutes, then, "Well, how's the old man?" And that was the way their conversation went, with pauses of a minute or more between each question and answer. It was hilarious listening to them.

It was common knowledge that their father had bludgeoned a son-in-law to death with an axe. It was quite a prominent case and was written up in the paper. Rocky and Jim were given leave to go back and testify at the trial. Someone asked Rocky one time if he had seen the incident. "Yeah," he said, "yeah, I did. He sure did squeal when the old man hit him with that axe."

We had been in training three weeks the day the Peewee Platoon marched up to the hut at four thirty in the afternoon for dismissal for the night and entered the barracks to find it a shambles. There were boots and things scattered all over the place. Scuttling along the rafters were two fel-

Mess line, Edmonton, August 1940. Note the variety of clothing, including the hated baggy fatigues worn by the two men with their backs to the camera. (Courtesy Margaret Atkinson)

lows, one of them laughing maniacally, and both dodging the boots, shoes and other missiles being fired at them by a third fellow on the ground.

And so we met Swede Schmitz and Shorty O'Neil. They had been transferred into our platoon from the reinforcement company while we were out training that day. Someone decided they would fit in, as they were about the right stature; but what that someone didn't realize was that those two would be behind any sort of devilry that developed from then on.

Shorty was the one who had been on the ground, firing boots up at Swede and the other poor, bewildered fellow. The two of them were buddies and went drinking together, but Swede made a habit of taunting Shorty, and it wasn't too hard to get Shorty riled up. He was 5′5″, black-haired, Canadian-Irish and as volatile as they come. Why we never got charged with damaging the barrack room I don't know, although we did get spoken to about it. It was a common occurrence that Swede would taunt Shorty until Shorty blew up and took off after him with his bayonet. Swede would tear down the whole length of the hut and out the door, slamming it just about the time Shorty got there, and the bayonet would go right through the door.

Swede never seemed to be happy unless there was some kind of ruckus going on, and Shorty was his willing accomplice. Between the two of them, they introduced a number of vile practices and so-called practical jokes to the Peewees. It did not take very long before they were joined by others who had a similar liking for devilment. You would be having a nap, lying on your stomach on your bunk, and all of a sudden you would become aware of an awful heat on your rear end. You would come instantly awake to discover flames three feet high rising from the seat of your pants. Somebody had come along and sprayed them with lighter fluid and set fire to them. Or you would be peacefully reading a newspaper and suddenly it would erupt into flame. If you hung your hand over the edge of your bed while you were having a sleep on a Sunday afternoon, somebody would come along with a pail of warm water and immerse your hand in it so you wet your pants.

I was more serious, I guess, and I could have got along without the silly pranks. I tolerated them, and I kept my temper. There were a couple of times I was ready to fight, but I backed off. I laughed and joked about some of the incidents, and, I admit it, I set fire to a few guys' pants, but I was never the practical joker Swede and Shorty were, and sometimes I thought that they went too far.

One fellow who got more than his share of abuse was Joe II (Joe Sequin), an Alberta French Canadian. Joe was the buffoon of the platoon, but he was a bit slow. You had to explain things to Joe a word at a time. I used to feel sorry for him because Swede used to pick on him a lot. He was always playing tricks on him, hiding stuff from him, setting fire to his bed or his pants. One time Joe had a big boil on the back of his neck, and Swede offered to cure it. He told Joe that the cure for boils was to heat a bottle and put the mouth on the boil. As the bottle cooled and created a vacuum, it was supposed to draw the matter out of the boil. They heated up a bottle good and hot and put it on the back of Joe's neck. For a while nothing happened; but then the air cooled, and the boil, along with a good chunk of Joe's skin, were pulled up a half inch or so into the neck of the bottle while Joe howled and squawked. Joe was an easy mark because he was gullible, but he never got mad. He would make more of an outcry than anybody else, but he took all the ribbing without ever retaliating.

Life was not dull in Peewee Platoon. I used to feel sorry for the corporals, who not only had to live through these goings on, but try to keep some type of order. For my part, I did my job and tried to keep out of trouble.

CHAPTER 3

Farewell to City Lights

As the weeks went by, our training got more intense. Parade drill was no longer strictly in platoons or companies; we did regimental drill, with every company in formation. We went on long route marches, ten or twelve miles out beyond the outskirts of the city and back again, marching in column of route: the three sections of a platoon marched abreast, tallest at the front, shortest at the back, one platoon behind the other with Headquarters Platoon at the head, and the companies marched one behind the other with Headquarters Company leading. The normal rate of march was 120 paces a minute with a 30-inch (76-cm) pace. A slow march, at 60 paces a minutes (still at a 30-inch pace), was done for ceremonies such as funerals and parts of an inspection parade for senior officers or dignitaries. In the slow march, the leg moves forward parallel to the ground; then, after a slight pause, the foot is placed on the ground with the heel and toe of the boot touching the ground at the same time. The arms are held by the side rather than swung as in the quick march. A double-time march, running in unison at 240 paces a minute, was done when it was necessary to move troops at a greater speed.

Everything in the military has to be done with precision, even to forming up on parade for morning inspection before carrying on with the assigned training for the day. Forming up for morning parade begins with the company sergeant major calling for platoon markers, usually a corporal from each platoon. They march to the sergeant major and halt in a line facing him with the marker for Headquarters Platoon in front and the rest in sequence behind. "B" Company markers, for example, line up with the marker for Headquarters Platoon in front followed by those for 10, 11 and 12 Platoons. The sergeant major gives the order: "Front marker, stand fast. Remainder, about turn." Then he orders the markers to count off seven paces distance at quick march. Each marker steps off the appropriate number of paces, calculated by multiplying the number of his position in line by seven. Thus, the marker for 10 Platoon counts seven paces, the marker for 12 Platoon, twenty-one. As each reaches his new position, he halts and about-turns. When the last has halted and turned about, the four markers are standing at attention in a row one behind the other, seven paces apart.

The company sergeant major then gives the order, "Company, get on parade." The members of each platoon move on their marker and fall in shoulder to shoulder, an arm's length apart, in three ranks, or rows, to the left of their marker. The remaining two corporals fall in behind the marker at the head of the second and third ranks. The company has now formed up in four platoons, one behind the other, with each platoon in three ranks of ten men abreast, and the platoon sergeant standing in front.

The company sergeant major asks the sergeants to report on their platoon conditions, and each in turn gives the usual reply, "All present and accounted for, SIR." The sergeant major turns the parade over to the officer in command, who then orders the platoon officers to fall in. They join their platoons, where each sergeant reports the platoon strength and any other necessary information, then salutes and moves to a position behind the platoon. The officer inspects the platoon for proper dress, clean rifles, morning showers and haircuts needed, and general appearance. When all platoons have been inspected, the officer in command says, "Platoon commanders, carry on." With that, the platoon commanders march their men away to their day's training, be it drills or lectures. In the case of a regimental parade, the formation and procedure are the same, except that after the company is formed up, it is marched to the parade area by the company sergeant major. There all the companies, under direction of the regimental sergeant major, are placed in alphabetical order in company formation to the left of the headquarters company, so that there are five company formations side by side across the parade area. The commanding officer of the regiment takes command from the regimental sergeant major, and it is the CO who orders the officers to fall in on parade.

In time, we became very proficient at parade drill. RSM Seal was part of the reason; but it was also because of competition between the companies on the part of the officers and NCOs. With each company having been formed from a different militia unit, pride in the parent unit dictated that each company try to produce a more efficient, better drilled, better qualified group of soldiers than any other company. That competitiveness may have filtered down to some of the men who had been with the militia for any length of time before they were activated, but most of us didn't have any affiliation, so it didn't matter much to us. However, with the company sergeant major out there saying that we were going to be the smartest soldiers this side of Buckingham Palace or he'd die trying, the end result was that the whole regiment benefited.

I hadn't been with the militia long enough in Wetaskiwin to feel any particular connection with the Edmonton Fusiliers. I just wanted to join the army. About a month after I enlisted I was called into the office one day and told that they had noticed in my records that I had been with the Edmonton Fusiliers, and did I wish to transfer to "C" Company, which was formed from the Fusiliers? I said no, it didn't matter to me. I was happy with the Peewees.

We made our acquaintance with the regimental medical officer when we began to receive an untold number of needles for various diseases. New recruits who had never been vaccinated got to know him first as they got their basic vaccinations, but after that there were periodic parades for hepatitis shots and other immunizations.

The MO's responsibilities with respect to the prevention of disease didn't end with giving us needles, however. He was also charged with protecting us from venereal disease. Short arm inspection was one of the methods at his disposal. That was quite the thing. Periodically, groups of us would line up naked in the regimental medical treatment room, and the Medical Officer would come along and inspect our genitals for signs of syphilis, gonorrhoea, crab lice, or any of a number of other conditions. It was usually done as part of a general medical inspection.

Sex education, aimed at discouraging us from exposing ourselves to possible infection, was another approach the MO used. It was pretty gruesome. We would be gathered under the direction of the regimental

medical officer and given a talk by the padre about how we were to behave and control ourselves and stay away from the loose women that we
were apt to encounter downtown. Then we were acquainted with the results of ill-advised liaisons, shown lurid movies of sex organs covered
with horrible lesions and given graphic descriptions of the consequences
of untreated venereal disease, or of the treatment you would suffer in an
attempt to arrest the progress of the disease. Just what they told us about
the treatments was enough to scare hell out of anybody. Sulfa drugs were
the only antibiotics available at the time; standard treatment involved a
device called a hockey stick which was inserted into the penis. The MO
made his descriptions as grisly and agonizing as possible, to impress on
us that the girls who look so beautiful at midnight after a few drinks look
different in the light of day, and that the wise man thinks twice before
doing something he'll regret some time later. He put it all in perspective
when he said, "When you're kissing a woman and getting all excited and
being tempted to throw caution to the wind, remember that all you're
kissing is a twenty foot tube with shit at the other end."

Army life wasn't all grub and grind and being ordered about. As well as
parade drill and combat training – and sex education – we had sports
days. There were track and field, boxing, team sports such as softball, soccer and volleyball. Once you were dismissed at 1700 hours, unless you
had special duties, you were free until lights out at 2200 hours, when the
company orderly corporal did a bed check to make sure that everybody
who didn't have a pass was in barracks. A pass to allow you to stay out
until midnight was available, as were overnight and weekend passes.
These were termed twenty-four hour or forty-eight hour passes. Saturday
afternoons, and all day Sundays after church parade, were duty free times
as well. There were a lot of different things you could do in the free time.
We played a lot of volleyball; every barrack had a volleyball net outside.
Some of the farm boys put up horseshoe pitches. I had my guitar, and some
of the other fellows had musical instruments. Corporal Darryl Robertson,
a professional musician, formed a band and wrote a couple of songs about
the regiment. I played chords with the band, and we played for a couple of
dances, including a regimental dance in the armoury. Eventually, Darryl
transferred to the Canadian Army Entertainment Company.

Different organizations would put on concerts and dances to entertain us. Darryl used to encourage us to go down and participate in some of the concerts. I went to Jack Prediger, an accordion player, and suggested that we work up a duet. At that time, "Beer Barrel Polka" had just come out and was a big hit, so Jack and I worked it up and went down to perform. Our turn came, and Jack played the "Beer Barrel Polka" while I chorded along on the guitar. The audience was enthusiastic and gave us lots of applause, more than normal, so I said, "Again, Jack, they want an encore."

So he repeated "Beer Barrel Polka." He finished, and we heard cheer cheer cheer, clap clap clap, shouts for more. I said, "Jack, they want another piece." Off he went again with "Beer Barrel Polka"! Three times in a row he played it! When he finished, I said, "Jack, we'd better quit while we're ahead. Let's get out of here!"

Jack was a good accordionist and could play other tunes. I don't know what happened, whether he had never heard applause before and went into a state of shock of sorts, but that night, it seemed like he was convinced that all the audience wanted was more "Beer Barrel Polka." I was waiting for the cabbages and the rotten tomatoes to start coming our way.

My guitar playing days ended between paydays when there was something I wanted to do and I was broke. With every intention of going back after payday and recovering it, I took my guitar downtown and hocked it for ten dollars, which was a good price at that time. I never did get it back. Not that I missed it; there were all kinds of guitars in the regiment. I expect that the rest of the fellows in the platoon were just as happy I didn't have it, because the majority of them liked the modern swing music, Glenn Miller and his ilk, while I was a hillbilly and played hillbilly music. Sometimes I was growled at while I picked away at one of my favourite western riffs.

With the city on our doorsteps, we didn't lack for recreation. We were within blocks of the centre of town, so it was just like stepping out the front door to go to shows or pool halls. The drinkers would go into the beer parlours and have a few drinks. I hated the taste of beer at the time, so the beer parlours never interested me. If I were on my own, I might go down to Waterdale Flats and find the old gang that I hung around with before I joined up, but most of the time I went out with a friend. You could catch a streetcar and a half hour ride would get you to Borden Park, one of the main parks in Edmonton. We spent quite a bit of time at the park. It had a zoo and some rides, including a roller coaster, and seemed to be a good place to meet girls. Sometimes a buddy would have a girlfriend who had a girlfriend, and the four of us would go out to Borden Park together.

I went to the Edmonton Exhibition at Borden Park with a friend in the platoon who had come in from a country town to join up. A girlfriend of his had come to Edmonton to visit him, and she had brought a friend with her. I was asked to escort her so he could be with his girlfriend. I readily agreed, and the four of us were off to the Exhibition. My date was a pretty girl and I was attracted to her, so I was happy as we wandered around the fair. I was a little uncertain when two fellows in civvies came along and called her over and spoke with her, but she came back to me. Us fellows had money to spend, so we were patronizing the midway, trying to win prizes by breaking balloons with darts or to make our fortune at the Crown and Anchor, generally being relieved of our money at all the booths and games. Suddenly the girl I was with took me by the hand and led me around the back of a booth, pushed me up against it, and started kissing me. I'm chagrined to say that I'd had so little experience with girls that I went into shock. Instead of responding to her like any good, hairy chested soldier, I was embarrassed. I pushed her away and stepped out from behind the booth. Suddenly, the evening turned very cool. "What's the matter with you?" she asked. "Those other guys invited me to go to a party, but I said no, I had a boyfriend here."

She was quite offended. Of course, I didn't know what to say. When I thought about it later, I realized she was probably quite a good time girl, and I must have embarrassed her by pushing her away. By the time we went home on the streetcar I'd woken up to the fact that maybe she did like me and I'd better respond, but when I went to sit next to her, she made sure that there was plenty of space between us and that I knew she was a woman scorned. I kicked myself for days afterwards; my one big chance, and I blew it!

One wartime institution that deserves mentioning is the hostess houses and canteens set up by various church organizations and women's clubs. They would be held in a church hall or basement or a room in the YMCA. Some put on dances once a week or so, but most of them just provided a place where a soldier who was away from home and didn't know anybody could go for tea or coffee and cookies or cake and have a friendly chat. The girls serving at the canteens, who were mostly the daughters of the organizers, would write a letter for you or do your mending, sewing on buttons and that sort of thing. There was usually a writing room and a library where you could sit and read. A lot of the fellows appreciated having a quiet place they could go to get away from barracks for a while, but I really don't think the hostess houses were valued as much they should have been for their efforts. They were pretty tame for the young fellows who wanted to have records playing and do some dancing after being out on parade all day.

Unless you had a pass, you had to be back in barracks by ten at night. The sentries had trouble recognizing us until we got our uniforms. We had no identification cards, so our army boots became our ticket through the gate. If you went out for the evening wearing ordinary shoes, you risked not being allowed back in. There were one or two fellows who took advantage of the situation and claimed that they were out all night because the sentry wouldn't let them in because they weren't wearing their boots. That ended when the sentries started checking that we had our boots on before we left.

As the summer wore on, the regiment was starting to shape up. When we went out on parade, we looked like soldiers instead of a raggle-tag bunch of misfits. We seemed to be pleasing our NCOs more often, because we weren't getting yelled at as much. Two months of intense "square bashing," as we called parade drill, had turned out a regiment that some said would have made a respectable guard for Buckingham Palace.

On August 15, 1940, we said farewell to Edmonton, and the regiment moved to Dundurn, Saskatchewan, for our field training. The people who had automobiles drove them down, but the bulk of the regiment was loaded on the train to Saskatoon, and then onto the branch line from Saskatoon to the hamlet of Dundurn. It was the rectum of the world. No city streets there; all there was in Dundurn, Saskatchewan, was a store of some sort and two or three shacky looking houses. I don't think you could even have called it a village. Gone, gone were the streetcars, the hostess houses, the movies, the cafés. Saskatoon, the closest civilization as far as we were concerned, was thirty-five miles away.

(Below) The South Alberta Regiment, wearing sun helmets, formed on parade for inspection by the Commanding Officer. Regimental Sergeant Major Chris Seal, in wedge cap, stands in front at the centre. The pouches on our chests were supposed to contain ammunition, but as we had none, we used them for carrying food, cigarettes or anything else we wanted with us. By this time, our once-khaki pants had been bleached nearly white by repeated washings and the Saskatchewan sun.

Dundurn camp. Marching at ease in column of route. "Marching at ease" meant that while we had to stay in step and in formation, we were allowed to talk and to relax our posture and movements.

Shaving parade at 0545, Dundurn Camp. In the centre of this group is a small fire heating a tobacco can full of water. All in this group shaved using the one can of water. Water was severely rationed.

Sergeant Alexander MacAskill at the ablutions table. The difference in skin colour between his face and his torso reflects the hours spent in the sun on the Dundurn sand hills. The wide leather belt he is wearing was not standard issue, but could be purchased at the dry canteen. As our pants had wide belt loops, that style of belt caught on and most of us bought them.

Private Galipeau at Dundurn, wearing the papier mâché pith helmet and smiling because no one has managed to bash it in – yet. No Peewee was allowed to wear an undamaged helmet for long.

Company cooks and kitchen facilities at Dundurn. The men wearing aprons or white hats are cooks. The others are on fatigue duty: peeling potatoes, washing dishes, serving meals, cutting wood for the cookstoves.

Meal parade at Dundurn. The hungry soldiers lined up on the right are carrying their square mess tins, one for the main course and another for dessert. Dessert might be rice pudding, custard or apple pie, baked in a large, square pan. Due to the water shortage, mess tins were scrubbed out with sand in the drainage ditch. The food was very plain; wholesome, I guess, but not delicious. The orderly officer, second from the left, waited to receive complaints and got quite a few about the food, but nothing much ever changed.

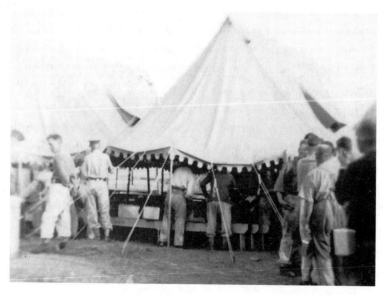

Some of 10 Platoon relaxing by the fire in the drainage ditch. Many fires were lit in the cool Dundurn evening to heat water for laundry and bathing.

Dundurn Military Camp, a few miles out, was built on an old dump. There was very little water, and what there was you couldn't drink. We slept in marquee tents, thirty men to a tent, and used four- and six-holer outdoor latrines. There was no hot water at all. You cleaned up at long benches out in the open with one cold water tap at the end. You filled a basin of cold water when you wanted to wash your face and hands. If you wanted to shave in hot water, you built a little fire of twigs and sticks in the big drainage ditch that ran around the outside of the camp and heated water in a can on top of the fire. It was quite common to see ten men shaving in a tobacco can of water, then running up to the cold water tap to rinse their faces. Every couple of days you went in groups to the showers. Because of the water shortage, you had two minutes: one to soap, another to rinse off, and that was it, get out and let the next guy in. An NCO stood there and timed you. Everything was sand and dust. We lived with sand day and night, sand in our clothes, sand in our food. In the morning we would shake all the dust out of our blankets and make up our beds nice and neat for the day. When we came back at night, the beds were all covered with dust again.

If you drank too much of the water, you ended up with the trots. I developed such a bad case I was put in the hospital tent for two days, where I learned a very valuable lesson. When I was admitted, I remember the Medical Officer telling the orderly that I was to get milk and toast for breakfast. When breakfast time came, I was served the usual mucky porridge which, with my stomach the way it was, I didn't feel like eating. Everybody else had been complaining about the food, too, so when the Orderly Officer came around, which he did at every meal time, and asked whether there were any complaints, I spoke up. I said, "Yes, Sir. When I was admitted I was told I was supposed to get milk and toast for breakfast."

He said, "Oh?"

I went on, "The food isn't very good anyway. The breakfasts are terrible."

He asked whether anyone else had any complaints, and there wasn't a soul spoke up. "No, Sir, everything's fine, Sir." That was when I learned not to be the spokesman for anyone. They'll be brave as hell until the time comes to speak up, and then they'll leave you hanging. From then on I made damn sure it was somebody else who opened their trap.

Dundurn Camp was where we began to get some training in field tactics. Because it was so hot and dry, we were issued with a sun helmet. The British army in India wore a proper pith helmet made out of heavy cork. We had much the same thing, only it was made out of papier mâché. You could always tell a Peewee, because where everybody else's sun helmets were in very fine shape, the ones the Peewees wore were kind of battered. It was a Peewee's joy and delight to beat up another Peewee's sun helmet and then watch the victim squirm while he tried to explain to the sergeant and the sergeant major and everybody else what had happened to it. Nobody ever beat up mine. I just stomped on it myself, because I knew my day was coming.

I don't know the size of Dundurn Camp, but it covered square miles of

Most of a section of Peewees. From left, back row: J.C. Smith, John Galipeau, unidentified, Abie Polsky, Sammy Marshall. Front row: O.J. Sequin, Ed Bradbury, Bill Morris.

The Peewees, waiting to be addressed by the colonel. The blond corporal in front is Ray Smith, who became a lieutenant and was killed by a sniper in the battle for the Leopold Canal in Belgium, which took place in 1944.

wild, open prairie with sand hills, scrub poplar trees and lots of cactus. We subsisted a great deal on cactus berries. The cactus blossomed in the fall, and produced a fruit that was good to eat and contained a lot of moisture. The regiment acquired a single truck that carried our noon rations out to where we were training. Our lunch was very skimpy, so far as I can recall. We would be given a couple of slices of bread, maybe an apple, some cheese, and a mug of tea, and that would be it, after marching three or four miles out and then spending the morning training.

It was here that we began to do field craft. We worked in platoons or sections and learned how to make use of the shape and slope of the ground to hide from the enemy, to get into the low areas and conceal ourselves behind shrubs. We learned how to judge distances and to follow directions to sight on a target. We started to learn something about compass and map reading. Working in small groups, we were taught how to make up the offensive and defensive formations that would be used in battle. Each section was under the direction of a corporal, who would have been told by the sergeant or the officer what his group was to do. Attack formations might have a couple of sections combining to form an arrowhead, or four manoeuvring to make a box. We practised how to form up quickly and move together in a coordinated fashion, or how to set up a defensive or holding position.

As well as the field craft, we were doing plenty of marches and runs to get us in condition. One exercise that really tested our mettle we were sure must have been dreamed up by a demented sergeant major. The whole regiment would be formed up in a single line across the landscape, stretching about a mile. We would march straight ahead for a while, and then we would be told, "Right wheel." That meant that the whole regiment pivoted on the position at the extreme right, until the line was marching at 90° or 180° or whatever the demented sergeant major decreed to the previous line of march. The people on the inside flank would be barely moving, while those on the outside flank were going as hard as they could go. By the time we left Dundurn, the regiment was in better physical condition than we had ever been before or, I think, ever were again.

Recreation at Dundurn Camp was limited. There was a wet canteen, but, of course, it was off limits to those of us who were under twenty-one. The army wasn't feeding beer to under-age people. Not that I really wanted to drink. I could never understand a guy sitting in the bar on a hot day guzzling that horrible, bitter stuff. The dry canteen had a little store where you bought incidentals; soap, toiletries, razor blades, chocolate bars, pop, writing paper, pens and pencils. You could go to the dry canteen to get out of the sand and wind and play ping pong, darts, card games, write letters. I was very poor at keeping in touch and only wrote home a couple of times, but I got letters from my sister and the occasional parcel with homemade cookies, which were always welcome.

The only respite we had from camp life was the occasional weekend pass into Saskatoon. We would catch the rickety old bus and clatter our way to town. The drinkers would head to the bars and whoop it up, but the majority of bars wouldn't risk losing their licences by serving underage soldiers, so the rest of us would go sightseeing, not that there were many sights to see. Besides, our minds were on other things than museums and libraries. We wanted to have a little feminine companionship, and so we paraded the streets looking for girls. In those days the girls seemed to accept the fact that if they were out on the street, guys were

"B" Company waiting for the train that will take us to the west coast, late
September 1940.

going to be trying to pick them up. If they weren't interested, a "Get lost,"
or completely ignoring the fellow, would suffice; nobody got pushy. If you
found a girl who was willing to talk to you while you walked alongside,
you were doing all right.

I only went into Saskatoon a couple of times. Once I went in with J.C.
Smith, and we did meet two girls, whom we took to the show and then
walked home. J.C. was obviously much more experienced with girls than
I was. He figured that the one I was with was available, but I didn't make
the right moves. For many a day following, every time the subject of girls
came up, J.C. went on at length about how Galipeau had had a girl who
was ready, willing and able, and he didn't do anything about it. My view
of the circumstances was quite a bit different from his. As I recall, it was
raining and wet. We were out in a grassy field someplace on the edge of
the city close to the girl's house and she wasn't feeling very well, so she lay
down under a tree until she felt better.

Life went on in Dundurn until the end of September. Then the good
word came: "You are moving, gentlemen. You're going to the west coast."

CHAPTER 4

From Sand and Cactus to Eden

A troop train took us from Dundurn to Calgary or Edmonton, depending on where our families lived, for a forty-eight-hour leave before we again got on the train, this time bound for Nanaimo, B.C. Our sergeant, then a man named Gordon Campbell, acquired a nickname on the trip out west. One of newspaper comic strips of the time had a recurring joke where somebody would be told, "You look like Maggie." As we were pulling away from a stop in a town along the way, Sergeant Campbell was standing in the half door of the train looking out. As the train went by, a couple of young fellows standing on the platform yelled out, "Hey, you look just like Maggie!"

Of course, from then on we called him Maggie Campbell, and the nickname spread throughout the company. Gordon Campbell was a well-liked sergeant, and accepted the name with good humour – but only off duty. On duty, an NCO was to be addressed only by his rank, e.g., Corporal or Sergeant, and sergeants major and officers were addressed only as Sir.

We left the train in Vancouver and boarded one of the CPR's *Princess* boats, which served as ferries at that time, and on September 30, 1940, we sailed into Nanaimo. We must have looked a pretty rugged bunch, suntanned and fit as hell, as we marched up through town in column of route. When we got near the camp we discovered the Duke of Connaught's Own Rifles, the British Columbia Regiment, lining both sides of the road as an honour guard to welcome us. The impression I had was that these fellows weren't too thrilled to see a regiment of prairie chickens marching into their town, invading their territory. "Prairie chicken" was a term we always felt was used with scorn to refer to the poor farm people and others who arrived in B.C. from the prairies with nothing but an old

47

The South Alberta Regiment marching to quarters in the Nanaimo Military Camp, September 1940. As we were on the coast and there was believed to be some danger of gas attacks by the Japanese, we were issued gas masks, which were carried in a large pouch on the chest. (Photo by Bob Forsythe, courtesy Ken Wright)

suitcase and the clothes on their backs. During the Depression many had moved to British Columbia, where at least they could grow vegetables and fruit and catch fish to eat, and B.C. had shipped food to the prairies for people who were down and out.

So far as we were concerned, Vancouver Island was a paradise. We'd never seen anything like it, and we were all taken with it. Even though the weather was wet and rainy during the winter, it was warm. There was an apple orchard just outside the camp and green grass all winter, in contrast to the burnt brown of the prairie.

Permanent quarters were supposed to have been ready for us, but they weren't, and once again we were housed in tents. For the first while we were in bell tents (a round tent that had been in service since before the First World War) with board floors. There were eight men to a tent, with the beds arranged like the spokes of a wheel. Since it was early fall, living in tents wasn't too bad. At least there was no shortage of water, hot or cold, and we didn't have to contend with sand in everything.

Our first job was building a parade square. Just outside the camp there was a huge slag heap left over from the old coal mine. We set up a production line: some people filling sandbags with cinders, some carrying the bags to the parade square area, others raking the cinders over the ground. The activity was reminiscent of an ant hill. The Duke of Connaught's were doing the same to build their own parade square in their part of the camp. Between us, over the course of about a week, we moved the whole slag heap. Anything that was left over we used to make paths between the tents, because the fall rains had started and the camp was a sea of mud.

Once the rains came, the bell tents were not the best accommodation. We had a terrible time getting ready for parade because everything was damp. As I recall, the officers and sergeants had wooden buildings for quarters. Our tents had one advantage over their quarters; although there was muck all around, the board floors of the tents stayed reasonably dry. It used to make us very happy when we heard about the water running a foot and a half deep through the officers' quarters during a heavy rain. Later on we moved into marquee tents with double bunks and stoves for heat, and we were able to get warm and dry. Construction was started on the permanent quarters after Christmas, and we moved into them for a short time just before we left in the spring.

Army food was never the greatest, but the food in Nanaimo was terrible. We complained and complained, but nothing happened until one night when we'd had enough and staged a riot. It began with one platoon, but spread like wildfire through the whole mess hall. We turned all the serving dishes upside down on the table, started throwing the food around and refused to leave until we were assured that improvements would be made. The food did finally get better.

Gunner Galipeau, Nanaimo. The Lewis .303 calibre machine gun shown here was a light, air-cooled machine gun with a rotating magazine, operated by the gas emitted during firing. It held 47 rounds, and had an effective range of 500 yards and a bullet velocity of 2,440 feet per second. The Lewis was taken out of service in 1941 and replaced by the Bren. When it worked, the Lewis was a good weapon, but it was subject to jamming.

The training we received was different from any we had ever had before. We began putting the skills we had been learning into a combat context. We did training exercises in a wide variety of settings: in the mountains, in the woods, around Nanaimo harbour. We attacked the town of Lantzville, captured the Nanaimo docks, marched ten or fifteen miles along backroads into the bush, did an exercise in tactics, marched back again. One group would establish a defensive position in a town, then the rest of us would attack and capture it. We did a lot of training around the Nanaimo waterfront, which was much less developed than it is today. We never seemed to disturb the residents; of course, the exercises were planned so as not to disrupt the town's activities.

Having drilled in the fixing of bayonets and practised our bayonet positions until we could do them in our sleep, we began the drill that would prepare us to use our weapons in combat. A gunny sack full of straw hung from a scaffold, another lay on the ground nearby. You would run up and thrust your bayonet through the upright dummy, then pull it out and pierce the one on the ground. This was real killer stuff, and again, we drilled until the procedure was automatic. There was a reason for this endless repetition. In those days, infantry both mounted and repelled bayonet attacks. When you were faced with an armed enemy, you didn't have time to think. You had to be able to react immediately and effectively, or you weren't going to survive.

Something that was unique to the South Alberta Regiment was that we made our bayonet charges in silence. From time immemorial, it had been the accepted practice that everybody would scream and yell at the top of their voices, in the hope of intimidating the enemy as they charged in toward their lines. Someone decided that in the SAR, bayonet charges would be silent. They felt that becoming aware of a line of men with bayonets fixed bearing down on them in silence out of the dawn mists would have a much greater psychological impact on the enemy than the screaming and yelling. To the best of my knowledge, we were the only regiment that adopted that practice.

As well as learning new uses for our bayonets, we were introduced to new weapons here and at subsequent camps in the coming years. We were impressed by the modern Bren machine gun, which replaced the Lewis gun. It could be either mounted on a vehicle or carried and fired from the hip. Each platoon was issued with one. We didn't fire it at first, but took extensive training on taking it apart, cleaning it and putting it back together. We drilled until we could strip and reassemble it in seconds. Since we had to be able to do this in the dark, we did a lot of our practice wearing blindfolds.

We were also introduced to the Boys Anti-Tank Rifle.* Had we realized it, the use of this weapon indicated just how unprepared Canada was for fighting a war. It was an oversized rifle of .55 calibre, with a bolt action the same as the standard issue Lee Enfield, but it weighed around thirty-six pounds. It was much too heavy to hold up to the shoulder, and could

---

* Donald E. Graves provided the following comments about the Boys Anti-Tank Rifle: The Boys ATR was a bolt-action rifle, .55 calibre, with a five-round magazine. It weighed 36 pounds and measured 5 feet, 4 inches in length. It would penetrate 24 mm of armour at 100 yards and 9 mm of armour at 500 yards. Effective range was 200 yards, maximum range was 500 yards. Fired prone with a bipod, supposed rate of fire was nine rounds per minute. It was absolutely useless for its intended purpose. However, the Long Range Desert Group used the Boys to great effect as an ambush weapon in North Africa against lightly-armoured and soft-skin vehicles.

only be fired from the prone position. It did have a bipod support, close to the muzzle end of the barrel, to hold it steady for aiming. Although we took some training on it, no one that I know of in our company actually fired a shot from it. Still, it provoked a great deal of discussion in the platoon, as to how much – or how little! – effect it would have against German tanks, and who would get stuck with carrying the horrible thing, let alone being placed in a position to fire at an enemy tank.

Three years later in our career, we were introduced to another bizarre weapon – though it would be more accurate to call it a plumber's nightmare. It was a British weapon called a PIAT, or Projector Infantry Anti-Tank. It served the same purpose as the American bazooka or the German *Panzerfaust*, both of which were essentially a tube, equipped with sights and a trigger, from which a rocket was fired; but this device was sort of a modern version of the crossbow. It consisted of a sheet metal tube with a heavy spring mounted in it. You put your feet on the ground on the butt end and pulled the handle up, and the spring would latch in place. Then you fitted a rocket-shaped projectile weighing two and a half pounds into the device, pointed it at the enemy tank and pulled the trigger. The compressed spring was then released, propelling the projectile towards its target. If you were close enough and accurate enough that the projectile hit the tank, it was quite effective, but it always bothered me that you had to be practically on top of the tank before you could use it, and arming it was a horror. As it appeared to me, the British and Canadian infantry fought tanks with a glorified popgun.

We got some training in unarmed combat, in which we were all interested. We learned how to disarm somebody who was attacking with a knife or a gun, how to throw an attacker, different holds to use to disable someone or take them prisoner. We were enthusiastic about the theoretical potential of these techniques, but I, for one, was skeptical about how useful they would be in practice. It was fine, I thought, that I knew how to take care of a guy's right arm with a gun in it, but what was he going to be doing with the arm on the other side? How effective were these techniques going to be for some Peewee if his opponent was a foot taller than he was? I could imagine myself hanging on the end of some big guy's arm, being flailed around with my feet off the ground. I guessed the training

Wakesiah Military Camp, Nanaimo, B.C., under construction in the spring of 1941, with the barracks for the South Alberta Regiment nearing completion.

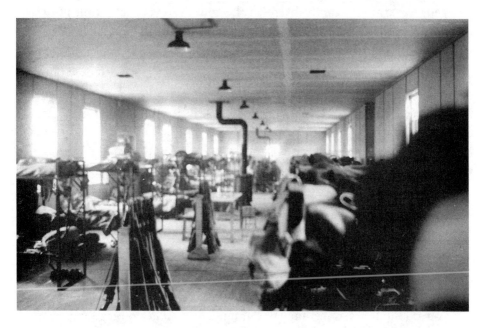

Interior of the new barracks. Three wood- or coal-burning stoves down the middle of the room provided heat, while double bunks lining the walls slept two 30-man platoons. I found the bunks fairly comfortable. The mattresses, stuffed with cotton waste, were certainly an improvement on the straw-filled sacks I'd slept on at logging camps. The racks in the centre held the rifles of a section ready for use, cleaning, or inspection by the company commander. From a winter in tents to this luxury on 31 March 1941.

A typical H hut, Nanaimo barracks. H huts were named for their shape. The two long sections at either end where the men slept were joined at the centre by a section containing showers, toilets, laundry facilities and coal for the stoves.

would help in a pinch, and it was better than not knowing what to do, but I had my reservations.

The one exercise that I did think was effective, and that stayed with me, was disarming somebody who was coming at you with a rifle. You used your left arm to push the barrel of the gun off to your left, while at the same time you grabbed the butt with your right hand, just behind the trigger guard, and pulled to your right. You then continued the motion to bring the butt up and smash it in your attacker's face. We practised both attacking and defending positions, and I was struck by how little control you had over your rifle when somebody employed this technique against you, even when you knew what was going to happen.

Another novelty was the gas mask. We practised putting it on in seconds as a rattle marked off the time. Each of us spent time in the gas chamber, which was a sealed building into which gas could be introduced in a controlled fashion. To demonstrate to us how effective and important the gas mask was in protecting us during a gas attack, the instructor would have us enter the chamber, wearing the mask, in an atmosphere containing tear gas, sometimes mixed with another gas called D & M which would cause mild itching and vomiting. The instructor would run you around the chamber for a few minutes to elicit heavy breathing, then have you take your mask off. No one loved that; as soon as the mask came off, stinging, horrible gas would hit your eyes. Then you would have to put the mask back on. Once the mask was replaced you couldn't remove it again, and occasionally – it never happened to me – a man would vomit in the mask. He would have to deal with it; if you took your mask off during a real attack, it could be the end of you.

A section of Peewees ready for a trip through the gas chamber. Wearing a gas mask was a much-disliked experience. The tight rubber face mask smelled of disinfectant and restricted vision, while the eyepieces were constantly fogging up. Once a week, we would be required to carry our gas masks in the big pouch on our chest all day. We had to put the masks on immediately at the sounding of a gas attack alarm and wear them for an hour as we carried out our duties.

The new guard, Nanaimo. Left to right, back row: Privates A. O'Neil, S. Marshall, J. Galipeau, unidentified. Front row: Sergeant Gordon Campbell, unidentified private, Private P. Marcotte, Private H. Wolgien, Private R. Gillies, Corporal I. MacIntyre. Private Gillies does not wear webbing and ammunition pouches, nor does he carry a rifle. As he was judged the neatest dresser, he was appointed regimental runner and relieved of sentry duty so that he could carry messages between regimental and company headquarters.

"B" Company taking a rest break during a 12-mile route march. The Peewees are in the foreground. We marched for 50 minutes and rested for 10 minutes. Nanaimo, 1941.

Tramping over the mountains and through the forests around Nanaimo kept us in shape, but there was also the assault course. This was an obstacle course with ropes to climb, barricades and fences to get over, pools of water to swing across, all as fast as you could go. Ours was not a very severe course, but it got us working. We were in pretty good physical condition. It wasn't very long before some of our more scrappy fellows were tangling with the lumberjacks in the bars downtown, and I guess many a lumberjack got quite a surprise.

The nightlife was great. We were within walking distance of town, where we found all kinds of pretty girls, a friendly population, and nice, warm bars and pool halls. The Eagles Club was lenient as to who they let in, and they served a good hot rum. It was wet and soggy in the tents up on the hill, and quite a few of us, including some, like me, who were underage, liked to go to town, see a show, and have a hot rum at the Eagles Club before we returned to the base. I never got drunk, but a couple of times I had maybe one or two too many.

Some of the fellows enjoyed dancing, but I didn't frequent the dance halls much. I would sometimes go to just sit and watch. Out in the backwoods we had danced to old-time music played on fiddle and guitar. I didn't know how to do the modern jive, and I was too ashamed to ask anybody to get up and dance my old-fashioned way.

Our beautiful infantry boots, which were about all we had to wear, presented a problem for the dance halls. Now, an infantry boot is a wondrous device when used for the purpose for which it was intended. It is a well made work boot, with sole and heel as thick as three quarters of an inch to stand up to long marches over any kind of terrain. We called them gravel crushers. They were fitted with hobnails, which were fine on grass and gravel roads, and even on asphalt, but they would ruin a dance floor. Consequently, every dance hall in town stationed a fellow inside the door with a pair of pincers. You paid your admission, then lifted your foot up so your hobnails could be removed. A lot of us took off the hobnails even if we didn't dance. Nanaimo's streets were steep, and the sidewalks were tiled. Walking on those tiles with hobnails was almost like being on rollerskates.

There were plenty of places to go and things to do. The colonel's wife organized some of the other wives who had come out from Alberta to join their husbands and started a little hostess house where we could go to write letters and have a cup of coffee, just to get away from the barracks. I think the older, married men frequented it, but there wasn't much going on there to attract the younger fellows. Some went bowling, a lot of us went skating. There was an arena, and while very few people in Nanaimo could skate, we prairie chickens were in our element. I understand that the first Nanaimo Clippers hockey team was formed from some young men from the South Alberta Regiment; we had two fellows who had played with the National Hockey League. The citizens of Nanaimo were very hospitable. Although most association was with the young women of the town, many of the fellows became acquainted with other young men in the town and became part of their group. They would meet their civilian friends downtown or in the pool hall or be welcomed into their family homes.

Unless you had a late pass, you were due back in barracks by ten o'clock. If you stayed out over time you couldn't go in through the front gate. You had to sneak in by walking up the road along the camp boundary and working your way through the three-wire fence into the tent area. There was a drainage ditch that ran along the perimeter of the fence around the camp, and there was many a time a fellow, myself included, suddenly found himself in the ditch up to his knees in muddy water as he tried to creep back into camp. On parade the next morning, you could usually spot the fellows who had been out late by the dampness of their lower pant legs.

Sunday morning there was church parade, which was compulsory unless you had a bona fide reason not to attend. Someone who could establish he was Jewish, for example, would be excused, but everybody else went. Services were conducted on the base by the padres for Catholics and Protestants. All who professed to be Christian, no matter what denomination other than Catholic, attended the Protestant parade. Two or three of our Catholic fellows preferred to go to Mass at a church downtown. We soon found out why. The Catholic church served bacon and eggs every Sunday morning after Mass. Next church parade, everybody had mysteriously become Roman Catholic. You've never seen so many people who had never been to church in their lives before they joined the army who suddenly decided to take up Catholicism. I was fortunate, because I'd been raised Roman Catholic and could justify my attendance at the church, but somebody did a quick check, and the number of Catholics shrank back to normal as suddenly as it had expanded.

The Peewees were in fine form in Nanaimo, up to the usual shenanigans with some new ones added. Certain members of the platoon contrived a new torment we called baptizing. Sunday afternoon, when we were sitting around in barracks doing nothing and getting bored, two or three of the fellows would get hold of some poor unfortunate, hold him down, face up, and pour water from the spout of a watering can over his face. I have no idea how a flower garden watering can came to be in an army barracks. The poor fellow wouldn't be able to breathe because of the water pouring over his face. So far as I was concerned, being baptized was worse than being blackballed.

Harassment was a common occurrence if you bunked with the Peewees. You might come in quietly late at night, trying to be a good guy and not wake anybody up, and all of sudden you would be on your knees on the floor seeing stars. Somebody in a top bunk had heard you coming and had taken his heavy army pillow, which was a sack stuffed with cotton waste and as hard as rock, and, waiting until just as you went by, brought it down as hard as he could with a clunk on top of your head. If it wasn't a pillow, it was a pail of water dumped on you as you came in. You should have known what you'd find when you finally made it to your bed, but you usually forgot and crawled in, only to discover that it had been short-sheeted. Then there were the guys who came in half cut after a night on the town and decided that if they were up, everybody else should be, too. They would go around to each bunk, shaking the occupant's arm and asking the poor guy if he needed to pee. Sometimes a bit of a skirmish would result, but it never became violent.

Sometimes Joe, the Indian, would have been into the booze when he came in from a midnight pass. He would be in a hostile mood, and would roam around in the dark until suddenly he would "go Indian," as we called it. He would start hunting for his bayonet, challenging guys to a fight, beating on the walls. Usually it would take four of us to get him into bed and hold him there until he settled down.

After we moved to Nanaimo some fellows transferred to other regiments, including my good buddy Sammy Marshall. They were replaced by new reinforcements who came to the SAR. I often wondered what these new guys thought they had come into their first few days with the Peewees, but it didn't seem to take long before they fit in. The poor corporals who had to deal with this crew had their work cut out for them.

There were a few of us fellows who used to go downtown together and we got to know some of the Nanaimo girls that frequented the same night spots we did, but I didn't have a girlfriend. One night I decided to go on my own to see *Northwest Mounted Police* at the movie theatre. I stood in line behind two young ladies who were chatting away, and I decided that here was a chance to see if I could make a pickup. I spoke to them, and they responded in a friendly enough manner and went on with their conversation. I followed them upstairs to the balcony, sat down behind them, and listened in on their discussion while we waited for the show to start. When I heard them talking about going skating the next day, I decided that I would go skating, too.

I showed up at the arena and skated around and around, watching until I spotted the pretty, blue-eyed girl who had been sitting in front of me at the show. I asked her to skate, and she agreed. Then, when it was time to go, I asked if I could walk her home. She was reluctant, but I assured her that I was the only trustworthy soldier in the whole Canadian army, and that she should have a fine fellow like me along to protect her from all the bad guys in the regiment. She finally gave in to my persistence and let me walk her home. The girl's name was Ivy Davies. She had been born in Wales, but had come to Canada with her family when she was about four and was now living with her married sister Flo in

Nanaimo. We started to see one another quite regularly after that, and before I knew it, I found I was falling in love.

Our first furlough was at Christmas, two weeks with an extra five days' Christmas leave, and I went home to Edmonton. I found myself in a dilemma. In those days, people used to have such a terrible time with my last name, Galipeau, that I often introduced myself as John Nelson, Nelson being one of my middle names; and that was how Ivy knew me. I knew she wanted to write to me in Edmonton, so when I got home I had to send her a letter telling her my real name, explaining why I'd deceived her, and asking her forgiveness. When Christmas leave was over I went back to Nanaimo not knowing how she had taken my confession. I don't recall what she said when I went down to see her at the hotel where she was working, but I managed to talk her into seeing me again.

It was shortly afterwards that I asked her to marry me. Before she would agree, she insisted that I write to her parents, who loved in Armstrong, B.C., and get their permission. I wrote what I hoped was a very appealing letter, making myself out to be a fine, fine fellow, which I was, telling them about the work I'd done and the places I'd been, assuring them I would look after their daughter when I came back from the war. I must have been convincing, because they gave their permission. Then I wrote and told my parents, who sent very nice letters to Ivy, saying how happy they were.

I also had to go through the process of applying for approval from the company commander, Major Wright. The monthly allowance soldiers' wives received from the Department of Defence was attractive, and there were quite a few instances where a girl would marry and send her husband off to war, only to marry another innocent young serviceman a month later. She would end up drawing two or three allowances under different names and different regimental numbers. Chances were good that not all her husbands would survive the war anyway, and if they did, she would deal with the situation when the time came. For this reason, when a military man applied for permission to marry, the fiancée had to be screened and approved. Ivy had to get letters attesting to her good character from two ministers. Of course, there was no problem, and we were given permission to marry.

Because the fate of the regiment was up in the air, we didn't set a date right away. We picked out a wedding ring, and I drew a new uniform from the quartermaster stores and put it away for the wedding. Then the regiment was sent down to Heal's Range near Victoria for target shooting and other training that would give us our qualifications on the rifle range. I don't remember, but I think we must have fired the new Bren light machine gun for the first time at Heal's Range.

While we were there, the Peewees got fed up with a fellow I'll call Pigpen. He was just plain dirty. He never, ever seemed to shower or wash properly. Even amongst a bunch of young fellows it was noticeable, and it irritated us. He could get away with it at Dundurn, where there was a water shortage and we all skimped on showers and washing, but when we got to Nanaimo where there was plenty of water, it got to us. More than once a bunch of us took him and threw him in the shower, clothes and all, and told him to wash up, but it didn't help. At Heal's Range there was an open sewer that ran along near the huts where we were quartered. In the hope that it would cure him, we took Pigpen one day and threw him in the sewer.

While we were at Heal's Range the word came that the regiment would be moving on. I wrote to Ivy and told her that we should get married because I was leaving in a week or so. She and her sister Flo hurried to make the arrangements, and on May 7, 1941, we were married in the manse of the Nanaimo Baptist Church. I asked my corporal, MacIntyre, to be my best man, but I didn't invite any of the other Peewees. I think some of them were put out, but I knew they would go out of their way to embarrass me. Since Sammy Marshall left, I had not been so close to anyone else in the platoon that I would want them at my wedding. Besides, how would I decide who to ask? It would be more than Ivy's sister could afford to provide for all thirty fellows at the reception. The platoon went together on a nice gift for us and gave us their best wishes.

Four days later, May 11, the South Alberta Regiment marched from the barracks down through town to the harbour. Our hearts swelled when we saw that the people of Nanaimo had lined both sides of the streets along our route to say goodbye to the regiment they had adopted as their own. There were not a few of us who had married Nanaimo girls, and so many fellows who had made good friends in the town. It felt like we were leaving home, and our families had come out to see us off.

(Below) Private J.A. Galipeau dressed for parade and inspection. I'm carrying a Lee Enfield .303 rifle, a weapon of British design and origin that, at this time, was being manufactured in Canada. My gas mask pouch is hanging on the front of my chest, while ammunition pouches are attached to the webbing shoulder straps.

My wedding day! May 7, 1941. Decked out in a fresh haircut and a new uniform, I was feeling excited, and happy that Ivy had finally agreed to be my bride. I think Ivy was wearing a blue dress, but her lovely blue eyes were all I could see. If it was raining, we didn't notice.

Noon break during exercises. Left to right: J. Galipeau, E.N. McDonald, R. Wear, H. McCleary, F. Moan, F. Sundstrom. We are wearing the usual dress for training and fatigues. Winters on Vancouver Island were mild, but cool enough to require the issue of cardigans made of khaki wool. Frankie Moan was killed in action in Holland in 1944.

CHAPTER 5

Land of Tourists and Canals

We marched onto one of the *Princess* ships and set sail for Vancouver. I felt so sad and low about leaving my beloved that I found a lifeboat, crept in under the cover and settled down by myself until we started to dock, when I climbed out again and went to find the platoon. They had been searching the boat for me. "Where've you been?" they said. "We thought you'd jumped overboard and tried to swim back to Nanaimo!"

We had a two day stopover in Edmonton to visit family, then got back on the train headed east for Niagara Falls. There we were to join two other regiments from Ontario, the Lincoln and Wellands and the Argyll and Sutherland Highlanders, to form a brigade. The three regiments were to rotate guard duty on the network of power plants and canals throughout the area between Lake Erie and Lake Ontario near Niagara Falls. One regiment would be training at Niagara-on-the-Lake while the other two were assigned to guard duty in different areas. Our job was to protect the canals and power plants from sabotage and infiltration by subversive elements. It was known that German saboteurs were moving into the country, and so from coast to coast, every railroad bridge, every power station, every portion of the vital transportation, communication and power systems that was vulnerable to sabotage was guarded. In the Niagara Falls area we were taking over from the Veteran's Guard, whose members were First World War veterans.

Niagara-on-the-Lake was predominantly a tourist town, about fifteen miles from the city of Niagara Falls, at the mouth of the Niagara River where it entered Lake Ontario. The town was very small, and there wasn't much there: a theatre and a few gift shops, but hardly anything in the way of entertainment. We were quartered in a military base camp large

enough for a regiment within walking distance of town. We had been sorry
to leave Nanaimo, but we were happy to be in a new situation where we
could expect new experiences. However, compared with our arrival on the
west coast, our arrival here was not very pleasant. It was hot and humid at
Niagara-on-the-Lake, and we were still wearing our heavy serge uniforms.

It wasn't long before we were issued with shorts and puttees, along
with a summer tunic that had brass buttons that required polishing down
the front rather than the plain front of the serge battle uniform tunic that
we usually wore. The new summer tunic was cotton cloth. Referred to as
"walking out dress," it was worn when going out of camp, or when full
uniform was ordered, such as for guard duty, regimental parades, company inspections or as specified by the Orders of the Day. On duty, the
normal dress was shorts, puttees and a cotton shirt
with the sleeves neatly folded to above the elbows. The
shorts were a source of great amusement to the American tourists; I remember overhearing one American
woman making a comment about grown men wearing
short pants. We still had our wedge caps, though we
wore our famous sun helmets with our fatigue dress
for training or guard duty on the canals and power
plants.

Puttees were a new challenge for us. They were a
length of woollen cloth about four feet long and three
inches wide, with a three-quarter-inch-wide tape
about two feet long at one end. You put your boots and socks on, then you
started at the top of the boot and wound the puttee around your leg in a
spiral to the top of the calf, where you wound the tape around a number
of times, tucked the end into the top of the last round of tape, and tight-
ened it as snug as you could. This held the tape and puttee in place. The
puttee was a standard item of dress used by the British army in the Middle East and other areas where shorts were worn.

It was not easy to wind the puttees so they came out looking right.
They were supposed to be wound evenly, each revolution overlapping the
previous one by half the width of the cloth. If you were really proficient,
you would cross the bandage at the front of the leg at each turn so you

ended up with a herringbone pattern. For some, mastering the puttee was almost impossible. We saw some very strange variations early on with puttees wrapped in different directions or with extremely uneven overlaps. I think there were some people who never really did get to the point where their puttees satisfied the sergeant.

We had one fellow who had an accent that made me think he was from central Europe. I don't know whether it was because he was cold, or whether he was modest and didn't want to show his knees, but he persisted in wearing his long underwear and winding his puttees over top. I suppose it was possible he was allergic to the melton wool of the puttees and it was irritating the skin of his legs. It was funny to the rest of us when he showed up like this on parade, but the platoon sergeant would not be happy about it, and this fellow would be sent back to take his long johns off.

For the first while, before we were sent out on guard duty, we spent our time parade square bashing and doing a bit of field craft. We were bored with the close order drill. It was the same old basic stuff we'd already done until we were perfect: right turn, left turn, marching back and forth on the parade square, and it was hot, terribly hot. One day we had been at it so long, and it was so hot, that as the afternoon wore on, we decided that enough was enough. We were at the peak of our training, and we couldn't see what we would gain by doing more. As we stood at ease, the word was passed right through the platoon, "Whatever the next order is, do not move."

The platoon officer, Lieutenant Tommy Barford, ignorant of the insurrection facing him, prepared to bring us to attention. He said, "Platoon," but we didn't straighten up. He said, "Attention!" but we didn't come to attention. He gave the order two or three times. We didn't move. He told Sergeant Jimmy Gove to take over. The sergeant gave the order. We didn't move. No matter what they did, we didn't move. We were standing in the sun, but we didn't care if we melted and collapsed in the heat; the Peewees had had enough, and they weren't going to budge. Eventually the platoon officer and sergeant gave up. I will recall to the end of my days the platoon standing at ease while Sergeant Gove stood under a tree and rubbed the end of a long stick back and forth on the ground and Lieutenant Barford slumped under the tree with his head down. Finally, quitting time came, and the sergeant marched us back to barracks and dismissed us.

I met Lieutenant Barford again overseas a few years later and asked him if he remembered the incident. "Oh, yes," he said. "That was one time I felt that I should resign my commission."

When we went on parade the next morning we had a new platoon officer, Lieutenant J.K. Smith, and a new sergeant, Howard J. Besson. Our previous officer was a small man, like we were, and he didn't have the presence, or the self confidence, that was necessary to impress a bunch of young guys. The new officer was a different type altogether. The first morning out somebody mumbled something when he gave an order. He was in the middle of the ranks right now, confronting this fellow nose-to-nose and saying, "What was that you had to say? You want to say something, come on out and tell me to my face." Then we got a lecture that gave us to understand that, so far as he was concerned, the kind of behaviour that had gone on the previous day would not be tolerated. If we tried to pull that kind of trick while he was in command, he and the sergeant would walk back to barracks, and we could stand there until next morning.

Sergeant Besson, too, impressed us. He was not a Peewee; he stood 6'2", weighed about 190 pounds, and wasn't going to put up with anything from us. We were not afraid of our new officer and sergeant, but we did have enough brains to realize that we'd better not mess with them. At the same time, I think the company officers realized that they had been pushing the close order drill too hard, and they eased up on the parade square bashing and gave us something less humdrum to occupy our time. We did more field craft and bayonet and unarmed combat drill. One part of being at Niagara-on-the-Lake that we found very interesting was our weapons training. Long Point Range, as I recall, was designed for anti-aircraft training, and we fired machine guns as anti-aircraft weapons for the first time. As I remember it, we fired from slit trenches so that the barrel of the machine gun was elevated. An airplane trailing a target some distance behind flew past the range as we fired on it. I felt the pilot of the airplane must be a very trusting type. There was no method of scoring hits; we were there to practice firing on a moving target.

The regiment also used another rifle range by the lakeshore. This one I remember for the pleasant duty it required one of us to perform. The targets were set up in a line parallel to the lake shore. Behind them was a high

Private Galipeau, in summer uniform, guarding a canal somewhere in the Niagara area, August 1941. American tourists laughed at seeing soldiers in short pants, but we didn't care – they were cool and comfortable. I had to answer to Company Sergeant Major Larry Blain for the damage to my pith helmet, which I had inflicted myself before any of my fellow Peewees could do it for me. Those are ammunition pouches on my belt, and the luxury accommodation behind is a bell tent.

(Right) Lance Corporal Galipeau with wife Ivy, Niagara Falls. You can see the lance corporal's single hook on my right arm. As I discovered, there was little advantage to having it.

(Left) Fooling around, Upper Decew Falls. I am threatening the photographer with a .303 calibre short magazine Lee Enfield Mark III service rifle fitted with an 18-inch bayonet.

Privates J.C. Smith and J. Galipeau sparring during time off from guard duty on the canals and power plants. I don't recognize the two onlookers on the far left, but the three in the background are (from left) Joe Sequin, John Bartlett and Frank Sundstrom.

mound of earth, called the Butts, to stop the bullets after they passed through the targets. For the safety of the public, one person was detailed to the shore behind the mound to keep the beach users away from the beach in that area. No one complained of this duty as most beach users knew to stay out of the danger area, so we could spend our time watching the girls browning in the sun farther up.

At the Long Point Range we were reintroduced to the Boys Anti-Tank Rifle, which we never did use. They didn't have the ammunition to let us fire this weapon, but to give us an idea of what it would be like, they had First World War Ross rifles that had never been cleaned, they told us, in their entire life. Each of us fired once, and that was enough. When you fired a regular rifle you got a jolt in the shoulder, but if you were holding the weapon properly, it didn't hurt. When you fired that dirty old Ross, you not only got a jolt – you were shoved back eight to ten inches.

Somebody in authority took a dislike to me at Niagara-on-the-Lake, or figured I was getting too smart for my own good, because I was promoted to lance corporal. At first, I was pleased as could be. This was it, I was on my way. Before long I would be General Galipeau, or at the very least I would have a regiment of my own. Those dreams of glory were quickly shattered. A lance corporal in the army, I discovered, is the worst rank in the world. If you're a buck private, you don't have to worry; you take your orders and do your job. If you're an NCO, you get your orders from up above and pass them on to the privates, and you have enough authority to get results. But a lance corporal has no friends among the privates, and he hasn't enough rank to give him any standing with the general NCOs. He's an in-betweener who is used by the corporal to do any dirty jobs the corporal doesn't want to do. The only advantage in being a lance corporal was a bit of a raise in pay, but it wasn't enough to make up for the hassle.

I recall once when we came in off the range after we had been out firing the rifles. Most of the time the 4 x 2, the piece of flannelette cloth issued by the quartermaster stores, was sufficient to clean the rifle, but if the rifles were used a great deal, there would be a buildup of metal in the barrel that required more drastic measures. The armourers used a small section of a material something like window screening, but much coarser. When it was pulled through the barrel, it would take out any heavy deposits. The screening would be issued as necessary, and then you were supposed to return it once you had cleaned your rifle.

Naturally, it fell to Lance Corporal Galipeau to try to collect the screening from the Peewees. And just as naturally, Lance Corporal Galipeau didn't have a lot of success. It was such a handy item that nobody wanted to turn it in. I went around the platoon asking for the screening, and got quite a variety of responses:

"Haven't got it."

"Lost it."

"You can't have it."

"Go to hell."

"Fuck off."'

"What the hell you want it for?"

"Give 'em a hook, and they think they own the goddamned army."

I went back to the corporal with the grand total of five pieces of screen from the whole platoon.

Such was the life of a lance corporal. He got no respect from above, and no respect from below. If your head started to swell when you got the promotion, it wasn't too long before you found yourself pleading with your buddies to do what you had been told to get them to do. A lot of men didn't want any sort of promotion. They were smarter than I was.

Military personnel are very democratic. The men will recognize those they feel are best suited to lead them and welcome their promotion. Anyone promoted by playing up to the superiors will find the men will not follow willingly. This was not the problem I experienced with my promotion; it was just that a one striper was in a sort of no man's land, neither private nor corporal.

The brigade received a number of Bren gun carriers, tracked vehicles on which Bren machine guns could be mounted, and a brigade carrier school was formed to train drivers for it. The two officers who were running the school, one from the South Alberta Regiment and the other from one of the other regiments, said that it would take a week before anybody would be able to drive one of these things with any proficiency, because it was set up backwards to what most people were used to. The engine and the transmission were behind the driver, so that gear shifting, which was done by means of a lever connected to a rod that went backwards to the transmission, was in reverse to the standard, familiar H pattern. Where low gear is usually in the upper left position, in a carrier it was at the bottom right.

We observed a regimental birthday party in July. The wet canteen was open, and there was quite a bit of celebrating. One of the buglers in the regimental band, well into his cups, wandered over to the compound where the Bren gun carriers were parked. Nobody had told him that he wouldn't be able to drive a carrier without two weeks' training, so he cranked one up, and away he went for a ride through the village of Niagara-on-the-Lake. He had a grand time roaring up and down the streets, taking out a couple of telephone poles and a street lamp before he ran into an oak tree.

When we were dispatched to guard duty, we left the base at Niagara-on-the-Lake and barracked either at an old glass factory in the Chippawa area, just outside the town of Niagara Falls, or in an old brick factory at Allanburg, near the town of Thorold, depending on our assignment. Each section of the platoon would spend nine days out on guard duty and then have three days' leave, so the barracks were only occupied by a third of the regiment at any given time. Even at that, the barracks in the old glass factory were quite a sight, because there was only the one, huge building, filled with a mass of double decker bunks. The brick factory was separated into smaller areas.

My company never was assigned to the Welland Canal, which would have been interesting because of the locks and the lift bridges where the big ships went through, but there were fifteen miles of Chippawa Canals to patrol, as well as the many little canals that carried water between the power stations, and the power stations themselves. When we were on canal duty we went out to one of the guard posts situated at intervals along the canals. Our quarters were a hut with five bunks, sleeping accommodation for half the men in the section. We had sentry duty around the clock, two hours on, four off, with the occasional eight hour break; so at any given time, some of the men would be on duty, some would be sleeping, and some would have time off. We were supplied with rations and did our own cooking. Usually somebody would volunteer to cook. The cook in our section was a Ukrainian lad who eventually ended up going to the kitchen and cooking full time. Nick used to roast chicken in a brown paper bag, old Ukrainian style. The first time he did it, we didn't know what to make of it: "What the hell you doing, Nick? Won't the bag burn?"

The bag didn't burn, and the chicken was especially good.

The area was rural, and there were little farms along the canals. When army rations became too dull and monotonous, one of our fellows would make a midnight raid on a chicken coop or turkey pen. I never went on one of these expeditions. I didn't have enough nerve, and I didn't know how I would explain it to Ivy if I came home with buckshot wounds. Our best chicken thieves told me that the thing to do was to carry a broom handle under your jacket, so it was nice and warm when you got to the chicken coop. You didn't cause a big commotion, you just slid the warm broom handle in amongst the chickens. A chicken would put both feet on this nice, warm roost, and you slowly withdrew the broom handle to within reach. Then you wrung the chicken's neck, and there was supper.

It didn't happen often that we took a chicken or turkey, but occasionally we would help ourselves. Somehow we didn't regard it as stealing. The army term is "scrounging," which means meeting a necessity by obtaining the required items. I feel guilty about it now; rationing was in effect, so the people we were depriving of their chickens were dealing with shortages of sugar and other supplies. Even at that, some would occasionally show up with a pie or a cake for the boys on the guard posts.

There wasn't a lot you could do during your off duty time, since you only had a few hours before you were back on the beat. You would sleep, read, play cards; sometimes we went swimming. We lost a fellow swimming at a place called Upper Decew Falls. There was a small canal with a dam that had a spillway at the far end through which the water went down into a valley to feed a small electrical plant. We used to swim in the water above the dam. One morning when I came off duty I decided I was going to go in for a swim. A fellow named Mullan said he would go with me. Then I decided against it and went to bed instead. I woke up about an hour later to learn that Mullan had gone too close to the spillway and had been sucked down into the gate and drowned. I couldn't help thinking that I was glad I had packed it in, or I could have gone down with him.

When you were on sentry duty you were outside any hour of the day, rain or shine, patrolling a quarter mile of canal with your rifle loaded and slung. We were warned not to shoot unless we were being attacked. There was a fence down the side of the canal, armed with electric eyes to detect anybody trying to get through. If the electric eye was triggered, searchlights would be switched on so you could locate the intruder. Sentry duty could

What we were guarding. The power house at Upper Decew Falls was one of many installations vital to war production.

get a little bit exciting at night, because almost anything would trigger the electric eye. A cat going through the fence would set it off, and even the fog could break the beam. On a foggy night, the damn things were lighting constantly. When the detectors triggered the lights they remained lit until switched off. By a quirk of fate, the switch would be at the far end of the sentry beat, which meant a quarter or half mile walk to turn the lights out.

There was one post the men told stories about. It had a house beside the canal where a young woman would undress at bedtime with the window of the room uncurtained and the lights on. My section never was detailed to that area.

It got pretty boring during the day, patrolling the same quarter mile of footpath for two hours at a time. Occasionally, to irritate the authorities and relieve the tedium, somebody would toss an old can into the water and left it drift down the canal. As it floated by the next guard post, there would be a great burst of gunfire. When the guard commander came rushing out to see what was going on, the sentry would claim that he thought he saw a mine in the canal. He knew perfectly well it was no mine. I believe there was the odd chimney in the area that got a bullet hole put through it as well. It was a good thing they never counted our ammunition.

Our platoon officer had a habit of checking to see how alert his men were. He would hide at the foot of a set of stairs or around a bend in the footpath, and then leap out with his pistol in hand as the sentry got near. He almost met an untimely end one night when he pulled his trick on a fellow by the name of Pete Winters. As he burst from his hiding place, he heard a rifle bolt go "*snick,*" then saw a bayonet coming at him. That stopped his foolishness.

You did have to keep your eyes open, not so much because of saboteurs and infiltrators, but because of possible encounters with headquarters staff. The sergeant major and the major would make unannounced tours of the footpaths to make sure we weren't shirking our duty. I had the pleasure of giving C.J. a little lesson in the dangers of shirking his duty when I went to relieve him outside a power plant building one night. He had gone into a glass telephone booth to get out of the rain and the cold and was hunched down on the floor sound asleep when I arrived. Putting my foot against the bottom of the glass door, I rapped loudly on the glass and said in my best NCO voice, "You're not supposed to be in there, Smith." He came to in a panic, grabbed his rifle, and went round and round in the booth about six times trying to find the door. He called me every name under the sun when I let him out.

There was one guard post located where a main road crossed a canal. This post was different from most because it had more buildings, providing offices, a kitchen and sleeping quarters for the company commander, company sergeant major and the staff of Company Headquarters. A separate building housed the platoon section on duty to guard and patrol that part of the canal. As a result, we performed our duties under the scrutiny of the Company Headquarters. A sentry box was located not far from the guard hut. One night Swede, who was on sentry duty at the lock, decided he was tired of standing in the sentry box – which he wasn't supposed to be in at all, of course – and looked around for something to sit on. He spotted a little fir tree, so he hacked it down with his bayonet, trimmed off the branches and jammed the trunk crossways into the sentry box to make a bar to sit on. When he was relieved after his two hours on duty, he threw the tree into the canal.

When the sergeant major came out on inspection first thing in the morning, he saw the stump of the little tree and the chips and branches from Swede's handiwork, and he very quickly figured out what had gone on. He found out that Swede had been on duty, and put him on charge for being in the sentry box and cutting down the tree without authorization.

I happened to be on kitchen fatigue near the guardhouse, and so could watch the goings-on. Flanked by an escort, Swede was marched in to the captain's office, which was in the guardhouse. The sergeant major explained the situation to Captain Lavoie and Swede stated his case, swearing up and down that he wouldn't think of cutting a tree, and in any case, there had been no tree to cut. In the meantime, every Peewee who wasn't on duty rushed out to where the tree had been. They dug up the stump and threw it into the canal, along with all the branches and chips, tamped the earth back down and covered it with the kind of debris you found on the ground in the area, smoothed everything over so the disturbed area blended in, and disappeared. The whole operation was done in about fifteen minutes. Shortly afterwards, a procession consisting of the accused, his escort, the company sergeant major and platoon officer left the Company Headquarters and proceeded to the scene of the alleged crime, where they halted. The sergeant major and the platoon officer walked up and down the path looking for the tree. They couldn't find it. They marched a little farther, turned around, came back. No tree.

Finally, the whole outfit made an about turn and marched back to the office. A short time later, out came Swede. In the absence of any evidence they couldn't convict him, and his case was dismissed.

Now, if I had any doubts that Captain Arnold Lavoie, who was second in command of the company at the time, knew exactly what had happened to Swede's tree, they were dispelled two years later in England where the regiment, now an armoured unit, was training in preparation for going over to Normandy. We had finished a scheme, or training exercise, and pulled into a country estate where there was a forest. During the war, many large landowners made parts of their estates available to the military, by order of the Crown under the War Measures Act. We were all busily cutting down trees and building fires when an order came through, practically from the King himself, that we were to cease immediately our vandalous activity. Further, we were going to have to pay £25 a tree out of regimental funds for those we had already destroyed. So what did Major Lavoie do? Exactly what the Peewees did, only on a larger scale. He got two or three tanks to hook big tow cables onto the remains of the trees and haul them off to where he'd had a bulldozer dig a big hole. All the trees, and all the evidence of their existence, went into the hole. Then dirt was pushed over them, and the whole squadron went out with tree branches and anything else they could find to smooth over the tank and bulldozer tracks and drag marks so you couldn't tell anything had ever happened.

A duty that I disliked immensely was policing. Each regiment had two or three regimental policemen whose duty it was to patrol the streets at night and see that no member of the regiment was behaving in an unsoldierly manner. Any who were would be collared, hauled back to camp and charged. The regimental police didn't deal with violations of civil law, the civil police looked after that, but they were on the lookout for behaviour unbecoming a soldier of the Canadian Army.

The rest of us would be detailed in rotation as company police in the various villages and towns near our barracks, places that the regimental police did not patrol. I never understood why they picked any of the Peewees for company police duty, because a fellow would have had to have been doing something way out of line before we would have arrested him. I found it the most deadly boring duty. I can recall twice going to a little village near the brick factory barracks near Allanburg. It was just a residential area, without as much as a coffee shop or a tea room, and very quiet. Nothing was moving. There were certainly no soldiers getting into trouble there, because there was nothing to attract soldiers.

I remember once I did police duty with a private from another platoon. We had never met before that evening, and we had nothing in common. We spent our four hours walking up and down the streets and sitting in a park making conversation about its statue and the fact that we were the only people there, feeling completely useless. It was even more boring than walking a beat on the canal at night.

When we weren't guarding canals, we were guarding power plants, which was usually a more interesting duty. The plants employed quite a number of civilian staff, many of whom were young women. They had to show their passes when they came through the gate, and there was a great effort among alert soldiers with good Canadian blood in their veins to try and catch sight of a girl's name and address or phone number from her pass. The girls weren't idiots, and there was many a smudged pass, or a strategically placed thumb, or a quick flash, or an offhand, "Come on, you know me!" as they went through the gate. It was the single guys, of course, who were most interested in the information, but if a married fellow had a chance to help a buddy out, he would be just as bad as anybody in his efforts to get the scoop on a girl that one of his good friends was especially attracted to.

I think the most popular post was the main power plant right at the brink of Niagara Falls. The other posts were isolated, but at the Falls there were tourists and townspeople walking by, and always something happening. When we were off duty we watched the visitors, or went for a ride on the *Maid of the Mist*, a boat that took passengers to the base of the Falls for a close look, or went down to the power plant below the Falls, where they let us in to see the generators and watch how the inflow water turned the turbines that drove them. At that time they had started to build a tunnel behind the Falls but work had stopped as soon as the war broke out and it was not open to the public. We used to climb along the river bank and enter the opening to the tunnel. Conditions inside were rough, with the wall and floor left just as they were after blasting, so it was a novel experience for us. The tunnel had large openings where you looked out at the water from behind as it fell. Today it is a tourist attraction with a nicely finished interior and elevators down to the tunnels.

The guards on duty at the main gate had an interesting time during the day. Sometimes vehicles carrying generals and dignitaries would come through, and you had to stop them and check their passes. On occasion, they would try to talk their way in without a pass. We weren't about to be fooled by any of that stuff. It didn't matter what kind of insignia you wore on your uniform, unless you had a pass from Regimental Headquarters, you didn't get through. Our guard at the main gate was very formal: two sentries out in front with fixed bayonets. We would stand for a certain length of time, then, on a quiet signal from one or the other, we would come to attention, slope our rifles, turn away from one another, march out so many paces, about turn, march back across to the other side passing one another in the middle, repeat the procedure until we decided we'd had enough, then come back to our positions, turn to face the front, order the rifles, stand at ease, and never move.

Sentries John Galipeau, left, and Ed Thorne on duty at the entrance to the power plant up-river from the falls. We are armed with Canadian-made British Lee Enfield rifles. Fixed on the rifles are 18-inch bayonets. The ammunition pouches on our shoulder straps contain five-round ammunition clips that can be loaded into the magazine of the rifle with the push of a thumb.

The American tourists loved it. They weren't at war, so our activities were a novelty to them, and they would stand and watch us by the hour. A group would wait for us to put on our show, and we would try to wait them out, remaining motionless until they left. They would shove one of their party in between us so they could take a picture, and we wouldn't say a word. One day a woman had a basket of plums and she was throwing them at us, trying to get us to move.

We younger fellows got a kick out of putting on the show for the tourists, and we became a bit possessive of main gate sentry duty. We would work the duty roster so that, as often as possible, two of us who felt the same way could work together, while the fellows who weren't quite as sharp had to stay inside handling the gate. At times they would moan about it, but we got our way fairly often.

Night duty was quite a different matter. After dark, it was a very lonely job. At two in the morning all the people were gone, the spray from the falls drifted over you, there was not even a cat walking by to break the monotony and ease your misery. We were not quite as sharp then. We were alert – you had to keep your eyes open – but occasionally we would find some place to sit down, or invent a way to while away the hours. I can remember many a night spent practising bayonet drill against a tree.

It wasn't until September that Ivy was able to join me. Before she arrived, I would spend my leave sightseeing in the Niagara region. I found the area very interesting, not just because Niagara Falls was one of the wonders of the world, but because that part of Canada had such an important place in the history of the country, particularly during the War of 1812. I hadn't paid much attention to history when I was in school, but I remembered enough to appreciate the significance of the locality. I went up to Queenston Heights and saw the big monument to General Brock and the plaques marking the sites of important battles, explored the remnants of an old fort at Niagara-on-the-Lake, and visited the grave of Laura Secord, who was buried at Niagara Falls. She had walked nineteen miles in the night through brush and swamp to warn the British outpost about a secret attack the American forces were planning. The British victory is credited to her efforts. I was interested to see the countryside in which these historic events had taken place. I also visited the museum where the barrels used by Red Hill, the fellow who was famous for going over Niagara Falls in them, were displayed, and saw my first four-lane highway, the Queen Elizabeth Way, which had just been built between Niagara Falls and Toronto.

Usually I had little money, so I had to look for recreation where I could entertain myself or be entertained at little or no cost. My financial distress was due to a great blunder I had made. I had gone to Niagara-on-the-Lake almost immediately after Ivy and I got married, and it never occurred to me until the first payday after I left Nanaimo that I might have had to make some kind of arrangements for Ivy. The army didn't let a man marry and then just leave his wife to make out the best she could. You had to sign over half your pay. I knew this, and expected it, but I had the notion that the paymaster would automatically look after the arrangements. What I didn't know was that I had to register our marriage, and they wouldn't send Ivy's allowance to her until I did. Since I hadn't done so, I was still drawing full pay. I had to write and ask her to send our marriage certificate so I could register, and then I had to repay the excess I had drawn, as well as the current month's draw, to pay up her allowance retroactive to the date of our marriage. As a result, there was a month's pay I did not receive. There was a rule that they couldn't give you less than five dollars a month, so that was what I got by on until I'd paid back what I owed. I felt so stupid that I never told any of my buddies what I'd done, and I never, ever told Ivy.

As a result, I was short of cash for a couple of months. I borrowed the odd dollar or two from the guys, and fortunately they were lenient with me and never needed their money back in a hurry, because I don't know how I would have repaid it.

One thing that helped was that I didn't have to worry about transportation costs. We hitchhiked everywhere. Hitchhiking was easy, because people appreciated that fact that we were soldiers serving our country. People were always buying drinks for us, and more than once we were eating in a restaurant and when it was time to pay our bill, the waitress would say, "That couple over there has taken care of it. They have a son overseas." So people were happy to give us a lift. We hitchhiked to Toronto a few times. One of our favourite places to go for a weekend was Fort Erie, where there was a big dance hall and amusement park by the lake. Even if you didn't have money for the rides, you could wander along the beach and watch everybody else have fun. If the weather was warm, you could even sleep on the beach and use the public washroom. Once I went down with a fellow by the name of Ed Bradbury, who was older than me and may have been bankrolling me a little bit. We were hanging around the amusement park when we were approached by an older gentleman who had a young woman about Bradbury's age with him. He introduced her as his daughter and said they were from Buffalo, New York, then explained that she wanted to go on the rides, but he didn't want to go with her. Then he said, "If I give her money to buy tickets, will you guys ride with her?"

That sounded fine to us, and off we went. We went on all the rides, which included what was billed as the greatest rollercoaster in the world. I guarantee you that once you rode it, nothing would scare you again. As the afternoon wore on, Bradbury and the young woman gravitated toward one another, which didn't bother me at all. As far as I was concerned, I was part of the deal, and it didn't worry me a bit if they sat in one car on the ferris wheel and I sat two behind, as long as my ride tickets were bought for me, along with the odd Coke and hot dog.

When it came near evening the father showed up again. He bought us dinner, then asked where we were staying. We hadn't made any plans, so he said, "I'll book you a room in the hotel."

This was great; we'd been at the amusement park all afternoon, we'd been fed, and now we had a place to sleep. Our good fortune continued the next morning, when an older couple at a nearby table picked up our breakfast check. We thanked them and made our way to the highway to thumb a ride back to the regiment. I amused myself on the way by telling Bradbury he had missed his chance to become rich by marrying the American's daughter. He hadn't even got her address!

C.J. was always off to Fort Erie to take in the sights and sounds of the amusement park. One time, however, he overstayed his leave and spent his trip back wondering how he was going to get out of being charged with being AWL (Absent Without Leave). He was hitchhiking, and the people who gave him a ride stopped along the way to pick up a young civilian. The kid seemed interested in what C.J. was telling him about military life, so C.J., being a good Peewee with a sharp mind, thought that if he could talk this young fellow into joining up and take him back with him, he would have an acceptable excuse for being late. He could say that he had been working so hard at recruiting the kid that he forgot when he was supposed to be back. He did talk young Reg Mavis into joining up, and he got away with it.

The kid was only sixteen, but he lied about his age and they put him in a uniform. C.J. was under-age himself, for that matter. For some reason or other Eddy Bradbury and I took Reg under our wing, befriending him so that he had someone who knew the ropes to lean on and learn from. He got his basic training with the Reinforcement Company before his mother finally spoiled his plans. He went home on leave proud as heck to be in uniform, and told his mother he couldn't get out. She wrote a letter to the colonel informing him that the boy was under-age and that he did not have permission to enlist, and she did get him out before we went overseas.

None of us heard from Reg again until he showed up at a regimental reunion in 1991 and came looking for me. He had joined the navy when he was old enough and was on a minesweeper sweeping the Normandy beaches on D-Day. He claimed that he represented the SAR on D-Day, because he went ashore with a landing party and was the only one who knew anything about infantry tactics, thanks to the couple of months he'd put in with us. He comes to all our reunions now.

The Canadian National Exhibition in Toronto that year featured the military in the opening parade and a special grandstand show. Each night after dark they staged a mock battle as part of the entertainment. It was quite a show. They had artillery guns, and set off a lot of fireworks and explosives. Each regiment in turn sent up a special platoon of nice, tall, impressive fellows to participate for a period of time. During the time the SAR was there, a couple of other Peewees and I hitchhiked to Toronto to take in the show and enjoy the Exhibition. We stayed at a barn that had been turned into a barracks for the military. The army billets were on the main floor, while the air force were in lofts that made up a second level. The open space between the two levels was fenced with wire mesh. There were a lot of stories about air force personnel getting drunk and bombing the army with beer bottles through the mesh.

What I particularly remember about the Exhibition was the Tommy Dorsey Orchestra playing for the dance. For the first time, I started to appreciate swing music. I also remember another incident where we were given a break. My buddy Butterworth and I were leaning on the fence watching the dodge-em cars when a well dressed gentleman walked up and asked us, "How's everything in the army, boys? Are you enjoying yourselves?"

We told him we were enjoying ourselves all right, but we had spent everything we had and were thinking of going back to the Falls. He gave us a ten dollar bill and a five dollar bill and told us to go and have a good time. He had a son overseas. We thanked him and, riding the rides and playing the midway games until the fifteen dollars was gone, wished the son overseas every good fortune in return for ours.

There was a lot of support from the people of Canada, and the United States. The First and Second Divisions were already overseas, so a lot of people had relatives who had left the country to fight. Others were of British extraction or had British kin and appreciated the Canadian Army's efforts to help. The States wasn't in the war, but most Americans supported what we were doing.

In September Ivy arrived and found work at the Metropolitan store in Niagara Falls. Then, of course, every time I was free I went home to her. Once I had just arrived home for my three days leave and we were walking down towards the Falls when a couple of fellows from the regiment came up and told me I was to report back immediately. I asked what was up, and they said that there was a strike at a power plant in one of the nearby cities. The authorities were afraid there were going to be riots, so the regiment was to go over and be ready to quell any insurrection. I told the fellows, "You didn't see me," and said to Ivy, "We're going home. I'm not giving up my three days, to hell with them. They can go and fight strikers if they want."

I was sorry afterwards that I hadn't gone, because it was something very different from our usual experience. The regiment went over in the Bren gun carriers in full battle gear, prepared to fix bayonets and quell a riot.

When the regiment came back, instead of waiting for leave to be up, they made an early change and went out on the guard posts. I arrived back at the barracks to find it empty except for a few headquarters people and the cooks and quartermasters. I found out where the company was and hitched a ride out with the ration truck. I reported in and was put on charge on three counts: AWL, failing to report for duty and breaking into barracks, which was a new one on me. My story, of course, was that I had gone home to my wife, and we had gone out and hadn't heard anything about any riots. We were at the larger post with the Company Headquarters, where there was a regular cook and kitchen, so the major gave me nine days kitchen fatigue. I spent my days peeling spuds and other vegetables and washing dishes and serving the CO's table, but once supper was served and the dishes were done, I had nothing else to do.

The guard post was by a lock gate where a highway road bridge and a smaller foot bridge crossed the canal. The sentries at the gate and by the canal were all Peewees. So after everything quieted down at night, I would take a walk across the foot bridge up to the gate where my buddy would be on duty, go out the gate and hike the two miles home. I would spend a couple of hours with Ivy, and then she would kick me out, much against my will. I hoofed back to the hut, arriving usually about midnight, and went to bed, ready to get up at five the next morning to help get breakfast ready. Between being short on sleep and doing a hell of a lot of walking, I got kind of tired, but I was home every night we were at that post. And nobody said a thing to betray my nightly sorties. Had I been caught, my punishment would have been most severe, but I had faith in the bond that united the Peewees.

Throughout our time at Niagara, rumours flew that we were going to be selected to go to Hong Kong. The Winnipeg Grenadiers had gone, and the scuttlebutt had it that we would be next. Of course, we were quite excited about going to such an exotic location, but the fates had it the other way, and thank heavens they did. I think we were well prepared as far as training went, but given the circumstances there, the best training in the world wouldn't have made any difference. Our move came at the end of November. On very short notice, we packed up and were off to Debert, Nova Scotia, a whole new area of the country, with new things to see and new things to do.

CHAPTER 6

Presenting "Fightin' Frank" Worthington

In December 1941, the SAR moved to the military camp at Debert, Nova Scotia, to join another brigade and eventually form the Fourth Division of the Canadian Army. The Lincoln and Welland Regiment and the Argyll and Sutherlands did not go with us. In late August 1941, the Argylls sailed for the West Indies and Jamaica, where they spent the next twenty-one months on garrison and guard duties. The Lincoln and Wellands performed arduous guard duties in Newfoundland from autumn 1941 to May 1943. Four units that would eventually form the Fourth Canadian Armoured Brigade were in Debert with the SAR. They were the Canadian Grenadier Guards, the Governor General's Foot Guards, the British Columbia Regiment and the Lake Superior Regiment (Motor).

Debert Camp was huge, with some 20,000 men, including many ancillary units such as military police (known as the provost corps), signals corps, dental corps, medical corps with nursing sisters, doctors and a field hospital, artillery, ordnance and service units, and many more that it would serve no purpose to list. Debert itself is a village with a couple of stores and a few houses, located outside the town of Truro. It's a sandy, pine-forested area, so we were back in the sand again, except we were in huts instead of tents, and we were heading into winter.

Truro itself, a half-hour bus ride from the camp, had nothing to offer most of the fellows. There was no doubt a theatre, but it was a dry town, so there were no beer parlours. On the weekends, the inhabitants of the largest military camp in Canada roamed the streets of Truro looking for some sort of amusement. I heard talk of some of the fellows heading for the black community outside town (which had been declared "out of bounds" to military personnel), where they could obtain a bit of bootleg booze.

I found myself in deep trouble with some of the platoon when we got to Debert. While we were in Nanaimo, a few of us had gone together to buy a radio for the barracks. It would go on first thing every morning, usually tuned to an American station that met with the favour of most of the fellows, and every morning, until I knew it by heart, I would waken to hear Kate Smith singing, "From the mountains, from the valleys, from the oceans white with foam; God bless America, my home sweet home."

When we left Nanaimo, the fellows told me to give the radio to Ivy to bring with her when she came to join us at Niagara. However, I had neglected to tell her that the radio belonged to others besides me. I had forgotten about it and didn't question Ivy when she arrived, and it wasn't until we got to Debert that somebody remembered the radio. I asked Ivy what had happened to it, and learned that her brother-in-law, who was with RCEME (Royal Canadian Electrical Mechanical Engineers) on the coast, had borrowed it and taken it out to his unit. I had to go back and tell the fellows that the radio was gone. They weren't happy with me. It took me a couple of paydays and a few pairs of polished boots to pay the guys for their share of the radio.

I wasn't in Debert very long before I was sent off to ski school in Megantic, Quebec. I was the only one who went from "B" Company; there were only two from the regiment. Ski school wasn't what I had expected. I had imagined a proper ski school, where we would be gliding down the slopes of the Appalachian Mountains and training in winter warfare on skis, like the Norwegian and Russian ski troops. It turned out to be a school for junior NCOs to upgrade their instructional skills and extend their knowledge, and to give them training in handling men and giving orders. We got a certain amount of instruction on great, big, heavy skis and snowshoes, wearing white winter camouflage suits, but we also did a lot of classroom work in map reading and tactics. I was bored silly, because most of it was stuff we had done before, over and over again.

I was less than impressed with one of our instructors, a young French-Canadian lieutenant whom I found to be childish. When we were out on an exercise and stopped for a break, he would run around making noises like a bulldozer and pushing over little spruce trees. His antics lowered my respect for both the course and the instructors.

Megantic was a French-Canadian town where very little English was spoken. The citizens ignored us for the most part. One evening the school arranged a social and invited some of the townspeople. It didn't do much for me, but there was dancing, and I think the fellows who weren't married enjoyed it. One thing that we liked very much about Megantic was that everything was open on Sunday. As soon as church was over, the beer parlours opened up. Furthermore, you could buy a beer or a glass of wine in a café, not just coffee. It wasn't so much that all of us really wanted to drink, but that it seemed so much more civilized. As far as we were concerned, Quebec was way ahead of the rest of Canada with the liberality of its liquor laws.

When ski school was over I went on two weeks' Christmas leave to Niagara Falls, bringing Ivy back with me to live in Truro. She found a suite to rent, got a job at the Metropolitan store (the Met was a chain with a store in almost every town), and made good friends with the wives of some of the other fellows. I missed a lot of the goings-on in barracks because I spent my time off with her, going for walks, picking blueberries when summer came.

On my return from my Christmas leave, I found the regiment had gone on with its winter training without me. I wasn't the only one who had been running around on snowshoes and learning winter warfare procedures. While I'd been sliding around the Quebec hills, the rest of the regiment had been on the flat and running through the bush. Nobody was interested in hearing about my experiences because they were full of their own escapades and the crazy things that had gone on while they were camping overnight in the snow and building lean-tos in the woods. There was no issue of special winter clothing, other than long wool underwear. We wore our leather boots with overshoes, the regulation great coat (overcoat), and a winter hat of melton wool cloth with ear flaps that came down and tied under the chin. They were much less effective protection against the cold than modern winter clothing.

The big news was that my ski training was all for naught. We were no longer an infantry outfit. Effective 26 January 1942, we were going to be converted to an armoured division. We were becoming cavalry, only instead of horses we would have tanks. We were no longer called privates, we were troopers, and we were organized in troops instead of platoons, and squadrons instead of companies. There were no lance corporals in the Armoured. I lost my hook and went back to being a trooper. I didn't cry about that. Instead of the South Alberta Regiment, which was what our shoulder flashes said, the records had us officially identified as the 29th Canadian Armoured Regiment (SAR). Only four of the regiments in the Fourth Division actually became armoured; the other four remained infantry regiments within the armoured division.

A number of people in the SAR were transferred to other units. An infantry regiment had five companies, while an armoured regiment had only four squadrons. To reduce the complement of men, the regiment surveyed the personnel. We were all asked whether we wished to stay with the armoured regiment or whether we would rather be transferred. Personally, I liked the idea of riding instead of walking, with nice, thick, steel walls around me. There were some people who were maybe a bit claustrophobic and didn't want to be "bottled up in a coffin," as they said. Some were transferred, but others were given the opportunity to take positions within the regiment that didn't involve being in the tanks – driving trucks and handling transport, for example, or working in the kitchen. There was an age limit for Armoured Corps personnel, so some fellows were transferred to other duties just because of their age. Many of the men transferred to the Ordnance Corps or Service Corps or to infantry regiments as they had no desire to become tank men.

The formation of four squadrons from five companies meant a change in commanding personnel as well. "A" Company was broken up, and two majors left the regiment. The new "A" Squadron, which included the Peewees, was commanded by Major Arnold Lavoie, "B" Squadron by Major Bob Bradburn, "C" Squadron by Major Albert Coffin, and Headquarters Squadron by Major Gus Miles. Major Lavoie, who had been second in command of "B" Company, had recently been promoted from captain. Major Howard Wright, who had been CO of "B" Company, became second in command of the regiment.

Coordinating our training and our conversion to armour was a new divisional commander, Major General Frank Worthington. "Fightin'

Fightin' Frank –
Major General
F.F. Worthington.
(Courtesy South
Alberta Regiment)

Frank," as we called him, was Canada's answer to General Patton, as far as we were concerned. He was the type of fellow to capture a young soldier's fancy. He had a rugged appearance, always wore battle dress and the black beret of the Armoured Corps, and carried an ivory-handled pistol in a holster on his belt. He had started out as a boy seaman, spent some time in Mexico fighting Pancho Villa and served in the First World War where he achieved the rank of lieutenant. He was a romantic figure to us fellows, the sort of man that young guys would follow. But he also had expertise. He was Canada's foremost practitioner in armour; in fact, I would say that he was one of the best that the Allies had. A review of his life I once read told of him, then a colonel, explaining to a meeting of British and American military officers how the German forces would bypass the Maginot line and drive a narrow front through the French lines to Paris. This took place before war was declared, and these senior officers were not prepared to listen to a mere colonel from Canada. When Germany did attack France in 1939, their strategy was precisely as Worthington had predicted.

Fightin' Frank took a personal interest in everybody under his command, and in everything that went on. He wanted results, so he didn't just stay in his headquarters; he went out and saw for himself how training was going and whether operations were running the way he wanted them to. Once he came upon a group of men who were learning to operate the Bren gun carriers. They had been out earlier in the afternoon and had returned to the compound with maybe an hour or so to go before four o'clock quitting time, which they put to use by cleaning the carriers. As Fightin' Frank stood nearby, he saw the soldiers hosing off the bogey wheels, then kicking dirt onto them and hosing it off again. He walked over to the building by the compound where the transport offices were, asked for the officer in charge, and told him in no uncertain terms that he did not especially want clean carriers; what he wanted was those men out on the training field *now* learning to operate the carriers, and if they were qualified, then the officer had better get some others out there and start qualifying them. They could clean the carriers when they needed cleaning, but they had better get dirty working. Immediately the class went back out to the training field, and they stayed out until they had completed their shift.

On another of his walkabouts, Frank was passing through the kitchen with a couple of aides. Some poor trooper was peeling spuds with his back to the door. Frank said to him, "Good morning. How's it going?"

The trooper answered, "What the fuck's it to you?" then turned around, and went white when he saw who it was. Frank said, "Never mind, soldier, carry on."

General Worthington was a man that we all admired, and even loved, in a way. He had a way of expressing things that made a fellow feel proud of who he was and what he was doing. He chose the South Alberta Regiment as the divisional reconnaissance regiment, for example, because, he said, we were all prairie boys, used to looking out over great distances, and so well suited to the demands of reconnaissance. Each division wore a different coloured patch on the shoulder, and Frank chose green for the Fourth Division because, he said, "This is going to be the division that will fight through the mud and the blood to the green fields of victory beyond."

As an armoured division, our head dress changed. We turned in our khaki wedge caps and were issued the black beret. I liked the beret; it was comfortable and it was distinctive. We were proud to wear it as, from what we had been told, it had an honourable history. We heard that the right to wear the black beret had been given by the French authorities to the British Armoured Corps in recognition of their valour in action during World War I.

I believed this story until recently, when the facts were related to me by military historian Donald E. Graves, the author of our regimental history. In 1943, the director of the Royal Armoured Corps issued a memo on the origin of the beret as head dress for armoured units. Apparently, World War I tank corps officers realized that their men needed a more practical form of head gear than the naval-patterned hat worn by most troops in that conflict. They particularly admired the beret worn by the French alpine troops, and therefore decided to adopt it. They chose as a model a style of beret worn by the girls of a particular private school in the U.K. The important thing about the beret was that it was comfortable under the awkward helmets worn by tank crews in World War I, and did not show the oil stains acquired inside a tank. Ours was black denim, and with it were issued black coveralls to wear as work dress for most of our daily duties in the tanks.

We had a khaki* web belt that we wore as part of our dress when we were walking out. In 1944, while in a holding position in Holland, many of us blackened our belt and gaiters instead of scrubbing them clean with soap and water. We felt the black webbing looked more appropriate with our uniform, and in the combat situation the authorities didn't seem to notice our improper dress, possibly because black web belts were worn by

---

* "Khaki" is from the Hindi word *khak*, meaning dust, and refers to the dusty colour of the army uniform.

the Canadian rifle regiments, including the Duke of Connaught's Own Rifles, which was part of the Fourth Canadian Armoured Brigade.

Our training schedule changed to a twenty-four hour day with three eight-hour shifts, same as if we were in a factory. All the services, too, went on a twenty-four hour schedule, so the kitchens served meals around the clock. During your shift you were in class, learning your new trade. When the shift was over, you were free, with a blanket pass, and could do whatever you liked until you were due back in class. Of course, I packed up and caught the bus into Truro to see Ivy whenever I could. If I were on the 0800–1600 shift, I could go home in the evening, then catch the 5 a.m. bus back to the base in the morning. If I had the 1600 to midnight shift, I'd stay in barracks, then go home in the morning, returning for my shift in the afternoon. No longer, at least for as long as we were going to classes, did we have extra responsibilities such as guard duty. They were assigned to others not taking trade courses. There was one miserable little duty, called fire piquet duty, that I didn't miss one bit. The huts were all heated from an attached boiler room, and somebody had to go around at night to each of the different boiler rooms to see that they were working right and that nothing happened to set the building on fire.

Those of us who were going into tanks were trained in one of three trades: wireless operator, gunner or driver-mechanic. A tank crew consisted of five people: crew commander, driver, gunner, wireless operator and co-driver. The crew commander, who would be a corporal or sergeant, not only had to learn how to command a tank and how to give effective orders when a tank was in action, but also had to have a smattering of understanding of all the trades. The driver learned how to perform basic mechanical repairs on the tank as well as how to drive it. The wireless operator was also the loader for the tank's guns, and so had to know something about gunnery. The co-driver, who was assistant to the driver, was a generalist. He could drive the tank, should the need arise. He manned the machine gun that was mounted at his position in the tank, acted as a foot messenger, did maintenance on the tank. Any odd tasks were usually given to the co-driver.

Each of the trades appealed to me, but I chose wireless because I thought it might be useful when I got back to civilian life. As it turned out, what we learned didn't have much application outside the military. Our instructors were signallers who were specialists in this area, and they gave us a lot of theory. They taught us about carrier waves and how to calculate wavelength and what length aerial wire you should put up for what frequency you were on and the different configurations that various aerials would require for shortwave receiving and sending. It was all very informative, but it had little relevance to our work in the tanks. I went for help to the Education Officer to build up my math skills, which were very weak. After four or five tutoring sessions on decimals and fractions and other areas that were difficult for me, I made it through. After spending a week or so on theory, we started to learn the procedures: how to use call signs and code words, the proper way to speak on the radio, the phonetic alphabet: each letter was assigned a word, Alpha, Baker, Charlie, etc., to avoid confusing one letter with another. I was particularly interested when we took a radio partially apart to see how it operated, and learned about minor repairs that we could carry out in the field.

We learned Morse code, and I did quite well at that. Morse is transmitted in a number of ways: as a series of short and long clicks, or tones, or flashes of light, or written in combinations of dots and dashes. When we were learning, we used "dit dahs," dit for a dot, dah for a dash. I remember us all sitting in the classroom going, "dit dit, dit dah dit," at each other, sending messages to impress the Morse code on our brains. I would often go through the alphabet thinking of each letter in dots and dashes while I was walking somewhere. The final training for Morse code involved learning to send messages using a telegraph key. It is simple to operate; a spring-loaded lever pivoting in the centre has a small pad on one end that is pressed intermittently with the forefinger to close electrical contacts and transmit the short and long electrical impulses that form the letters and numbers. I found that with Morse code you had to be listening ahead to the signals coming in while you were writing down the ones you had just received – rather as when you're playing music, you read ahead of what you're actually playing. That seemed to come easily to me, and I don't remember too many having trouble with it. To qualify as wireless operators we were required to send and receive messages in code, without mistakes, at the rate of thirty words per minute.

Barracks at Debert Camp, near Truro, Nova Scotia. The buildings were covered with tarpaper, probably because they were not expected to be permanent.

(Left) My bunk made up for inspection. Most Saturday mornings, we cleaned our quarters for inspection, scrubbing the floors, washing the windows, dusting every corner. Our blankets, folded neatly, were laid on the doubled mattress, with the pillow on top of the pile. Our spare uniforms had to be hung at the head of the bed and our personal items stored tidily on the shelves above the top bunk. Our shoes and Lee Enfield rifles, both well-cleaned, were placed neatly on the beds.

(Right) Lance Corporal John Galipeau at Debert. Soon afterwards, as part of the unit's conversion to armour, I lost my hook and became plain Trooper Galipeau. That suited me. Note the neatly-wound puttees above the boots, holding the bottom of the pant legs in place.

Then we did some work with the Aldis lamp, which sends Morse using flashes of light released when a shutter is moved, and the heliograph, a mounted mirror that was used to transmit messages in the First World War. Proficiency on the Aldis lamp and heliograph were skills that we did not need, but the infantry signallers who instructed us worked from their precis and Signal Corps manuals.

Once we had a basic understanding of sending and receiving messages and operating the wireless, we went out in radio trucks. These were quarter-ton trucks, a small military-style utility vehicle that was later replaced by the Jeep. The backs of the radio trucks were covered with canvas and equipped with radios, and with four operators to each truck, we travelled around practising sending messages to one another. We used to go out at night, park the trucks between the barracks and take turns on the radio.

It was on one of these exercises that I had my first experience with driving. I'd had my turn on the radio and had nothing to do, so I climbed in the front of the little quarter ton and was fooling around, starting it and messing with the gears, and I thought, "Well, here I am, let's see if I can make this thing go." I put it into first gear, let out the clutch and stepped on the gas. Of course, I didn't ease up on the clutch and down on the accelerator the way a well trained person would. I snapped the clutch and jammed on the gas, and all of a sudden the truck careened forward, heading for the side of a hut. I turned the wheel as hard as I could, and the truck started making circles in between the two huts. Luckily, because it was in first gear, it couldn't go too fast. The truck made three revolutions before I got my brain working enough to put in the clutch and step on the brake. I don't think I'd ever been more scared; but what amazed me was that the guys in the back never reacted a bit! Never said a thing! It was as if they hadn't even noticed.

While I was getting my wireless training, of course, my buddies were getting their training in driving and gunnery. The gunners stayed at Debert. The drivers were sent off to Camp Borden in Ontario, where they completed a driver-mechanic course that qualified them to do regular servicing on the tanks, every morning and every night, as well as emergency repairs. The course included instruction in the replacement of bogey wheels and suspension springs as well as repair or replacement of broken tank tracks, a task that, under the driver's direction, every member of the crew would assist with. Swede, Shorty and C.J. were among the drivers from the Peewees. As a part of their training they had to learn how to use a file very precisely, and so were given a metal block that they were to file square to within ten one-thousandths of an inch. As I understand it, there was not one Peewee who ever achieved his square block. If he left it in the vise for a moment while he went away for something, when he came back, it would have mysteriously been filed off the square, or some other terrible tragedy would have befallen it. I never heard of drivers from any of the other troops being sabotaged that way. Luckily, wireless training wasn't vulnerable to sabotage.

When we had completed our basic trade training, we all had to learn the basics of the other trades so that any of us could take over a position in an emergency. We spent a short period of time in the gunnery school, learning how to take the tank's big six-pounder gun apart and identify what could go wrong to prevent it from firing, gaining an understand of the firing mechanism and sighting. We learned to receive fire orders, which are the instructions given to the gunner by the crew commander to direct fire to a designated target. He would order the turret traversed right or left, then give reference points: "Fir trees, middle distance, 200 yards," then, finally, describe the target. Training aids included a diorama on the wall that you would look at through a gun sight, which was a telescope with scales marked on it, and a tabletop model of a landscape with miniature fields and houses. In either case, you would identify the target indicated by the troop commander's firing orders and aim the telescope gun sight at it. There was a blade of metal on top of the exterior of the turret

With Herb Roulston (on the right) in a Truro park. Herb and I were posing for our wives, Ivy and Vi, and Herb's two boys, aged four and five, during one of our infrequent family outings. Herb was awarded the Military Medal in 1944.

along which the crew commander sighted so he would know when the
gunner had traversed to the target location.

We had other new weapons to learn besides the heavy rifle, which is
what the six-pounder is properly called. The Ram tank that we were soon
to meet also had two .30 calibre Browning machine guns, one mounted
in the turret in a fixed position aligned co-axially with the six-pounder,
and the other in the front, or bow, of the tank for the co-driver to use. It
was in a fixed mount with some traverse. We had to learn how to take them
apart, clean them, and take corrective action if they failed to operate.

The Sherman tanks that we used after we went overseas also had a .50
calibre Browning mounted on the top of the turret for the crew commander to use. When we got to France we found that the .50 calibre Brown-
ings were a pain in the neck. Conditions were so dusty and dry that the barrels and mechanism got full of dirt all the time and the guns wouldn't fire
properly. It was almost impossible to keep them clean. We immediately
made a present of them to the infantry, who mounted them on the Bren
gun carriers and were as happy to get them as we were to get rid of them.

When the regiment changed to armoured from infantry we turned in
our rifles and were issued a .30 calibre Smith & Wesson Police Special pistol as our personal weapon. The co-driver was given a submachine gun as
his weapon. The co-driver was the fellow that usually had to get out of the
tank and do any ground work, such as carrying a verbal message or going
out on reconnaissance, and the submachine gun was a more effective
weapon for that type of duty.

Finally, there was driving training. Very few of the gunners or operators were trained on tanks in Debert, but we all were taught to drive motorcycles and trucks. I had three days on a motorcycle; I think the fellows
who were becoming drivers received more time. We had Indian motorcycles, which we had to kick-start – no such thing as an electronic ignition.
It needed all your weight to jump on the starting lever, and then the moment it reached bottom, you had to move your foot to the side out of the
way before the lever, which was spring-loaded, kicked back to its starting
position. If you weren't quick enough, the lever would give you a real
good whack. When the motorcycles were cold, you might have to jump
on the starter three or four times before the engine caught, and you could

be sure that somebody would be a little bit slow and end up with a painful bruise on the leg.

Once we learned to start the things, we had to learn to ride them. They were hard to balance until you got the hang of it, and we all wobbled a bit when we first put them in gear and started to move. We then took the motorcycles to an area out in the field where we rode around in a circle. The instructor had raced motorcycles, and he used have a little fun with us. You would be riding around and around nice and quietly, and he would come right up behind you and push you to go faster: "Come on, come on, come on, get going." Everybody talked about that instructor chasing you around the bowl. The fellows that had longer training on the motorcycles went out on the road in convoys, but I never made it out of the field. I didn't train on the Bren gun carriers, either; most of the drivers did.

I pity the poor guy who gave me my first lesson in the truck. We were driving what we called 30 hundredweights, which is the military equivalent of a two-ton truck. The military trucks at the time had right-hand drive because we were going to take them overseas to England, where we would be driving on the left side of the road. Since most people had to get used to shifting with their left hand rather than their right, everybody took driving instruction, whether they knew how to drive or not. I suppose there might have been others like me who couldn't drive but never admitted it.

Our instructors were the regular drivers. The fellow who taught me was a very laconic person. He sat in his seat and never said a thing except to tell me when to shift gears or which way to turn – no real instruction. He started out by saying, "OK, put her in first and let's go."

I had figured out where first was, so that part went all right. We were driving in an open area where we couldn't run into anything. He had me drive around for a while, then told me to shift up, shift down, shift up again. I had to learn to double clutch. When I got to the point where I was shifting fairly well, we went out on the road in convoy, a number of us together. I didn't know how to take advantage of the natural tendency of a vehicle to maintain a direction once it has been put in motion, so I was holding the steering wheel in a death grip, trying to correct every minor deviation and keep the truck on the road by main force. I wasn't doing too well, and I knew it, but couldn't figure out what was wrong. Finally, after about a week, I got a new instructor. We went out on the road and the convoy was leaving us behind, because I was afraid to go too fast since I couldn't seem to steer properly. My new instructor told me, "Don't steer the truck, guide it. Let go and let the truck do the work."

I tried it, and he was right. Momentum kept the truck going in a straight line, and I only needed to steer if we were taking a curve or making a turn.

The gunners and drivers didn't need to know all about radio repair and theory, but they did have to learn how to take messages on the radio and cover radio watch, as the radio was never shut down if you were in action. Somebody decided it would be a great idea to have the newly qualified operators teach radio call procedure to the drivers and gunners of our own troops. This was one of the most frustrating experiences I've ever had, rivalled only by my time as a lance corporal. We were to gather our crew, or maybe a couple of crews, in the barracks and teach them the procedure used to keep messages short, precise and clear to avoid having all the radios netted (tuned) to the same frequency blocking one another's transmission. Code words and terms are used to identify the station coming on air, whom they are calling, when the transmission is ended, and whether a reply is expected, among other information. To give a simple example, consider Tank 1, call sign Baker Four, calling Tank 2, call sign Baker Four Able, to find out whether fuel is needed. The exchange might go as follows:

Tank 1: "Baker Four, Baker Four Able, message, over."
Tank 2: "Baker Four Able, pass your message, over."
Tank 1: "Baker Four Able, what are your fuel requirements, over."
Tank 2: "Baker Four Able, will need twelve jerry cans, over."
Tank 1: "Baker Four Able, roger, out."

Only the "Baker Four Able" call sign would be used during the conversation. The participants wouldn't get confused, because each knew who he was, but any unauthorized listener, such as an enemy radio operator, might well get mixed up as to who was calling whom. "Message" means, "I have a message for you, awaiting your reply." The word "Over" means "I am finished talking." The term "Roger" means "I understand," and "Out" means "End of transmission; I have nothing more to say." The total discussion would take only two minutes or less air time.

I gathered four or five guys together sitting on a bed and tried to teach them call procedure. They were not terribly cooperative. It wasn't that they were having fun with me, it was a lot of plain ordinary bitching, for the most part.

"I don't need this BS."

"What's this crap for? That's for the stupid operators to do."

"I don't need this, when am I going to be on the radio?"

"Well, guys," I'd say, "if something happens to the operator, what are you going to do?"

"I don't care, let the gunner take over."

Just like when I was a lance corporal, I ended up pleading with them: "Well, I gotta do this, fellas, we've gotta put in the time, you might as well learn it."

"OK, go ahead, what do you want to tell us?" So I'd explain the procedure, and they would look at each other and start making up their own system. I finally gave up and said, "Well, OK, you guys, I don't care how you answer the radio, just make sure you know who you're talking to."

It was the drivers and co-drivers who were the least obliging. The gunners were usually a little more cooperative. It didn't last more than two or three sessions, anyway, before they called it off. I suspect I wasn't the only one who ran into trouble.

Once we had finished our classroom training and everybody had achieved an acceptable level of proficiency in his trade, we went back to normal routine: reveille at six, some PT and a bit of close order drill to go with our continued training, the usual fatigues. Finally, we got some tanks. I understand our tanks were pilfered by General Worthington from a load that was slated for the Fifth Division. They were a Canadian-built tank called the Ram. General Worthington had a great deal to do with designing it. He incorporated the best features of the American and the British tanks, including an American air-cooled engine. The Ram was a good tank; the fellows liked it, and it could move quite quickly. Out on the road, it would do about thirty miles per hour. The one feature that was not too popular with the drivers was that every morning before the engine was started it had to be cranked by hand fifty times. The Ram had an eighteen-cylinder radial engine, and overnight the engine oil would settle in the bottom cylinders. The cranking distributed the oil throughout the rest of the cylinders so the engine wouldn't blow a cylinder head when it was started. Even at that, it gave out great belches of blue smoke.

We were assigned to crews, and began to learn to work together as a team. I was in Sergeant Simon MacKenzie's crew when we received our first tanks. Mac had joined the Peewees about the same time as General Worthington took over the SAR. He was a Scot in his early thirties, with a family of six youngsters at home. He handled the troop as best he could, and had less trouble than anybody because he was easy-going and didn't let our antics bother him. All the crazy goings-on just sort of bounced off Mac.

After we went overseas, I was moved to the troop officer's crew, but on some occasions I would be back in Mac's tank. We became very good friends after the war. He had a farm outside Red Deer and looked me up when I moved there from Wainwright. I used to drive by his daughter Margaret's place on my way to work, and one day, at his urging, I stopped in to meet her. She told me that her dad talked about me all the time and had wondered where I was. I asked, "Why me especially?"

She said, "Out of that whole troop, the one person that would do something when he was asked, without any complaining, was you. He said you were his most willing soldier."

Mac and I had the same birthdate. Margaret arranged a birthday party for us and gave us each a little toy tank as a memento; I have mine to this day. Mac died in 1993. He had a number of strokes and ended up in a care home. He hardly knew me when I went to visit him, and it broke my heart to see him like that. I still keep in touch with Mac's family. Ivy and I became friends with his sons and daughter during the time we lived near them. Since we moved away, we make the effort to visit Mac's widow, Kate, whenever we are in the area. Simon MacKenzie will remain in my mind forever as one of the finest men I have known.

When we began training in tanks, I was a little apprehensive about how I would react to being encased in thirty tons of steel, because I was a little bit claustrophobic and I was prone to motion sickness. For the first few hours I suffered some of both, but I overcame it and I was happy that I was able to. In fact, I found the tank to be a surprisingly comfortable vehicle. The most amazing thing about it was that it was the smoothest ride in the world. Each track ran on three double sets of bogey wheels, and

"Betsy," our first tank, a Canadian-made Ram Mark II. My note on the photo at the time says, "Our pride and joy. She's kinda big and powerful but we can handle her." The driver, Bob Kerr, is seen cleaning mud from the track rollers. By his head is a canvas folder with pockets that held wrenches and other tools used for maintenance and repairs. When not in use, it would be rolled up and stored in the box with the open lid, seen just above Kerr's head. The tank's tow cable is hooked onto the hull behind the tool box. A carbon tetrachloride fire extinguisher can be seen on the side of the hull just beneath the turret, with the rolled-up tarp farther back. Protruding from the turret is the tank's six-pounder (57 mm) gun, which fired a six-pound projectile. The slot to the right of the gun accommodates the gunner's telescopic sight.

each wheel had its own arm and big coil spring, so that it moved up and down independently of the other wheels according to the terrain. All the bumps and potholes got evened out so that you were hardly aware that you were going over rough ground. There might be the odd lurch when the tank dropped into a hole or heeled over to one side, but as far as riding along in normal conditions was concerned, the smoothness of the ride in a tank was the biggest surprise in my life. The intention, of course, was that you would be able to use your guns while you were travelling. You couldn't sight in a gun if you were bouncing all over the place.

We trained on the tanks and Bren gun carriers in an open area about a mile long. During the winter when the snow was heavy the fellows used to love to take a carrier down the length of the training area, driving as fast as they could go over the bumps to jump the carrier off the ground. One day after a fresh snowfall, C.J., who was a driver, took his carrier, not down the usual road area, but a little bit off the side. He went roaring down, over a jump, and instead of landing on solid ground, he went completely out of sight under the snow into a gully ten feet deep. The snow had blown into it overnight so it looked level with the rest of the terrain. They had to dig C.J. out of the gully and haul out the carrier with a bulldozer. It took him a while to live that one down.

When spring came, we began to do a little tactical training. We would go out with three or four tanks, sometimes a squadron, travelling around the Nova Scotia countryside on what the army called "schemes." Americans called them wargames. The purpose was to get everybody used to travelling in convoy with the tanks and carrying out attack and defence manoeuvres. While we were on a scheme, each tank crew was a little unit on its own within the convoy. Our days were spent travelling together in a confined space. Each crew cooked its own meals and ate together, cleaned and looked after the tank together. If we were out overnight, we bivouacked together. It was something like being a crew on an aircraft. We had to learn how to get along in close quarters, and as a result each crew formed a bond.

We were amused by our first training as crews, which was somewhat like infantry playing at being tanks. Lengths of 2″ x 2″ lumber had been fastened together to form a letter H configuration. The troop was paraded to an open space within which we could march from place to place. Each crew was presented with one of the H-shaped structures and told to arrange ourselves in the positions we would occupy in a tank, with the driver and co-driver holding onto the front crosspiece and the operator and gunner behind them holding the back crosspiece. The corporal or sergeant commanding each crew fell in to the rear of his crew, as did the troop officer with his. We were now imaginary tanks, and under orders from the troop officer, we walked hither and yon over the area forming tank battle formations such as arrowhead, square and line abreast. The crew commander received orders for each move from the tank officer and in turn had to direct his driver to the correct position and his gunner to fire on targets. As can well be imagined, these exercises were accompanied by a chorus of grumbling and muttering, drivers' imitations of running engines and crashing gears, and a goodly amount of laughter. It is possible the exercise had some beneficial effect on our subsequent training, though at the time we could not determine what. We only did it three or four times before it ceased for good, to our great relief and satisfaction.

The summer was taken up with general training. We did schemes around the province, sometimes in the tanks, other times in convoys of trucks. It was on a wireless scheme working from trucks that I learned first-hand about barnacles. It was a hot day in June or July, and we stopped by a little cove. I thought, "Oh, great place to go for a swim," peeled down to my shorts, and in I went. The swimming was fine, the water wasn't too cold, and I enjoyed myself until it was time to get out. There was no beach, just some rocks that were steep enough that I had to climb, scraping my stomach and chest up against them. That was how I discovered barnacles. The rocks were covered with them, and I got scratched up. Of course, none of us prairie guys knew anything about barnacles, and we had no idea what this growth was all over the rocks.

Such was the capability of our general that in six months we made the transition from an infantry division to armour. We were not ready for action yet, but we were definitely ready for the next step and larger training operations. A number of our officers and NCOs were sent over early to the Canadian Armoured Corps Reinforcement Unit in Britain, where they attended the Armoured Corps school in preparation for arrival of the rest of us. In August 1942, our time came. We packed up the regimental stores and orderly rooms and boarded the train for Halifax, bound for England. Going overseas was an adventure – it was what we had joined up for – but I think that leaving Ivy was the hardest thing I had ever done. I recall getting out of bed at home about four thirty in the morning and catching the five o'clock bus to go back to the camp, and it was the saddest day of my life. It was all I could do to keep from crying. I knew that where I was going, there was no chance that she could come with me. I was glad that it was dark on the bus to camp so no one could see the state I was in.

It could well have been that everyone felt the same, for no one spoke, and we rode into camp in silence.

CHAPTER 7

And So To England

On August 22, 1942, we marched aboard the troop ship *Strathmore* in Halifax harbour, weighed anchor and sailed for England. The sea was calm, and the crossing was quite uneventful. We were travelling in convoy, escorted by navy ships, and the only incident that I can recall that was at all alarming was when one of the transports collided with a corvette and the collision set off three or four depth charges. All of a sudden in the middle of the night there was all this banging and crashing, and we all rushed up on deck to see what had happened.

However, the conditions we lived in were miserable. The ship was grossly overloaded, as were all of the ships taking troops to Britain. There were 10,000 troops, as well as some civilians, a company of the Canadian Women's Army Corps and a detachment of military nurses, all officers; all nurses were given commissions. A few of the people, especially the officers and the civilians, had cabins. The CWAC were quartered on the upper decks and may have had cabins. I never found out as enlisted men were not permitted on the top three decks unless detailed there on duty. The rest of us had nothing of the kind. The men of the regiment lived and slept on mess decks on one of the lowest levels of the ship. During the day, there were eight-foot-long tables to eat at and benches beside them to sit on. Food was brought from the galley in large pots and pans by a fatigue detail. At night, we unrolled the hammocks that hung from the ceiling and climbed in. There was no space between them. As the ship rolled, a hundred men hanging from the ceiling swung back and forth together. Water for washing was very limited; we had to make do with a rough sponge bath. The mess decks had no ventilation, and the air was putrid. I was sick from the minute the ship left the dock, and it wasn't so much seasickness as it was the stench of the mess deck.

I tried to stay on the outside deck as much as possible. Whenever we could, we slept on the open deck. The only disadvantage was that in the morning the crew washed down the decks with hoses pumping sea water, and the only warning you would get would be a small East Indian coming along saying, "Wasser coming, wasser coming" as he walked. You had better have your blankets picked up and out of harm's way by the time he got out of earshot, because the fellows with the hoses were right behind him. The crew were mostly East Indian and seemed very devout. We found it interesting to watch as some of them rolled out prayer rugs each morning and prayed facing to the east and Mecca. For most of the trip there wasn't much for us to do. We had some PT, and at one point they had us carrying the biggest damn sacks of flour I'd ever seen up six sets of narrow, steep gangways from the hold of the ship to the galleys. I strongly suspected the mind of a sergeant major behind that exercise. It seemed like the kind of thing a sergeant major would dream up for a bunch of guys who were just sitting around playing cards or reading books, not keeping busy and not keeping in shape.

Those of us who were qualified in wireless were detailed the odd duty on the bridge to operate the Aldis lamps. Since we were travelling in radio silence, the Aldis lamps were used to transmit messages between ships. Under the supervision of the ship's signaller, we would send messages to and receive them from the other ships. The ship's signaller watched what you did when you were sending and took the messages down at the same time you did when receiving. If your performance wasn't up to minimum specifications, he would relieve you and that was that. I seemed to do all right, and I was glad to do it. It made me feel a little bit important and broke the tedium. The messages that we handled dealt with army business and were always in code, so we did not know the content. Messages for the ship's captain or officers were received and sent by the ship's crew.

The rest of the time, all we had to do was hang around. Sections of the ship were out of bounds: the upper decks where the civilian passengers were, and the section where the service women had their quarters. The women's quarters had great attraction for some of the single guys, who would stand nearby, longingly hoping for some contact with the girls. There was only one fellow, as far as I know, who ever managed to attract one or two of the CWAC to the gate at the top of the outside gangway past which the army fellows could not pass, and that was our friend Pigpen, the guy we threw into the sewage at Heal's Range. He was always after the girls, and somehow, in spite of his lack of personal hygiene, he had more success than any of us ever thought possible. It amazed me how the women would spend time talking to him when we shunned him. We used to wonder what the women found so attractive about him. Thinking back, I realize that he was the only one to make any effort at personal contact. The rest of the fellows probably could see no future in it, and so didn't bother.

We landed in Glasgow on September 2, 1942. Everybody was on deck, trying to get up to the rail and have a look at Britain. Down on the docks we saw a group of soldiers loading and unloading cargo. Somebody said, "So that's the famous British Tommy."

We weren't overly impressed. We'd heard so much about the British Guards that we had expected all the British military to be spit and polish brass and shiny boots. These fellows were anything but. The knees of their uniforms were so baggy they looked like they were smuggling coconuts, and their boots were scruffy. We particularly noticed it, not just because of the contrast with our expectations, but because the Canadian soldier prided himself on his appearance. We envied the Americans their uniform, which was dressier, more like what our officers had, than our battle dress with its blousy jacket and straight pants, but we did our best to make what we wore look as neat and presentable as possible. We polished our boots and pressed our pants and jacket. It seemed like the British Tommy didn't make any effort at all.

To illustrate how the Canadian soldier felt about his appearance, consider how we wore our gaiters. The bottom of our pant leg buttoned over, using a tab with a button hole sewn to the cuff on the outside of the leg that fastened to a button on the inside of the pant leg so it wrapped around close to the ankle. On parade we wore a canvas gaiter that wrapped around the ankle and the top of the boot. When we put on the gaiter, the pants developed a double fold that held the pant leg up instead of allowing it to drop down over the gaiter in a neat, blousy fashion. To our mind, the pants didn't look right. Then some bright soul had a bright idea. He took a number of 9 mm pistol rounds, pried the bullets out of the casings, strung them onto a shoelace, and tied the ends of the lace to make something that looked like a small necklace four to six inches in diameter. Before he buttoned his pants, he slipped one of these necklaces up each leg, then buttoned his pants over top and put on the gaiters. The weight of the bullets on the shoelace pulled the pants down so they bloused over the gaiters. He came out on parade with his pants neatly bloused, while everybody else's pants had the funny looking vent up the front. It didn't take long before the practice spread through the whole unit. After the war, the army took to issuing the troops with a length of chain to serve the same purpose.

To be fair to the Tommy, just as the Americans had what we considered a better looking uniform than ours, we had a better looking uniform than theirs. Ours was a better quality serge in a slightly darker colour. Where their buttons were exposed, ours had a flap covering them. Our boots were plain toed and polished up beautifully, while the British had an ugly looking shoe with a heavy toe cap. To us, they looked like real clodhoppers. The British troops liked our boots so much that they used to try and get them, while any Canadian who went to the quartermaster stores for a new pair of boots and got shoes with toe caps immediately started complaining. I can't recall any instance when anyone in the SAR was issued a pair of the English boots with toe caps. However, I do recall on one occasion seeing some of the Second Division Infantry that had been issued boots with toe caps. When I asked where and why they had been issued, the men said that there had been shortages of Canadian boots, due to the loss of shipments when transport ships were sunk by enemy action. They were doing their best to wear the British boots out so they could turn them in for new Canadian ones. Wearing them out was difficult; if the tops were all right, it was normal practice to have the regimental cobbler just put on a new half sole. I had no doubt that the boots these fellows wore would soon suffer "accidental" cuts and abrasions to the tops to render them unwearable.

Armoured Corps troops, who had to walk and climb on the slippery metal tanks, were issued regulation boots with a rubber grip tread sole. They may have been what saved us from the good old English gravel stompers.

Our time in Britain didn't begin on a very positive note. The five divisions of the Canadian army were, in effect, under the British high command, as if Canada were still some backward colony, and we were deemed to be British troops. This arrangement had a number of rather irksome consequences for us. In consideration of the British troops, we were required to give up certain things while we were in England. We were paid more than they were, so the single men who were drawing full pay had their pay cut (and the cut portion held until they came home) to bring them down to the same level. As a married man, my pay was already cut, so I didn't suffer any further reduction. We didn't have to give up our boots, but when we were in Canada we had been issued with a cotton khaki shirt and a tie that we could wear with tunics open at the neck when we were going out. The British army didn't have anything of the sort, so our shirts and ties had to go. If my memory serves me right, there was many a shirt and tie just went in a fellow's kit bag, to be brought out when he was going on leave. There were lots of rumours about Canadian uniforms and other equipment getting sidetracked. Everything that came from Canada for the Canadian forces went from the docks, where it was unloaded from the freighters from Canada, to a British Army Ordnance Corps service depot. Some people swore that they had direct evidence that some of what was sent over for the Canadians never did reach us.

As much as we resented these circumstances, we had enough sense not to blame the British soldiers. I doubt that any of us even mentioned it to them. We knew about the shortages in Britain and the tough time the country was having. But what we couldn't understand was why our country couldn't provide for us the way the Americans provided for their troops. The Americans had no cut in pay, and they were paid more than we were to begin with. We used to ridicule the canteens the Americans provided for their men, but I think it was mostly envy. The American canteens had everything: ice cream and chocolate bars, hamburgers and fries, all things that were in short supply for us. Our canteens were run by the English NAAFI (Navy, Army and Air Force Institute). NAAFI was a civilian organization that provided tea and crumpets, sawdusty sausages, a writing room, pretty basic facilities. We used to talk about the NAAFI tea, which was a very strange-looking concoction with milk and tea all mixed together. The NAAFI canteens mirrored the shortages Britain was experiencing, while the American canteens, which were supplied from the States, reflected the abundance available there. The Americans went all out for their troops, and we didn't know why Canada didn't do the same for us. Depriving us wasn't going to change anything for the British troops.

Looking back with the perspective that comes with age, I realize that these were the thoughts of young men who had not taken the time to consider the magnitude of the war effort the Canadian people were making to bring peace back to the world. We had no real justification for our attitude, which arose mostly, I think, from envy of the plenty the Americans enjoyed.

Fortunately, we didn't lose our washing machines when we went to England. We had a regimental fund, called a canteen fund, created from the profits of the wet and dry canteens. At one point, money from the regimental fund was used to buy every squadron a gasoline operated washing machine with a little Iron Horse engine you had to kick-start, much as you started a motorcycle. It was a real luxury to do laundry using a washing machine instead of the old scrub board. Of course, having a washing machine added another duty, but nobody really complained. One day a week would be designated laundry day, when everybody in the troop would have their laundry marked and in a bag ready for the poor soul whose turn it was to do the wash. When it came time for us to go overseas, the washing machines were taken to the quartermaster stores and packed in big wooden crates marked as kitchen equipment, boots, anything about that weight and size. The creative labelling was necessary because the washing machines were not military equipment, and would not have been taken on the ships had the authorities known. As far as I know, we were the only Canadian regiment in Britain that had their own washing machines.

On top of everything we gave up or did without, we also had to go back to the classroom for a couple of weeks. All the training we'd had in

Canada turned out to be for nothing, because we had to repeat what we had done in Debert all over again to satisfy the British military command and requalify under British standards. Except for some minor details, the training covered exactly the same basic material. We might has well have missed Debert and come over six months earlier. It was a waste of time, as far as I was concerned.

Another aspect of being under British command that irked us once we got over to France was that the Canadians never got credit for their efforts and accomplishments. You would see a report in the paper with the head-line, "British Troops Make Gains," and when you read it, you would real-ize that the action referred to was in the Canadian sector, and it had been our fellows who had made the gains. I fault our authorities in Canada, or maybe the Canadian attitude. Every time the Americans were involved in some little skirmish, they let the world know what their troops had done. Too much so, really. We didn't want an exhibition made of what we did, but at the same time, we wanted our contribution to be acknowledged as Canadian, not as British, and we wanted the Canadian people to be aware of their army's achievements. We weren't happy about being left in the lurch by our Canadian politicians who didn't stand up for us and let us be an entity on our own; but, being soldiers, we did what we were told. We could do little else.

It wasn't easy to adjust to life in England, either. We were quartered in a military camp in a village called Headley in Surrey, some thirty-five miles south of London. The regiment was dispersed in squadrons to sur-rounding areas, with "A" Squadron right in the village. Our accommoda-tion was little tin Nissen huts, what are now called quonsets, along the side of the road. We had a new language to learn, because none of us found it easy to understand the accents in that part of the country. There was blackout every night, and there were shortages of everything, like coke for heating. What coal there was went to the kitchens for cooking. We had very little heat in our billets, though the weather was always wet and cold. And the food – if we went to a little café, there was no such thing as a hamburger or a hot dog, or steaks or roast beef, the things we were used to. They were making do with sausage and eggs, and usually the sau-sage was something like sawdust and the eggs were powdered. The Germans had a good word for the make-do wartime food containing substitutes for the normal ingredients. They called it *ersatz*. I liked the flavour of the sawdust sausages, but missed the meat they lacked.

The one thing it seemed England had plenty of was mutton. You could smell mutton cooking a mile away. We weren't used to it. I don't think our cooks were either, and they didn't know what to do with it. On every table at meal time there was a large bottle of HP Sauce with which we would drown the mutton while we prayed for a parcel from home. It was a big event when the parcels from home came in; everybody had cake and cookies and tins of meat.

The saving grace, the godsend to us all, was the good old English pub, which we took to wholeheartedly. We had a pub called the Holly Bush at the end of our group of huts that was run by a woman called Sally, a good, old, motherly lady who must have weighed 300 pounds. I think every soldier who ever stayed in Headley Camp would remember Sally and the Holly Bush. Sally used to tell us how she used to play with the Canadian soldiers during the 1914-1918 war, and that now their sons had come over, she worried about her daughter playing with them. Sally was as rough and ready as any sailor. She could swear and curse and be as raw as

The Holly Bush, our local pub, photographed on a regimental tour in 1997. (Photo by Dianne Graves)

any guy we had ever known, and throw out any man who got out of line; but the pub was the place you went to for warmth and comfort and companionship. There was always somebody playing the piano. We had fellows who could play, and if one of them wasn't there, one of the locals who played would be. You would play darts and shove ha'penny, sing, play cards; there was always something going on. I think the beer must have been a little weaker, being wartime, because there was lots of moaning by our connoisseurs that they missed our Canadian beer, but the pub had it all over the Canadian beer parlour where you had women in one section and men in another, and you just sat there and drank and squabbled.

The Holly Bush is still there, run by Sally's daughter. A group of our fellows went back in 1989 and found it.

It was on our way back from a pub in a village three miles down the road from Headley one evening that we made the acquaintance of another British institution, the Home Guard, consisting of civilians overage for the regular forces who were trained and armed with shotguns or their own hunting rifles and patrolled their districts to catch saboteurs being parachuted into the country. Three or four of us had decided to take a shortcut through an orchard. Suddenly, out of nowhere, appeared a shotgun-toting Home Guard. Now, he was serious. We were just walking quietly through the orchard, but we had no business being there. He said, "Halt!"

One of us asked, "Who are you?"

"Never mind who the bloody hell I am. What are you doing in here?"

Dim as the light was, we could see that this fellow had a double-barrelled shotgun pointed at us, so we didn't argue with him. We just explained that we were taking a shortcut back to our quarters.

"No bloody shortcut through here, fellows. Where are you from and who are you?"

"We're Canadians."

"How am I going to know that?" The Home Guard didn't trust anybody. He paraded us out of the orchard and interrogated us, asking which was our regiment and where were our barracks and so on. I guess we convinced him of our innocence, because he finally let us go, telling us, "Stick to the roads, lads, or else you're going to be in trouble."

Another time we ran afoul of the British air raid warden. We were living on what I guess had once been a village green. There was a mess hall in the centre and a row of the infamous Nissen huts down the side by the road. We slept on single beds rather than double bunks, with mattresses consisting of a thin pad filled with cotton waste or horsehair. One of the Peewees was making his bed one evening, and somebody else pulled it apart on him. That started the usual ruckus. In no time, all the beds were being pulled apart, and soon afterwards the mattresses were going out the door, followed by a commotion of laughing and hurrahing and wrestling Peewees, half of them trying to retrieve mattresses and the other half trying to prevent their retrieval. All of a sudden from the darkness a voice thundered, "Close that bloody door!" Startled, we stopped dead as the voice continued, "There's a bloody war on, you fellows, and there's a blackout."

The voice belonged to one of the air raid wardens who patrolled the streets to make sure that no lights showed to give bombers a target. As we stood there like bloody fools, he told us what he thought of us, in plain language as only the English can, and every bit of what he said was true. We scuttled back inside the hut with our mattresses and kept the door shut. Of course, we were giggling and laughing about it the whole time.

The war was new to us. We knew it was on, and what that meant started to sink in. We could hear the bombs dropping on London, and our area too was being bombed. It wasn't long before we came to recognize the German aircraft when they were flying over on bombing raids. Their engines made a sound that was distinctly different from the sound made by the Allied planes; they pulsed, while the engines of our planes made a steady drone. The regiment had been dispersed, with the squadrons quartered two or three miles apart, to reduce the concentration of facilities so that it would be harder for the enemy's air reconnaissance to identify our location. All these things – the precautions, the bombers flying overhead, the blackout, the presence of the Home Guard – all of them together brought home to us that the war was getting closer, and that it was only a matter of time before we were going to be right in it.

We had a lot of preparation to do, though, before we would be ready to go to war. We had Bren gun carriers and did some training in them, but since our tanks hadn't arrived yet, we followed normal routine, including foot drill, route marches, map and compass work, and fatigues. In addition to our regular PT, we were encouraged to get involved in sports to improve our conditioning. I never got very deeply involved with the sports, because I somehow wasn't well coordinated for team sports and had no talent for track and field, but I would go to inter-squadron meets and put up bars for the high jump and rake the long jump pit, mainly so I could cheer for "A" Squadron athletes. The greater emphasis on sports throughout the regiment had followed a change of regimental sergeants major. RSM Seal transferred out of the regiment while it was still in Canada. To fill the position, Company Sergeant Major John McKenzie,* who was sports-minded, was promoted to regimental sergeant major.

During the conversion to armour, "A" Squadron had had a change of squadron sergeants major that resulted in one of my more memorable sporting experiences. Company Sergeant Major Blain had been transferred to a reinforcement training depot in Alberta. His replacement, Squadron Sergeant Major S.H. Patterson, at times displayed a strange sense of humour. I particularly remember one football game he organized at Headley. He marched the squadron out to the middle of a field with a goal post at either end. He lined us up higgledy-piggledy, no particular organization, then went down the middle and numbered us off, dividing the eighty or so men into two teams of forty each. Then he put a soccer ball in the middle of the field and said, "All right, now, here's the game. You lot on that end will put the ball in that goal. You lot on the other end will put the ball in the other goal. How you get there doesn't matter, there are no rules. Now go to it."

It was a free-for-all. You didn't have to kick the ball, you could carry it or throw it to pass, and if somebody picked up the ball and tried to run with it, you could pick him up with the ball and take them both to the opposition goal line. You could do anything to put that ball into the opposition's goal, and to keep it out of yours. At first I was worried about what might happen, and tried to remember who I might have insulted so I could avoid them; but nothing of that sort happened. It was a rough game, but a good one. I ended up on the sideline with a badly kicked shin,

---

* Sergeant Simon MacKenzie and RSM John McKenzie were brothers. One of them changed the spelling of his name to save confusion!

in company of a few others with similar injuries, but I'll remember that game to the end of my days when I think of Sergeant Major Patterson.

RSM McKenzie placed an emphasis on competition between squadrons, and had a special interest in the teams that entered inter-regimental competition in the Fourth Division. The regimental boxing team came under his personal supervision. Throughout the regiment there were fellows who had boxed semi-professionally, or even professionally, and we had a few fellows in the troop who were with the regimental team and boxed quite extensively. I had fooled around doing a bit of boxing when we were at Niagara-on-the-Lake, so when it was announced that classes would be run on sports days, I and others who were interested wandered down to find out something about it. We spent some time learning the proper stance, the proper way to deliver a punch, the different punches (such as straight, hook and cross), how to move our feet, and some other techniques of offence and defence. Then we squared off wearing big ten-ounce gloves and sparred. It was good exercise, and if you were a good boxer and had the desire to pursue it, you could end up on the regimental team. The fellows on the boxing team were fed the best of food and were matched to fight the boxers in other regiments. If you were good enough, you could work your way up: Brigade Champion, Divisional Champion, then Army Champion, and ultimately, try for the Allied Forces championship. One of the Peewees who fought on the regimental team, Archie McLellan, was a light heavyweight, and maybe with the right spirit and the right attitude he would have made a champion. He was a fine boxer and won many fights, but he lacked the brute or killer attitude needed to beat the divisional or army champions.

I went into it originally just to get some self defence training. I didn't know what I was going to run into when I went on leave in the London pubs. I enjoyed sparring and boxing, but I didn't have the spirit to be a serious competitor. I did win at least one inter-squadron fight, through sheer tenacity as far as I know. I have no doubt that Sergeant Major McKenzie, whose baby the boxing team was, was looking for men who could move up onto the regimental team, because when I came out of the ring after that fight, C.J., who was my trainer, said to the sergeant major, "What do you think about him?"

The sergeant major replied, "Well, can you get him down to feather-weight?"

The jockeying for position in a weight class would have finished me, if nothing else had. At 135 pounds I was a lightweight, and I really didn't want to see myself light enough to make featherweight, but because I was at the lower end of the lightweight class, most of the fighters that I was going to have to beat were six inches taller than me and had longer reach. I suppose it's just as they say, it's not the man in the fight, it's the fight in the man, and it was not my greatest desire to discover how much fight there was in this man. Attitude wouldn't help to heal the bruises.

We spent Christmas at Headley. We had Christmas turkey dinner and our first parcels from the Salvation Army, containing hand-knit socks and bottles of hair oil. All the pubs were doing their best, but there was a shortage of booze. Some of the boys got to the condition where they would drink anything, and one of them wondered out loud how much alcohol was in the hair oil. They asked the Medical Officer, and the MO said, "Whatever it is, I've got the antidote, so go ahead," and a few bottles of hair oil were drunk.

It was quite a party. There were a few little dustups in the pubs with an Ontario unit called the Elgin Regiment, but nothing very violent. The truth is that it was a happy time for everybody to let their hair down, the way that Canadian troops can do.

CHAPTER 8

Darts, with Mild and Bitter

Just before Christmas 1942, we got tanks, three per squadron. Though we used the Canadian Ram tank, mounted with a six-pounder gun, for most of our training, we never went into action with it. Sometime in late 1943, we started to get the American Sherman. All the Allied Forces made the switch. Even the British used it in most cases. They mounted flamethrowers on their Churchill tanks, which were a larger tank with a wider tread that made them better in mud, and kept them for special uses, but for the most part we all used the Sherman. The only place the Canadians didn't use the Sherman or the Ram was the Dieppe raid, where the Second Division used the big British Churchill.

I'm not sure of the reason for the switch to the Sherman, but I suspect that it had to do with standardization of parts for the factories and speed of production. Locomotive works in Quebec produced the Ram, which had a cast iron hull. The Sherman was built with a welded hull, which I imagine would be much quicker to manufacture. I doubt that Canada could have kept up with the demand if we had continued to use the Ram.

Later on in Normandy, they took the turrets off the Ram tanks and used them as infantry carriers. They were the forerunner of today's armoured personnel carrier. In the case of rapid movement by armour, infantry is left behind unless you have a way to move large numbers of men over variable terrain. We adopted the practice of riding infantry on the back deck of the Shermans, but that put the men in a very vulnerable position. In the turretless Rams the infantry were better protected until they got to where they would dismount and support the armour.

Now that we had the proper equipment, we began more serious and advanced training. On January 15, 1943, we moved to Aldershot, which

Training with a Ram tank in Britain. That's me on the barrel, with Corporal Reginald Pickard (left). Driver Wilf Taylor appears to be filling in his daily driver's report. We are dressed for the English winter in coveralls, knee-high rubber boots and the leather gauntlet-style gloves that were issued to tank crews for a while. Cpl. Pickard is wearing the special windproof coat that was issued to crew commanders. Wilf has on the leather jerkin drivers wore to protect them from the cold air drawn in through the hatches. On the left, the radio antennas can be seen rising from the turret. Just beneath is the pistol port, which the wireless operator could open to eject spent shell casings.

became the base from which we travelled all over England on training schemes. It was at this time that the title "Recce," for Reconnaissance, was added to the name of the 29th Canadian Armoured Regiment. We were designated as divisional troops, which meant that although attached to the 10th Brigade, we were under command of the division and could be sent wherever we were needed.

We didn't mind Aldershot. We were in a town, with pubs and theatres close by. However, we weren't happy with the barracks. They had been built around the 1800s, and the only heat was from a tiny fireplace at one end of the barracks, which were fifty feet long. It was winter time, and *cold.*

Some interesting things happened in Aldershot between schemes. For a while our drivers were testing a new, secret, two-man tank. The rest of us never saw them. Each day C.J. and Swede and two or three others would go out and run these tanks around. The experiment ended the day C.J. got in his tank and started it up, and it exploded. He came back to barracks with a very scorched face and no hair or eyebrows.

Four Troop (the Peewees) was involved in testing the infamous Sten gun. We went out on the range, fired them, and then, on orders, we threw them in a mudhole and fired them some more; or tried to. Some worked and some didn't. Everybody felt ridiculous dropping them in the mud, and we were all giggling when we tied lengths of cord to them and dragged them along the ground like pull-toys before trying to fire them. Unfortunately, those cursed pieces of piping must have worked well enough that they were accepted, because we ended up with them instead of the American .45 calibre Thompson submachine gun we had expected to have.

We found the Sten gun to be a very unreliable piece of equipment. It was originally made to drop to the Free French and other underground forces in Europe. It was little more than a piece of pipe with a short rifled barrel screwed into it. The breech and firing mechanism were of simple design. The breech was made up of a length of steel tube about a foot long with the barrel attached to the front. The device that held the magazine was placed on the left side, close to the end of the barrel. The firing mechanism was a round steel block the diameter of the breech tube with a firing pin machined in one end. It fitted into the breech with a length of coiled spring behind it to force it up against the end of the barrel. A slot some four or five inches long was cut in the right hand side of the breech, as was an opening to allow the spent cartridge casings to be ejected. The steel block that served as the bolt was fitted with a steel pin that protruded through the side slot to be used as a handle to cock the weapon. In the firing position, the bolt was held against the compressed spring by the trigger. When the trigger was pressed or pulled, the spring forced the bolt forward to place a cartridge in the barrel and fire it at the same instant. When the cartridge fired, it drove the bolt back against the spring, at the same time ejecting the spent casing. The bolt then moved back to compress the spring, which would then force the bolt forward again to fire another cartridge, and so the cycle went until the trigger was released. We had any number of people wounded by them. There was a safety mechanism, but if you happened to drop the Sten and the safety hadn't been locked, or if you slammed the weapon down hard, the bolt would slam back and the gun would fire. We hated the thing.

Out on schemes, our training took on a larger scale than ever before. We began doing exercises that simulated what we would find in action. The regiment would be split, with half taking the defending position while the other half attacked. The exercises were then expanded to include more than one regiment, and then more than one division. At times, the scheme would involve as many as four divisions, with 20,000 men in each division and 250 tanks in each armoured division. All these schemes had umpires, officers from various regiments who were designated to evaluate the tactics and actions and determine what the outcome would have been of any particular action. My greatest desire at times, and I think this was true for the infantry boys, too, was to be taken prisoner or declared dead, because then you would be out of the action and could take life easy in a make-believe prison camp or lounge around as a make-believe corpse – or so I imagined. I might have had my assumptions rudely challenged had I ever been picked as a prisoner or casualty, but I never was. The schemes simulated battle conditions, so they were quite extensive, and quite rugged. You went without food and sleep, you went without a wash or a shave. I can recall one scheme where 4 Troop was in a holding position. It was cold, and it was wet, and the only shelter we had was the tarp that covered the tank. As I recall, we had no blankets with us, and trying to sleep on the cold ground under that tarp was not pleasant.

For these large schemes we went to the northern part of Britain, which was much less settled than the south, and the terrain was more open and natural. This was where we were threatened with trouble for cutting down trees, and Major Lavoie demonstrated how well he'd learned from the Peewees. When we were travelling to or from these exercises, the tanks were put on trains or on truck transporters to haul them the long distances. After one scheme, "A" Squadron was left behind waiting for transport to move us back south. We were in a farming area where they were harvesting sugar beets. Somebody came in and said that farmers were paying, if we wanted to go pick beets. We had nothing to do, so we thought we might as well make a little easy money. We went out to the beet field in the morning and set to work. One person would go along pulling beets and laying them in a row all down the length of the field with the stalks and leaves pointing out either side. Behind him, somebody else came along with a special knife and cut the tops off. We thought we were in pretty good shape, but we weren't used to this kind of work, and after a few hours there were some aching backs. The aches weren't the worst of it. What was really discouraging was that working in the same field were some Land Army girls. The Land Army took over most of the agriculture when the men went off to war. Those girls went along with no moaning, no groaning, and the quantity of beets that they picked was far greater than ours. They put us to shame.

If we admired anybody in Britain, we admired the Land Army girls, not just because they were girls, but because of the work they were doing and the dedication with which they did it. The English winter was like a Canadian west coast winter; it rained and rained and rained, and they were out in the mud and the cold doing what had to be done to keep the country fed. On a regular route march we would march for fifty minutes and rest for ten, and it happened on one route march in the south of England that when we stopped, there was a group of seven or eight Land Army girls in the field right beside us. They came over to talk to us, and we noticed right away that they had very little protection for their hands, which were all red and raw. Some had no gloves at all, others had gloves that were completely worn out and had nothing but fingers left. One of us asked, and the girls said, "Well, we just can't get gloves."

As the troop marched away, there wasn't one of the guys wearing gloves. I have no idea how we explained our lost gloves to the quartermaster, who was one of the strictest quartermasters in the regiment. If you wanted a new pair of socks, your old ones had to have darns on top of the darns before he would give them to you.

We always did a lot of maintenance on the tanks after a scheme. They would be unloaded in the parking area, then the rolled tarps would come off the back deck, the tools would come out and we would undo bolts to open the back decks to get into the engine compartment. The driver and co-driver would change the engine oil, put clean oil in the carburetor air cleaner, clean dirt off the engine and look for anything that needed the attention of the fitters (mechanics) who tuned up the engines. The guns would be stripped, cleaned and oiled. The tanks would be cleaned inside and out and the tracks and all parts checked for loose nuts and bolts. Everything was given a general servicing. My baby, of course, was the radio set. I had to perform tests to make sure that everything was working properly, and make sure that I had spare valves, which is what the British called the vacuum tubes that were an essential part of a radio before transistors were invented. Every operator had a box of valves, all packed nicely in foam, and I had to check whether I needed to renew my stock. I was also responsible for the gasoline-operated Homelite generator with a one-cylinder motor that was mounted in the tank to keep the batteries charged and the radio powered when the tank engine wasn't running.

It amazes me when I think of it now, but we washed everything in gasoline; or petrol, as it was called in Britain. We would take one of the square five gallon cans gasoline came in, cut it off to make a pan, and fill it with gasoline to use for cleaning. We used it because it dried quickly and was effective in removing grease spots. I remember being inside the tank washing down the interior of the turret with gas. You hear today about people who sniff gasoline to get a high. I couldn't say it was a high I got, but after some time spent breathing gasoline fumes, I would feel a little strange. It strikes me now that it was a pretty stupid thing to do, and I have to wonder why it was allowed. If somebody had happened to turn on a switch or cause a spark in any way, I don't know whether the fumes would have been so rich that nothing would have happened, or whether there would have been a great *whoosh!* and a fire in the tank.

We used gasoline like water, despite the rationing and all the messages the public heard about saving petrol. We were issued two uniforms, one of which we kept for dress, and a suit of black coveralls that we wore for working around the tanks or for similar duties. Our work uniforms didn't go to the cleaners when they got dirty. We used to take three or four gallons of gasoline, slosh the uniform around in it, and then hang it up to dry. I don't remember smelling of gasoline the next time we wore them.

Archie McLellan, the Peewee who boxed on the regimental team, had been assigned, at his request, to the kitchen before the regiment left Canada, but after we got to England he decided he'd had enough of the kitchen and he wanted to get back with the guys he'd trained with, so he was reassigned as Swede's co-driver. Archie was a little slow mentally, and Swede was always one to capitalize on another's limitations. The first morning he had to do tank maintenance, Archie, in his trusting way, asked Swede, "What can I do? What do you want me to do first?"

Swede said, "Well, we've got to get water for the radiator. So Archie, take these two five-gallon buckets and go get water. It'll take about six buckets, Archie."

Off Archie went with the buckets, and began bringing back water. Now, the Ram, which we were still using at the time, had an air-cooled engine, and it didn't need water; so I don't know what Swede did with the water, but he poured it down through someplace into the hull and sent Archie off for more. Finally Swede told him, "That's enough, Archie, we don't need any more," and Archie went to see if he could help somebody else. And he saw that nobody else was putting water in the radiator.

"How come you guys aren't putting water in your radiator?" he asked. "Swede just had me pack about six pails of water for the radiator."

"Archie, that's an air-cooled engine," they told him. "It doesn't take water."

There was a bit of a scuffle when Archie got back to the tank and found Swede.

The maintenance period between schemes brought an interesting phenomenon to our attention. When we were on a scheme, as long as we threw gas and oil in the tanks and cleaned the guns when we fired them, the tanks ran with no problem whatsoever. After a session in camp when we had cleaned everything up and the fitters had tuned the engines, for the first couple of days there would be tanks stalled all over the place. Of course, we grumbled that we would be better off if we left the damn things alone. After being driven for a day everything seemed to correct itself, and the tanks would run smoothly again.

At this point I want to say a special word about a man named Bill Christie. Bill was our Tech Stores corporal. Just as we got our clothing from the Clothing Stores, tools and equipment were issued from the Tech Stores, and it was Bill's job to make sure we had what equipment and supplies we needed for the tanks, and to keep track of it once it was issued. When we came in at night we did a last parade when we topped up the fuel and engine oil, did any lubrication that was necessary and carried out any maintenance needed so the tank would be ready to drive off next morning. Everything we used had to be accounted for, so Bill Christie would be there with his clipboard, recording the usage.

The patience and endurance he displayed was beyond belief. The drivers had a funnel they used to put oil in the engine. When they needed oil, they would draw a couple of quarts out of the barrel, then pour it into the engine through the funnel. The funnel would invariably get left either on the track of a tank or Bren gun carrier or on the ground, where it got squashed. Then the drivers would moan at Bill about having no funnels. Bill would try to get them to look after them and put them where they would not get damaged, but it was hopeless. Every night, the drivers would be snarling at Bill, "Where's the damn funnel?" and Bill would tell them, "If you'd look after the funnels, you'd have them. If you guys don't smarten up, I'm not going to give you any more funnels." But he'd have to, of course; we couldn't service the tanks without them.

It was always the troops that went into action who got all the accolades, but nobody could have done anything without people like Bill who kept us running, and suffered a great deal of abuse for their efforts.

Our drivers really came into their own in England. In Canada, the tanks had been fitted with tracks with rubber pads on them. For battle, steel tracks were used, and it was when we got to England that they were issued. The steel tracks were fine going across country, but they would slide all over the place on pavement. Once the tanks built up some momentum they would roll along just fine, but there was many a time that the people in Britain found they had a tank in their front yard or came upon one in the ditch after the steel tracks slid off the paved road. We had some excellent drivers, and they used this tendency for the tanks to slip on pavement to develop a technique all their own. You steer a tank with two long levers called tiller bars, square metal rods with rubber hand grips on the end, which essentially operate the brakes. When you want to make a turn, you pull a tiller bar, slowing the track on that side, and push down the accelerator so that the track on the other side powers you around. This was too tame for our Peewee drivers. They decided they didn't need to slow down for a corner. They would come to an intersection or corner and pull on the tiller bar without slowing down so the tank skidded around the corner like a sports car doing a four-wheel drift. When the tank was pointing in the right direction, they would jump on the accelerator again, the tracks would grind and chew, and away they'd go. It was terrifying.

There was quite a lot of minor damage done by the tanks. Besides what they did to ditches and front yards, you could always tell when the tanks had been through the towns, because the bricks on the corners of the buildings on those narrow roads were all chipped out about six inches deep. I used to admire the way the guys could go through the little villages where the streets were only twelve to sixteen feet wide, and full of people on bicycles and mothers with baby carriages. The drivers could only see ahead. They couldn't see much to the side at all. I would have been creeping along, but it never seemed to worry them a bit, and the villagers didn't seem in the least disturbed. I can't recall anybody ever being hurt, but up in the turret peering out of my periscope at bicycle riders who seemed unconcerned as these thirty-ton monsters rumbled by only inches away, I was always apprehensive.

We were out on a scheme when I finally got my chance to drive a tank. We were finished for the day and were coming in from the training area back to the harbour,* which was what the area where the tanks were parked at night was called. The driver, Bob Kerr, asked me whether I would like to try driving. I said sure, I'd like to, and got in the driver's seat where he gave me my instructions. They were fairly simple. The gear shift was standard, except it was much bigger than a truck's, and the clutch was three feet long and took all your strength to push it down. There were four forward gears and a reverse gear, and you double-clutched both gearing up and gearing down. Before long, I was rolling around just fine

---

* Tanks were originally developed by the navy and a lot of naval terminology persisted, including: "harbour" for the parking area, "tiller" for the steering mechanism, "hull" for the body of the vehicle, "hatch" for the entrance and "sponson" (a projection from the side of a warship through which a gun can be trained fore and aft) for the storage area on the inside wall of the tank.

out in the open where I couldn't hurt anything. There was a fairly long hill down into the harbour, and when I started down the slope, Bob reminded me to watch the tachometer and keep the engine at 2,500 rpm.

Naturally, as we were going downhill, the tank had a tendency to speed up, and so I hauled back on the tiller bars to slow it down, all the while keeping the rpm at 2,500. We got to the bottom of the hill and I went to make a turn, and the tank would barely respond. I didn't know what was wrong. Bob never said a thing except, "I guess we have to call the fitters."

Then it struck me what I'd done. I had burned out the brakes. Instead of letting the engine slow the tank down, using the brakes only when needed, I'd had the engine running in high gear to hold it at 2,500 rpm. In effect, I had been using the engine to overcome the brakes. What Bob had meant was to keep the tank from turning the engine over the 2,500 rpm limit. I felt so stupid, but there were no repercussions, and I smartened up when I got a chance to drive after that.

As it happened, I drove tanks quite a bit following that incident and became quite comfortable with them. I didn't get into a truck until after the war was over, by which time I was a sergeant. We were billeted in a village in Holland and went to a church parade a few miles away. The men rode in the back of a truck while I rode in the front with the driver, Tommy Semple. On our return, he said, "Drive it back, Sarge."

Everything was fine until we came to the turn from the main road onto the sideroad that led to the village. I shifted down and turned the steering wheel, but just as the truck got into the turn, by reflex action, my foot went down solid on the accelerator as if I were driving a tank. We didn't make the turn. Right away I realized what I'd done and eased off on the accelerator, but we were already thirty feet off the road headed for a great, big oak tree. I slammed on the brakes, almost but not quite in time, and we hit the oak tree with a bump! It wasn't a violent collision and nobody was hurt, but I dented the bumper on the truck.

I felt terrible, because Tommy loved his truck. It was his baby. He had used the same truck all through the war, and there hadn't been a mark on it until I ran it into the oak tree. I got it back on the road and drove into the village, where everybody unloaded. Then I went back to talk to Tommy. While I had been occupied with getting everybody settled,

Ram tank being transported on a Royal Canadian Army Service Corps flat deck trailer pulled by a ten-ton tow truck. Tanks were often moved from one training area to another this way. Towing cables front and back secured the tank to the trailer. The tank is fitted with rubber tracks to prevent damage to the pavement when travelling the roads during training. The number 45 identifies this tank as one belonging to the SAR. The headlights have been fitted with a cover that permits only a small amount of light for driving during blackout, and the poles at the side of the road have been painted white at the bottom to make them visible to "blacked-out" drivers. I'm sitting in the co-driver's hatch, with the tank's six-pounder gun and the driver's hatch to the left of me. The rest of the crew were travelling on the back of the truck and took the picture.

Tommy had quietly taken a logging chain, gone off someplace and found a tree, and pulled the bumper straight.

Yet another lesson in how experience is the best teacher.

Not all of our training consisted of travelling around the country on schemes, of course. To make sure we didn't get too far out of condition, once a month the whole regiment would get out of the tanks and do a forced march, twelve miles in two hours. There were a lot of blistered feet when the march was over. Everybody would pull off their shoes, and the

Medical Officer would go around and treat blisters. Some fellows had a little time off duty because their feet were so bad.

On one or two occasions we participated in firepower demonstrations with the artillery. These were exercises in which the artillery fired a barrage, and the armour and the infantry followed the barrage precisely as we would in action. I was a little worried during these operations; not for myself, because a shell would have to hit in just the right place to really damage a tank. I worried about the infantry. Those fellows went right in behind the barrage, and any mistakes on the part of the artillery would have been disastrous. It was an effective way of giving us a feel for what it would be like in action. On other occasions we had smoke demonstrations. Each tank had a two inch mortar that could fire high-explosive shells, smoke shells or flares. We would lay smoke by firing a number of smoke shells, and the tanks would advance through the smoke so we could see how effective a method it was to screen our movements.

Our squadron went north to an area near Ledshot to practise on firing ranges. We had a terrible time. I disliked the area immensely. It was raining, and everything that wasn't under water was a sea of mud. Our quarters were Nissen huts with no heat. The pathways between the huts had duck boards on the ground, but even they were under water. We preferred the southern part of England, where we spent most of our time. I will always remember the white cliffs of Dover, not for the cliffs themselves, but for the chalk that they are composed of. It extends quite a way inland, as we found out when we tried to dig slit trenches to prepare defensive positions. You couldn't shovel chalk. Every inch of our trenches had to be broken with a pick-axe before it could be shovelled out.

I always wanted to use gun cotton to make my slit trenches. Gun cotton was a solid, white block of an explosive material that looked like moulded cotton. It had been used extensively in the First World War to blow up bridges and railroad tracks and roads and so forth. It would have been very handy for blowing holes for trenches. I had learned about gun cotton when a number of us took an explosives course. Learning how to set dynamite and use explosives was very enjoyable for us young fellows. We used to make grenades by taking plastic explosive and moulding it into a form the size of a hot dog bun. Then you wrapped it with a length of fuse with a detonator, stuck the detonator in the end of the plastic explosive, split the fuse at the end, inserted a match head to make sure it would light, then lit it and threw it like a hand grenade. These were to be used against the enemy if you were out of hand grenades, not that they were very effective.

Everybody had their favourite explosive device. Mine was an instantaneous fuse that would explode the moment you lit it. It was the greatest thing for cutting down trees. You would wrap three to four lengths of fuse around a tree, attach a length of regular fuse for safety, and light it. When it burned to the instantaneous fuse, it exploded, and down went the tree.

When we went to France, each tank was issued with an explosives kit, a box four feet long, eight inches deep and ten to twelve inches wide, filled with explosives. A lot of the fellows were frightened of having all those explosives around and hated the thing, but ours rode along quite nicely on the back deck of the tank.

It was on the Downs, as they called the hilly open areas near the coast in the south of England, that an incident took place that became legend in the regiment. We were on a regimental exercise where each squadron operated within its own area. One of the tanks in "C" Squadron stopped on a slope, and the crew dismounted and walked a little way away from the tank. They turned around to discover that the driver had neglected to set the hand brake, and the tank was rolling down the hill. As the force of gravity took over, the tank gathered speed until it was moving faster than anyone had ever seen a tank move before. At the bottom of the hill there was an eight-foot stone wall. I can imagine the images that went through that driver's head as he visualised what would happen when thirty tons of tank hit the wall. I would be wondering how much I was going to have to compensate some farmer for damage. However, as luck would have it, just prior to reaching the wall, the tank came to a place where the slope levelled out. Just as if it had gone over a ski jump, the tank cleared the wall and whomped down on the other side. There was minimal damage to the tank and none at all to the stone wall. The story of the flying tank was told and retold for months afterward.

CHAPTER 9

Corporal Galipeau

During our training on the South Downs in Sussex we were in a number of towns at different times, including Worthing, Brighton, Haywards Heath and Hove. There were other places very rural in nature, consisting of a cluster of houses, a pub and possibly a community hall. Their names I cannot recall. Only the landscape comes to mind, very quiet and pleasant. Other than the "local" there was very little in the way of entertainment in the evenings and on weekends. To see a movie or find a more lively pub it was necessary to catch a bus to one of the nearby towns. Sussex was a nicer part of England than the Midlands and northern training areas, and of all the towns around the South Downs training area, I liked Brighton best. Brighton was a larger city and had a skating rink, theatres and lots of good pubs, all amenities lacking in the other places we'd been.

There were no barracks in Brighton. The tanks were parked in one section of a major city park, far enough away from our billets that we were taken to them by truck when we went to do maintenance or drive them to the Downs for training. We stayed in private homes left vacant when the bombing started. The fact that we were in houses didn't mean that we enjoyed any of the finer things in life. We slept on the floors in our underwear, no mattress, no pillow; you spread one blanket on the floor and pulled the other two over you. Your pillow was your small packsack. It was cold sometimes, but we were young and fairly rugged and used to being outside, so we survived.

One of the quiet rural towns where we were quartered was East Grinstead. Two houses held a troop, with the remainder of the squadron occupying a big, old mansion. Because there was room for most of a squadron in the mansion, there was only one troop at any given time sleeping in the houses. The mansion was laid out something like a hotel, with bedrooms upstairs and larger rooms downstairs. The large entrance hall had a huge, circular, marble mosaic on the floor, and when I was hut orderly I used to mop that floor three times, making sure the mop was well rinsed each time, because I liked the mosaic so much I wanted it to be shiny clean. The mansion intrigued me. I used to wander around the overgrown gardens and walks or sit on the neglected patio and wonder about the rich former occupants. Who were they? How far back did the family go? Had they been important? I guess it appealed to the romantic side of my nature. Growing up in Canada, I had heard all about the English nobility from my English-born mother, and here I was living where English nobility had lived.

While we were at East Grinstead, somebody in authority got the bright idea that the troops should plant a Victory garden at one of the houses. We were told to get shovels and picks out of the tanks and set to. The enthusiasm on the part of the fellows was far less than overwhelming, especially when we tried turning over soil that had never been broken and was covered with quack grass that went down a foot and a half and hadn't been cut for years. Fortunately, Mac, our sergeant, could get things out of the guys that nobody else could, and our Victory garden did get dug, more or less, and planted. We sowed seeds and put up sticks for the peas and beans to climb. I don't know whether anything ever grew. The soil was never raked; it had been turned over with shovels and batted down to break up the lumps, creating a sad looking mess of dirt with quack grass sticking out of it which was then left for nature to reclaim.

It was April 1, 1943, that I was promoted to corporal. I had been uninterested in promotion. I didn't think I was held in high enough regard by that gang of rowdies I was with to be an effective NCO, for one thing, and I didn't want to put up with the kind of resistance to authority some NCOs got. The guys weren't that bad, but they did resist authority, and I didn't want to have to deal with it.

Finally there came a day when I was on kitchen fatigue. Since the time I had been a kitchen flunky in a logging camp as a teenager, I had had no love for kitchen fatigue. There I was, up to my neck in big, greasy pots and

Corporal John Galipeau in the black beret of the Armoured Corps, 1943. The badge on the beret is the regimental crest, showing the provincial crest of Alberta with the words "The South Alberta Regt" on a scroll at the bottom. It had to be kept polished and shiny. Just above the two stripes designating my rank as corporal is a "wireless bug," depicting a radio tube producing radio waves, representing my trade as a wireless operator. The cord around my shoulder is a lanyard in the regimental colours of black and gold, an accessory that was added to the uniform by the troops when we were in Nanaimo. The end of it was usually attached to an item that was kept in the jacket pocket, such as a pocket watch or jackknife.

pans and faced with stacks of carrots and turnips and bags of potatoes to peel, when somebody came in and told me, "Get your jacket on, they want you in the orderly room."

When I got to the orderly room, Major Lavoie told me that there were positions for five corporals. The wireless operator in the troop leader's tank was to have the rank of corporal so he could take over command of the tank if something happened to the lieutenant. The sergeant, who had his own tank, could take over the troop, but this way there would be an NCO in each tank when the lieutenant wasn't there. Then Major Lavoie asked me if I was willing to accept the promotion.

I looked at Major Lavoie, but I didn't see Major Lavoie. What I saw was a stack of peeled potatoes and a big, greasy pot. I thought, "Two stripes will get me out of that damn kitchen." And I said, "Yes, sir, I will accept the promotion."

I received no special training to go with the two stripes. I could have used some instruction in personnel management, but the army didn't bother to give that sort of education. More than likely, they worked on the principle that if you had been assessed as able to do the job, you would go ahead and do it. I knew what to do, and most of the time, there wasn't much to it beyond following the regular routine. I made sure the guys were up and dressed, and I would fall in the troop to march to mess hall. I was supposed to keep order in the barracks. If the sergeant wasn't there a corporal was in charge, and if the guys were misbehaving or doing something wrong, it was up to him to take control. Most of the time in barracks, there was no distinction between a corporal and a trooper. The men knew the routine and carried it out, and a corporal had to do very little to assert his authority. There were three corporals in a barracks with each troop, and the senior corporal would be the one to take charge should the need arise.

The nightly bed check was the orderly corporal's responsibility. By ten o'clock, everybody who didn't have a pass was supposed to be in. When we were in barracks at Aldershot or in the Nissen huts at Norfolk, ten o'clock was lights-out time. As orderly corporal I had a list of all those who had passes or were away on leave, and had to check that everybody else was where they were supposed to be. If somebody was missing, I had to report them.

Bed check became a little trickier when we were stationed at Brighton, where we were scattered around. Instead of two troops to a barracks we would be eight men to a house, which made it harder to keep track of where everybody was. I had to go house to house to do the bed check, and I'd commonly find four or five fellows missing who didn't have passes. I was supposed to turn in their names to the orderly sergeant, but these guys were my buddies, and I really didn't want to see them get in trouble. On the other hand, if I turned in a report that said they were in and they got caught downtown, I would be in deep trouble. I told the fellows that I wasn't going to take the heat for them. "If you're caught out downtown after ten when I've reported you in," I said, "you tell them that you were here at ten and you sneaked out afterwards. You take the load, don't dump it on me."

I have no doubt that the sergeants major knew what was going on; in fact, they had told us, "You better make sure that if any of these fellows you've marked in gets caught downtown by the military police, they swear that they were in when you checked and they sneaked out afterwards." In fact, it did happen that guys would show up for bed check and then sneak out to go back to the pub or to meet a girlfriend. As it turned out, none of the Peewees ever got caught downtown. They used to say they were too shifty to get caught, and I had reason to believe them.

As for keeping order, it wasn't always easy. That bunch of ruffians didn't always know when to stop. I remember that Joe Sequin, the French Canadian, got picked on something terrible. Once on kitchen fatigue the fellows were messing around, and somebody took a hot poker and put it across Joe's butt, burning him badly. Another time, in a house at East Grinstead, they put paper on his bed and set it on fire, then blocked the windows and doors so he couldn't get out. They all thought it was funny, but I had to step in and tell them that enough was enough.

When we were in houses rather than barracks the guys had to be in by ten, but the lights-out rule wasn't enforced. The shenanigans would start when the guys who had been at the pub came staggering home. Anybody who had been lying on his bed relaxing or reading soon found himself outside chasing somebody who had antagonised him.

Joe Spence, the Indian from Hobbema, had himself quite a time in England. Indians got a raw deal in Canada, where they weren't allowed to drink in beer parlours even after the war.* There was no such discrimination in England, and Joe made the best of it. Joe was not issued a pistol as a personal weapon. I don't recall his position in the tank – possibly co-driver, in which case he would have been issued a submachine gun instead of a pistol. He may also have been a scout for the squadron, which meant he would have been issued a rifle. Thank God Joe didn't have a pistol, because when he was in his cups he could get pretty wild. He would come in after an evening in the pub and say to me, "Corporal. Give me your pistol."

"What's up, Joe?" I'd ask.

"I got a spy."

"Where's your spy?"

"This guy down in the pub was asking me all about our rifles. He's a spy. I'm going to take him out and shoot him. Gimme your pistol."

"Where is he, Joe?"

---

* Nanaimo was an exception. Those under twenty-one and Natives could not drink in beer parlours, but a couple of private clubs, such as the Eagles, overlooked the regulations for soldiers, and there were places in Chinatown that would serve anyone in secrecy.

"Oh, I'll get him."

"No, no, I'll go down and see him, Joe. Tell me where he is."

Eventually Joe would tell me where he had left his spy, and I would go down and find him. I'd say, "Are you waiting for Joe?"

"Yes, he brought me up here," this poor unfortunate would tell me. "He said you fellows had something special he was going to show me."

"Please," I would say, "just leave. Joe has the notion that you're a spy. Now, maybe you are, and if you are, I want you to get out of here anyway, but if you're not, I suggest you go, because Joe can get kind of strange at times." And he could; if he got really drunk, he would come in wanting to spill blood.

Joe didn't find a spy every night, but I could bank on it that a couple of times a week, I'd be sitting around at ten thirty shining my shoes, and Joe would saunter up to me and say, "Corporal, can I have your pistol?"

"What's up, Joe?"

"Gotta spy."

"Not another one, Joe!"

We were entitled to a nine-day leave every three months. We would save our pay so that we had a bundle to spend when we went on leave. Fellows would visit relatives if they had any, tour Britain if they didn't, go to places they had read about and wanted to see. I travelled to Wales two or three times and visited Ivy's sister Elizabeth, and twice I went north to Hartlepool to visit my mother's relatives. I didn't like going to relatives too often because they were living on rations and I didn't want to be a burden. We usually tried to take something with us if we were going to be staying with people, and we were given a ration coupon book so that our hosts could purchase extra essentials such as butter, eggs and meat if we were going to be staying any length of time. The amounts were small and quickly devoured by a healthy young soldier. I went to Edinburgh twice and really enjoyed it. I didn't go to Glasgow; very few fellows went there unless they had relatives. It was a very rough city, and word was passed to avoid it. They said there were districts in Glasgow where even the cats walked down the centre of the street at night for safety.

Most of the time I spent my leaves in London. London offered everything I wanted. The first two or three times, I went to London on my own.

There were some very good clubs there for soldiers on leave, and the Canadian Legion had set up two hostels where service personnel could get a bed for the night. There were many other hostels, operated by British organizations, for troops on leave, but the Canadian Legion Service Club provided better quality accommodation and food. I enjoyed myself just exploring. Like any other tourist, the first thing I did was to visit Trafalgar Square and 10 Downing Street, Buckingham Palace and the Tower of London. I would spend my nine days exploring the city, riding the Underground, sightseeing, going to the theatres at night, and I came to know London very well.

The London underground railway, or tube as the Londoners called it, was a marvel to me. It was possible to travel anywhere you wished, and it was hard to get lost because there were maps of the system on every station platform and in each rail coach. The tube was my magic carpet, whisking me from one historic site to another throughout the greater London area. At night it was a haven from the German bombs for thousands of London citizens who moved into the stations with blankets and pads or cots to sleep the night in safety on the platforms. By nine o'clock each evening you had to pick your way through family groups snug in their blankets to reach the edge of the platform and board the train. At such times, I would think of my wife, my mother, my father and others at home in Canada, and be thankful they were not having to endure the same plight.

In Brighton we were right under the flight path of the German aircraft going to bomb London, but I never had close experience with bombing until I was in the city. There, air raids were such a part of nightly routine that when the planes came over and the air raid sirens went off and the bombs started falling, the guys staying in the service clubs would just grunt and turn over and go back to sleep. Not too many bothered to get up and go down to the air raid shelters. It would have meant getting dressed and dragging our packs with us, and it was not worth the trouble. In the movie theatres they would flash a sign on the screen when bombing started saying that there was an air raid in progress and anybody who wished to leave to go to a shelter could do so. Not many Canadian or British military personnel left; however, it was a matter of some discussion that the majority of those who did leave were wearing American forces uniforms.

By this time the Americans were stationed all over England, and a source of great amusement to the other Allied forces was the number of medal ribbons the American soldiers wore. It seemed like an American could have three rows of ribbons before he even got into action, because every time he passed a course or qualified on a particular skill, he was given a medal. There was a story that went around about two Americans who were in a movie house when the air raid announcement came on the screen. The Americans stayed, and one fainted and the other one received a medal.

We didn't think much of the American custom of giving out medals so freely. We received the Canadian Volunteer Service medal sometime in 1943, and we were happy to get it, but we thought it was too easily given and it didn't mean that much to us. If we were going to have a medal, we wanted to feel we'd done something to earn it. At the time, the Canadian government had defeated a vote on conscription by a large majority, but had enacted a program that required men to take thirty days' training in the armed forces, after which they were released. We called these fellows "thirty day wonders." The purpose of the program was to establish a pool of men who at least had some training and were ready to integrate into the forces if need be. Some of them did decide to stay on and come overseas, but they couldn't be sent over against their wishes. The idea of the Canadian Volunteer Service medal was to acknowledge those who had volunteered before there was any form of compulsory service.

Eventually, I became quite friendly with another corporal, Danny White. We liked to do the same kinds of things, so we took leaves to London together. Herb Roulston, also a corporal, was entirely different in nature from us. I don't think he could find anybody who wished to go on leave with him, so he asked if he could go with us. We said he could, but we ended up regretting our offer. Herb was a heavy-duty drinker. He was just about the only one of us who would get so drunk that he became obnoxious. He could be quite belligerent when he was drinking, and when, on leave, he couldn't find someone else to fight, he would challenge Danny or me. After the first couple of times we tried to leave him behind, but he always managed to come along.

When we went into battle, Herb proved to be one of the bravest and finest soldiers in the regiment.

This was when I really learned to drink beer. The pubs were warm, dry and friendly, and going to the pub was an agreeable way to spend time after hours and on weekends and leaves. We had a favourite pub, the Orange Tree in Euston Square, but we didn't restrict ourselves. The three of us covered London pub to pub and did some wild and wonderful things. The pubs had broken hours; most opened at eleven, closed from noon to three, then opened again until about ten. I can recall coming out of the pub one evening and seeing an elderly woman selling flowers. We were in a state where we were feeling good and loved everybody, so we bought every flower she had and went down the street giving them away to ladies standing in the theatre lineups.

Danny and Herb used to give me a hard time about not being able to keep up with their drinking, and they were right, I couldn't. I used to eat something every couple of hours as well as drink, and I would get so full I couldn't drink any more. Danny had been in the Edmonton Regiment and had gone through the same experience with the hard drinkers in that unit, and he told me that he just used to go to the toilet and put his finger down his throat, get rid of what was in his stomach, then come back and start over. I couldn't do that just to keep Herb and Danny quiet.

During afternoon closing time we sometimes wandered down to Covent Garden. Before the war it had been a theatre, but it was used as a dance hall throughout most of the war, and would hold thousands of dancers on its huge floor. It was frequented by servicemen from all the Allied forces. I finally broke down and started to dance. There were plenty of dance partners. People thought nothing of a married women going to a dance and leaving her husband at home, or going out dancing while he was away at war. To our minds, that made British husbands very broad-minded, but all the women were going for was just to dance. It was perfectly respectable. That suited me. I wasn't looking for romance; I was married and I wanted to be straight about it. But I did enjoy going to the dances, and my dancing began to improve, or so I thought; at least, I was no longer self conscious.

Sometimes Herb, Danny and I rode the Underground to an outlying pub. We were standing in the middle of the subway car headed back into the centre of town one night after one of these expeditions, not really arguing, just quibbling a bit the way three half-drunk guys will. After a while I noticed that there was no one around us. We came to station after station, and nobody sat down near us. I looked at the other end of the car, and it was jam packed; the seats were full, the straps all had people hanging on them, but no one came down to our part of the coach. It struck me that they were scared of us. I thought it was kind of funny. We were noisy, but we were not going to hurt anybody.

At one station a woman got on and leaned up against the wall not far from us, looking out the window. Danny wanted to know where we were, so Herb said he would go see. He walked over to where the woman was standing and said, "Can I look out your window?"

"I'd prefer that you jumped out," she replied. That cracked us up. We laughed about it all the way back to the Canadian Legion, where we were staying.

Herb, as I've mentioned, could be belligerent, especially where American soldiers were concerned. One afternoon we went to a theatre. When the show was over we had a few pints of beer, then went to the dance hall on the second floor of the building next door. It was filled with Americans, big, brawny guys. As soon as we got in the door, Herb had his jacket off, ready to take on the lot of them. "Oh, God, we're dead," I said to Danny. Fortunately, the Americans wanted no part of it. Herb was a tough looking fellow, about 5′6″, but there were at least 200 Americans there. We were escorted back down the stairs and out into the street, where our American escorts offered to accommodate any of us if we still wanted to fight. Danny declined their offer and said we would be on our way; so off we went, with Herb telling Danny and me how chickenshit we were.

Sometimes, after pubbing all afternoon, I wanted to have a good meal for supper and go for a quiet walk beside the Thames to clear my head, or sit in Trafalgar Square and people-watch. One afternoon, having heard about a small theatre in the Elephant and Castle district that had an excellent musical variety show, I told Herb and Danny that I was going to have supper and go to the show, and I would see them later. "Later" turned out to be when we woke up in the Club the next morning. Heading back to where we were staying in Euston Square, I got off at the wrong stop. As I walked down the way I heard music coming from an upstairs

hall, so I decided to go up and see what was going on. The hall was full of
civilians. There was a little tea cart in the corner, so I ordered tea and a
crumpet and sat down to watch the dancing. I had just finished my tea
and was thinking about leaving when the orchestra played the last dance,
so I started down the stairs with the rest of the crowd. Well, I thought I'd
somehow got in among seventy-five Herb Roulstons, every one of them
looking for a fight. I got bumped from the side, bumped from behind. It
was pretty clear I wasn't welcome. I soon realized from their accents,
which were so thick you could cut them with a knife, that I had fallen in
with a bunch of Irish workers who had been brought over to do war work.
As far as they were concerned, I was a British soldier, and Irish workers
did not like British soldiers. The Canada badge didn't mean a damn thing
to them. Being the biggest coward in the world, I reached the bottom of
the stairs and did double time down the street. I hailed the first taxi that
came along and told the driver to take me to the Canadian Legion Service
Club. I had my fill of Irishmen that night!

One place that interested me greatly was Canada House, which was
open for troops during the war. There was a reading room and a lounge
and the world's largest crap game, played on a snooker table. That table
never saw a pool ball, but it saw an awful lot of dice. I never counted, but
I'm sure there were close to a hundred men, from every regiment as well
as the air force and the navy, standing two or three deep around the table,
either shooting craps or watching the game. I never did get my hands on
the dice, because it took hours for them to go around the table, but, along
with most of the other fellows, I bet on whether the fellow rolling the dice
would make his points.

There was usually a card game going at night in the barracks, and on
Sundays and in the afternoon if it was close to payday. Some of the fellows played bridge if they could get together a foursome and a place to
play, but usually it was a penny ante poker game or a game called stook.
Stook resembles blackjack, in that the object is to acquire a hand totalling
as near twenty-one points as possible without going over. However, in
blackjack, the dealer plays against the whole table. In stook, he plays
against each other player in turn. The dealer places a pot in the middle of
the table to act as a bank, and each player places a bet in any amount up

to the value of the bank. The dealer holds the deal until the bank goes broke, or until three rounds have been played, at which time the deal passes to the player on the dealer's left.

The troop really got into dice when a character we all knew as "Needles" joined us. His real name was R. Nield; I never knew what the R stood for. He had been a rumrunner on the east coast during the Depression, and he fit right in. His personality seemed suited to his former profession; he was never perturbed, no matter what the situation. Needles always had a pair of dice in his pocket, and he didn't miss an opportunity to take them out and get a game going. When we stopped for our ten-minute rest every hour on a route march, Needles would shake his dice, and it wasn't long before there would be four or five guys on their knees at the side of the road shooting craps.

I enjoyed playing dice, and I was fairly lucky and did all right. When I went home I asked Ivy if she wanted to learn how to play. I never made a pass, and she made every point! That humiliated and cured me. I stayed away from gambling after I got home, especially when I joined the Legion. Some of the fellows carried on and got in over their heads and lost a lot of money. Years later I played what we called Depression Poker. There was a four-dollar limit that you put in, and if you went broke, you kept playing. We played in different homes, with the host providing sandwiches and beer. The most it would cost you to play all night would be four dollars. If you had a lucky night and cleaned up, your total winnings could be thirty-two dollars.

All during my time overseas, Ivy and I were writing back and forth; at least, Ivy was writing. She was very faithful. She wrote conscientiously at least once a week, and I got lots of letters and packages from home. Those letters and packages meant a lot to me. I am very much ashamed to admit that I did not keep up my letters in return. I had a terrible time writing. The other fellows seemed to be able to sit down and in fifteen minutes, they'd have three letters written. I couldn't do that. When there was a letter to be written I'd procrastinate, and poor Ivy was lucky if she got a letter once a month.

Parcels from home usually included cartons of cigarettes. We all had lots of cigarettes, because the tobacco companies offered a deal where if you sent them a dollar they would ship 300 cigarettes overseas in a carton. Most of us got our people at home to order cigarettes for us, either in the carton of 300 or by the thousand, from a cigarette company, which would parcel them and mail them to the regimental address. If you ran short of cigarettes, you could also go up to Canada House and get a carton of 300.

We spent the summer of 1943 out doing field exercises, often up in Norfolk firing on the ranges. On November 1 we moved to Maresfield Camp, a little north and east of Brighton. Instead of being scattered in squadrons, we were together again as a regiment in proper brick barracks, with a room at the end for the corporals. Our schemes continued, and then on December 23 the regiment went to Lydd Ranges for firing practice, and that was where we spent Christmas. On December 31 the regiment went back to Maresfield, except for "A" Squadron. We went up to the Moorcock Ranges near Norfolk, a fine place to spend New Year's. It was raining, and Moorcock was nothing but a big sea of mud and tin Nissen huts. We fired our tanks, and on New Year's Day, 1944, headed back to Maresfield.

The regiment went through a number of changes in senior officers over a short period of time. We got a new colonel, Lieutenant Colonel G.D. de S. Wotherspoon. I never knew what the initials stood for.* We learned after the war the other officers called him "Swatty," though not to his face. At first we missed our old colonel, but it turned out to be lucky for the regiment. Wotherspoon took us through the war, and we couldn't have had a better colonel. He was a brilliant man and knew what he was doing. It was often said that the Brigadier consulted with him when we were in action with the 10th Brigade.

Shortly after Lieutenant Colonel Wotherspoon arrived, Fightin' Frank retired. We all felt a bit shaken up at losing him. His replacement as divisional commander, General George Kitching, visited each regiment to introduce himself, and I remember the day that we gathered in a big hall to meet him. I can't say we were overly inspired by our first impression. We were used to Fightin' Frank in his black beret and battle dress. The man who stepped out on stage was a well dressed, tall, distinguished-

---

* I have since learned that his full name was Gordon Dorward de Salaberry Wotherspoon.

looking fellow with British-style moustache, British bearing and British decorum. He was a graduate of Sandhurst Military College and wore the dress uniform with a Sam Browne belt; all in all, the image of a perfect King's general. In stark contrast to General Worthington's plain speech and rough and ready fashion, he spoke to us in proper English manner, complete with the proper English accent. His appearance and presentation did little to inspire admiration in the minds of the wild colonial boys of the SAR. We figured we'd been saddled with a wimp.

General Kitching took us into battle, and I guess he was a well enough trained and experienced fellow, but I feel Frank Worthington deserves most of the credit for how prepared we were for action. Not only did he make sure we got the training we needed; he took pains to prepare us psychologically, as well. There would be a debriefing after a scheme, and if he thought we weren't performing to the standards he wanted to see, he didn't mince words. He would stand up on the back of a truck and tell us, "You fellows are living on borrowed time. The average life of a tank crew in action is fifteen minutes. So you'd better smarten up, or you're not going to make it very far."

I'm not entirely sure why Worthington was retired. Age may have been a factor, but I can't help but think that military politics had something to do with it. Frank was a go-getter who knew his business, and I think the higher-ups may have felt somewhat threatened by him. With his knowledge and ability, and his determination to go in and get what he felt he needed, he'd be a little bit hard to handle. He would say what he thought, and do what he thought right with his division. I think everybody felt that he should have been given the chance to lead us into battle, because of the kind of person he was and what he'd done to bring the Fourth Division to the standard it was when he turned it over to General Kitching.

Another new addition to the regiment was someone who gained a lot of respect from the men, our new padre, Honorary Captain Albert Silcox. He was a fantastic man. Everybody in the regiment loved him. He was not sanctimonious, he was down to earth, just one of the fellows. If you needed help, he was there for you. Poor Ivy had to get in touch with him the following winter when we were in action in Holland. She wrote to Captain Silcox and asked whether there was anything wrong with me because she hadn't heard from me for so long. He came and had a talk with me, and I tried to explain that I would sit down in the tank intending to write a letter, but I could never figure out what I had to say. I didn't want to talk about battles, and there wasn't much of anything else to tell her, other than to say I was fine. I can understand why she was concerned, but I just found it very hard to write. To this very day, I am ashamed when I think that if I had written even just a few lines, it would have relieved her anxiety.

It was while we were in Maresfield that I got a letter from Ivy that disturbed me very much. After the regiment left to go overseas, Ivy had gone back to Nanaimo, where she'd got a good job as an accountant at the Plaza Hotel. She wrote and said that she'd been asked if she would be interested in joining the Women's Auxiliary Air Force (WAAF), which would bring her overseas. I discouraged her. None of the fellows really advocated their wives joining the forces, though it did happen in many cases. In general, the women that joined the Canadian forces received a great deal of criticism from the rank and file. There was really no reason for it, except that it seemed that we never had contact with women in military service. Except for the nurses who were in the field hospitals, the servicewomen were always put someplace where only the officers had contact with them, or so it seemed to the lower ranks. We used to say, "Yeah, they're only here for the benefit of the officers," never considering, in our ignorance, that the servicewomen, being employed in military headquarters as clerical staff and drivers, always worked in areas frequented by officers, and naturally were quartered near their work places, as were the headquarters officers. The criticism was undeserved, and it was very wrong of us, but I didn't want to have my wife being put in this position.

Then, too, I knew that I was soon going over to France and wouldn't see her anyway, so there didn't seem to be much point in her joining up. When I think about it now I realize that there would have been advantages for her. With her education, she would have had a commission. She would have been able to visit her sister in Wales, whom she hadn't seen for years, and she wanted to do her bit for the war, like anybody else. However, I was swayed by how the other fellows talked about the women in the services and convinced her not to enlist.

It was that same attitude that led to my final break with Sammy Marshall, who had been my buddy when I first joined up. We stayed in touch after he left the regiment when we moved to Nanaimo. He had been married since then, and while I was overseas he wrote to say that his wife was joining up. I, foolishly, wrote back saying that I thought he should try and persuade her not to go into the forces. I got a letter back from Sammy, chastizing me to say the least, and, to my regret, I lost touch with him after that.

On April 25, 1944, all leave was stopped, so we knew things were getting serious. Our letters were all censored by the troop officer, which didn't go over well with some of the fellows who felt it was an intrusion into their privacy. I don't imagine the troop officer was any happier than they were, but with the deadline for the Allied invasion of Europe drawing near, we had to make sure there was nothing said, in all innocence, that might give information to the enemy.

By this time, England was overcrowded with Allied troops. Every corner that wasn't filled with British troops was occupied by Canadians or Americans or Poles or Australians, as well as French, Norwegian and other troops that had escaped when the Germans invaded their countries, all waiting for the Second Front invasion. The country was packed. On May 21 we began waterproofing the tanks so that if the landing craft were not able to get close enough to shore to allow us to unload on dry land, we could drive them through water. This meant sealing the muzzles of the guns and all the openings where the guns met the turret and the turret met the hull with gun tape, which was similar to what we now call duct tape. At the back of the tank we fastened a square duct made of sheet metal rising maybe four feet above the back deck, open near the bottom for the engine exhaust pipe, so that the tank would continue to run even if immersed to within a foot of the top of the turret. The air for the carburetor and for cooling the engine was drawn in through the turret hatch. We caulked every seam and crack on the hull and covered them with gun tape. Small explosive charges were set, to be detonated electronically when the tank reached dry land to remove the gun muzzle sealing and the duct from the back deck. When we were done, we tested our workmanship by driving the tanks through a depression in the ground filled with eight feet of water and checking for leaks. A number of tanks were picked at random and taken to the beach training area, where they were driven out into the ocean to test the waterproofing in the salt water and waves.

On May 21 we started waterproofing the tanks, and on May 22 we stopped waterproofing the tanks and took them out on the ranges for a final firing check. The tanks we had were new Shermans, and somebody suddenly realized that we had better make sure that the guns were sighted in before everything was sealed up. Once the waterproofing was done, the tanks weren't moved until we left for the continent, although we did go down each day, start up the engines and perform our regular maintenance checks. For the next while we killed time with small arms practice on the ranges, firing pistols and the infamous Sten guns, playing team sports and going out on route marches.

Finally the big day dawned: D-Day, June 6, 1944. We heard about it on a German broadcast somebody had picked up at seven in the morning. We were all excited now that the Allied invasion had really begun, and we were relieved we weren't part of the first assault. Maybe we should have wished that we were among those who led the way, but we knew what the fellows leading the invasion had to face, and we were just as glad we weren't there. We knew it was just a matter of time before our turn would come.

At night we heard the German bombers fly in on their raids, and on June 16 the first buzz bombs passed over our camp. The German V-1 flying bomb was nicknamed the buzz bomb because it sputtered along like

(Facing page) The Sherman was one of the great tanks of the war, and it was the Sherman, in its various versions, that took us into battle. Crews were pleased to find the interior larger and more comfortable than that of the Ram. The model shown here is a Sherman V (M4A4). Its body was about 19 feet long, almost 9 feet wide and 9 feet high. It was armed with a 75 mm main gun plus two .30 calibre Browning machine guns. The engine produced 450 horsepower at 2400 rpm. Fuel consumption was one mile per gallon. It had a crew of five: driver, co-driver, gunner, wireless operator and crew commander. The British fitted a number of Shermans with a high-velocity 17-pounder gun in place of the 75 mm (which was outclassed by 1943), eliminating the co-driver position to make room for the larger shells. The Sherman was used by the SAR from January 1944 until the European war ended in May 1945. (Drawings by Chris Johnson)

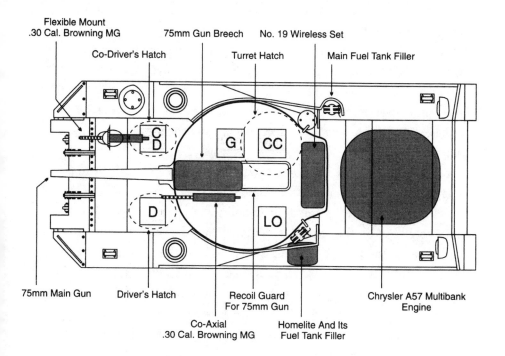

Flexible Mount
.30 Cal. Browning MG

Co-Driver's Hatch

75mm Gun Breech

Turret Hatch

No. 19 Wireless Set

Main Fuel Tank Filler

75mm Main Gun

Driver's Hatch

Recoil Guard
For 75mm Gun

Chrysler A57 Multibank
Engine

Co-Axial
.30 Cal. Browning MG

Homelite And Its
Fuel Tank Filler

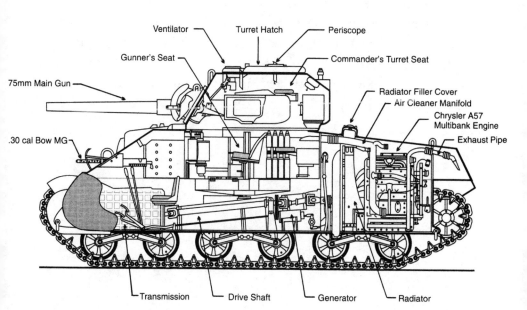

Ventilator

Turret Hatch

Periscope

Gunner's Seat

Commander's Turret Seat

75mm Main Gun

Radiator Filler Cover
Air Cleaner Manifold
Chrysler A57
Multibank Engine

.30 cal Bow MG

Exhaust Pipe

Transmission

Drive Shaft

Generator

Radiator

a motorcycle. It was jet-propelled. When the engine quit, the bomb dove into the earth and exploded. They were fired at London from the continent, but sometimes the engine quit prematurely and they came down much sooner than intended. I understand the Germans were afraid of them because of that flaw. In the evenings we used to sit up on top of the barracks, where we could see more, and watch the fighter planes go out to intercept them. Some would fly up beside the buzz bomb and try to just clip the wing to throw it off course. Most pilots tried to explode the bomb in the air using gun fire. Since the V-1 flew faster than most of the fighter planes, clipping the wing was not easily accomplished, and there was no way to control where the damaged bomb would fall.

On July 18, 1944, we were on our way. We were to go in convoy to the docks in London, from where we would cross the Channel to France. We left after dark. Earlier in the day the tanks had been brought into line ready to go out on the road in a column. The "A" Squadron tanks were right outside the main door into the NAAFI canteen. When the command came to mount up, we all knew that this was a one-way trip. We'd spent two years fighting a make-believe enemy. In a few days we were going to see the genuine article face to face. As we left the camp, on our way to leave England, the NAAFI girls stood in the doorway of the canteen, with tears in their eyes, and waved to every tank and truck that went by.

That departure brought the future into focus for me. From here on we were going to be living day by day, moment by moment. I never thought about being killed. What I worried about was whether I was going to be able to stand up to the terror of battle. After an hour on the road, of course, my reflective mood was gone, and we were on just another dreary drive through England in the dark.

CHAPTER 10

Baptism of Fire

We drove all night. We hadn't been told our destination, but come first light I could see we were in London. It was early morning and there was nobody on the streets. We were on our own.

It must have been quite something to see the column of tanks making their way through the streets of London, but I suppose Londoners were used to it by the time we came through. Troops had been moving through to the docks for several weeks; the Fourth Division was the last Canadian division to go to the continent. When I thought about what a massive movement of personnel had taken place in a short time, it seemed to me that Britain must have felt very empty all of a sudden. I've wondered since how the English really felt when we all left. The country had been jammed with troops, every hole and corner, and suddenly the English people had their country back. I wonder whether they missed us.

It was daylight when we got to the docks and pulled up in column in our assembly area. We did a last parade on the tanks and went to bed. We slept until noon, then went to the mess hall for dinner. We spent the night with our tanks, prepared for loading the next day. We were supposed to stay put, but, being good, resourceful Canadian soldiers, we were able to find an opening in the fence where we could get out and have a final last fling down the road at the local. It was a nice evening, and a few of us sat out on the grass outside the pub. I was talking with a fellow from the British Columbia Regiment who knew Ivy, so when the guy I had gone to the pub with decided to go back early, I told him to go on without me. "I'm fine," I said. "I'll just have another pint."

I left just as it was starting to get dark, about ten o'clock at night in mid-July, and somewhere along the way I took a wrong turn. The staging area was huge. There were American troops, Canadians, British, all in large fenced enclosures, and I couldn't find the right one. I went up one road and down the next, trying to locate my regiment. Midnight passed and I was soaked with sweat and practically in a panic, because reveille was at first light and we were going to load. I knew that when your regiment is ready to go into action and you're not there, you're considered a deserter. I was just about to give up and make a real break for it when suddenly, there was the hole in the fence and the "A" Squadron tanks. I slipped in through the hole and into the wee tent we had set up with a tarp at the back of the tank to catch a couple of hours sleep before we moved out. At that moment, I was the happiest man on earth.

The next day, the tanks were loaded by crane onto the decks of Liberty ships, which were freighters the Americans built for transport of supplies to Britain during the war. Crossing the English Channel took two days. My troop was lucky. By the time they got to us, the decks of all the Liberty ships were full, so half the squadron, our four tanks and the tanks of the headquarters troop, were put aboard an American LST (Landing Ship Tank). This was a vessel that could be run up on the beach and had a front ramp that could be dropped to load or unload. Everything about the landing ship was typically American. When the Americans wanted a ship, they decided what kind of a crew would be needed, and then they built the vessel to accommodate them. An American LST would hold at least twenty or more tanks; as we had only eight on board, there was a great deal of empty space. How it came to be I will never know, but 4 Troop and HQ Troop travelled first class across the English Channel.

We had heard rumours of how the Americans lived, but this was fantastic. There was everything on that ship, including automatic washing machines, which we saw then for the first time (we'd just seen wringer washers before), and bunks with mattresses. By this time, a mattress was quite a novelty. Much of the time we had been in England, when it was time to sleep you spread a blanket on the floor, pulled a couple more over top of you, and that was it. The floor can be the most comfortable bed in the world to sleep on once you get used to it. When I came home and started sleeping in a bed again, it didn't feel right. It was so soft I sometimes had a back ache.

However, they had proper three-tiered bunks on this landing ship, and the food! We couldn't believe it. When we went up for breakfast in the morning there was a cafeteria line to go through with scrambled eggs and bacon, and the eggs and bacon kept coming as long as you held your plate out. There was orange juice, hashed brown potatoes, everything you could have wanted. It was heaven. They didn't have a large crew on the ship, so to show our appreciation, we went below and mopped everything down: the area where we slept, the latrines, or heads as they called them, the laundry area; we scrubbed and cleaned so it shone. They were very pleased. One of them told us, "We never hauled Canadians before, but I see you are the guys we should have been carrying all along."

He said that most of the time they had been carrying troops who were not Americans or Canadians down into North Africa and Italy, and the degree of help and cooperation they had received had been totally different. Where we helped out by cleaning up or in any other way we could, the foreign troops, as they were referred to, did not.

The final meal was a revelation. It was steak, T-bone steak. I don't know how long it had been since we had seen steak. Since rationing had begun earlier in the war, not even the people back home in Canada were getting T-bone steaks on a regular basis. We all went in the food line and took a big steak, and instead of eating inside, we took our plates out and sat on the deck to eat. It was quite rough and the ship was rolling, but we didn't want to be inside. When we were finished, one of the mess crew came out and said, "Another steak for any of you guys?"

Back in we went for more, and we were sitting there like a bunch of bloated pigs when the steward came out of the mess with a big pan of cooked steaks. There must have been twenty or thirty steaks in the pan, and he just threw them overboard. We were shocked at the waste, but I don't suppose there was much else they could do with them. To avoid sickness due to spoiled food, regulations prevented them from keeping leftover meat to be served at another meal.

The next afternoon, July 25, 1944, we landed in France on Gold Beach, at a village called Courseulles-sur-mer, near Bayeux. The LST took us right up to the beach, so there turned out to be no need for the water-proofing and all that work had been for nothing as far as we were concerned, but nobody knew ahead of time under what conditions we would be landing. The tanks that had been loaded on board the decks of the Liberty ships landed somewhat differently. The ships anchored some distance from the beach. The tanks were unloaded by cranes from the open deck to landing craft that ferried them, two tanks at a time, to the beach. Whether they drove off onto dry land or had to go through water I never bothered to find out. I learned that the fellows who had shipped over on Liberty ships had not had as pleasant a trip. They had slept on the decks with their tanks and had eaten from combat ration packs. I am firmly convinced that no other soldiers in all of the Allied armies travelled to France in the luxury that the Peewees and Headquarters Troop of "A" Squadron enjoyed.

As soon as we landed we moved across the beach onto some high ground, where we formed up and spent the night, sleeping beside the tanks. We were in close proximity to the line of action, and the reality of what we were up against started to sink in. We heard some German planes come over and wondered whether we were going to find out right then and there what it was going to be like to be bombed or shelled or strafed, but they didn't bother us. We didn't need a visit from the enemy planes to tell us we were in the war zone. We could see the devastation, the shattered buildings and the bombed-out country, we could hear the artillery at the front line not far away, and the air was thick with the stench of death.

We moved a little way inland the following morning and harboured the tanks in a large, unploughed field, where we removed the waterproof-ing and made sure they were ready for action. The front line was only four or five miles away, and we could clearly hear the sounds of battle. One of the men who had been transferred to the Service Corps when the regi-ment went armoured came riding a motorbike down the road out of no-where. We recognized him, now a sergeant major, and he stopped for a moment to kibitz with us, saying, "What are you guys doing sitting here? They need you up at the front!"

Unlike the poor fellows who had arrived on D-Day and were thrown right into the thick of the fighting, we were eased into battle. On July 29 we moved up to the city of Caen, which was a terrible mess. The only way the Allies could drive the Germans out was by bombing so extensively

The destruction wrought by the Allies in driving the Germans from Caen, France, was beyond belief. I couldn't imagine how it could possibly be cleaned up and the city rebuilt. This photo, taken months after the action that caused this devastation took place, shows the residents going about their daily affairs among the ruins. Where possible, Allied forces avoided such extensive damage, and Caen was the worst I saw – until we entered Germany. There, our artillery and air force bombers purposely and systematically set about the destruction of the cities of Cleve and Emmerich. Like other invaders throughout history, I, and I believe many of my comrades, relished giving the enemy some of his own back on his home ground. (SAR)

that the city was destroyed. We were only there for one day before we moved to relieve the Third Division from their position on the line. "A" Squadron went to a position near a village called Bourgébus in support of the Lincoln and Welland Regiment. We saw signs of battle everywhere. Nobody had had a chance to bury the German dead, and the fields were littered with their bloated corpses. We noticed immediately all the corpses were barefoot. Apparently, the French people in the area, who had been without boots for so long, were not about to let the big, beautiful jackboots that the Germans wore go to waste.

There wasn't much happening as we sat alongside the road. I was dozing off when I was startled awake by the appearance of the biggest tank I'd ever seen. It was three times the length of a Sherman and twice as wide, with a double turret and four guns. It looked like a battleship coming down the road. When the supertank went by, I saw that it was a fake, manufactured out of sheet metal welded like a parade float onto a regular Sherman. Close up it wouldn't fool anybody, but from a distance it would really look impressive. It was taken up on the hill overlooking the front and driven back and forth with the idea of intimidating the Germans by showing them what they were going to have to deal with now that the Fourth Division had arrived. I don't know how much it frightened the Germans. I suspect they probably said, "Bring it on! We want to see how good it is!"

The manufacture of this false supertank served to bring to light something that always bothered me, and I think bothered a lot of people. The German armour was much better equipped than the Allied armour. Their tanks were so heavily armoured that the shells from our low velocity 75 mm guns didn't penetrate at all on a frontal attack; they just bounced off. Germans I met after the war told me that they called our Sherman tanks "Ronsons" or "cigarette lighters," because the 200 gallons of gasoline they carried for fuel, along with all the ammunition, meant that they were very likely to go up in flame when they were hit in a vital spot. The German tanks were diesel, which didn't ignite as readily. The 88 mm gun that many of the German tanks carried was far superior to our 75 mm. The 88 was an anti-aircraft gun that they had brought down from its overhead firing position and adapted so it could be fired over sights on level ground. One model was made to fit the tanks. The projectile wasn't much bigger, but the power behind it made the 88 a much more effective weapon. The muzzle velocity was fantastic, faster than the speed of sound. The first time we encountered it, we found that the shell would hit and explode before the sound it made when it was fired reached us.

The Shermans had some advantages over the German tanks. Our turret, for example, was powered by a hydraulic motor, and all the gunner had to do if he wanted to traverse the turret was turn a hand grip lever. The turrets in the German tanks were all traversed by a crank. They used to say if a Tiger started firing at you, you could back around and get out of the way before he could crank his turret around to catch you. But we

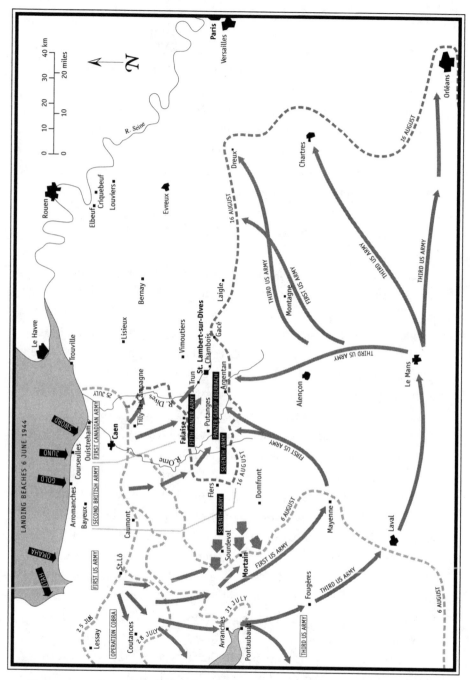

The map shows the progress of the Allied armies from the landings on June 6, 1944, to August 16. It shows clearly the Falaise pocket formed by the advance of the British and Canadian armies from the north and the Americans sweeping around to the south. (Adapted from *South Albertas: A Canadian Regiment at War*)

weren't very happy about the lack of armour when we were in combat with the 88. It had the power to punch right through the tank, in one side and out the other. Once we got into battle and found out what we were up against, whenever possible we would have the fitters weld old tank tracks from both German and Sherman tanks that had been destroyed in action on the front and the side of our tanks to give us more protection.

I could never understand why the most industrialized nations in the world, Britain and the United States, could not provide us with a tank to at least equal the one produced by the Germans. I guess a deciding factor was that the Americans could turn out Shermans by the thousands, so the Allies chose quantity over quality.

"A" Squadron drew the distinction of being the first squadron of the 29th Armoured Regiment to go into action. We were attacking a town called Tilly-la-Campagne, which was a well-fortified stronghold that the Germans had held against repeated attacks. They had underground tunnels, so when we started shelling, they could just disappear until we were out of ammunition. I don't think we were expected to be any more successful in our attack on Tilly than anybody had been before us, but it provided an opportunity to ease us into battle.

It was in the late afternoon while we were preparing for the attack on Tilly that we suffered our first casualty. The Germans would fire airburst shells over our positions. An airburst shell is a shell that explodes 50 to 100 feet up in the air above you and fires down shrapnel. We were loading the tanks, and we had one fellow up on the back packing the bedrolls and placing gear in the storage box fastened to the back of the turret (it was called a blanket box, but was used for general storage) when he was hit by an airburst fragment. It shot down from above and tore through part of his shoulder, digging a gouge through his chest an inch or more deep, while smaller fragments hit him in two or three other places on his arm. He went down, and everybody went into shock and just stood there; except for an older fellow who quietly climbed up on the tank and took control. He started giving first aid to the wounded fellow and telling us what to do, and we managed to regain our senses and begin to function again.

We became acquainted with another wonderful weapon during the assault on Tilly, one we called the Moaning Minnie. It was a six-barrelled mortar, with the barrels arranged in a circle like the cylinder of a revolver. It could fire six bombs at once, and each of the bombs made a strange howling sound as it flew through the air. The beauty of it was that at least you could hear it coming and could take some kind of cover. It had a devastating effect on infantry. We considered it another German weapon from hell.

We moved on Tilly that night. The Lincoln and Wellands made their attack, supported by 2 Troop and 3 Troop of "A" Squadron. As had happened before, the attack got part way in and ran into heavy firepower and the troops had to retreat. Our squadron commander, Major Lavoie, received a compliment from the colonel acknowledging how well "A" Squadron had acted to help bring the Lincoln and Wellands out.

That night 4 Troop, my troop, was held back in reserve position alongside a railway embankment, ready to go in if needed. One troop was always held in reserve so that if any of the troops in action got into trouble, there was someone to assist or provide cover for them. It was a late attack, and dark. One of the other tanks called on the radio and said they were having trouble with their intercom system, would I go back and help find the problem? I walked maybe the length of a city block back to the tank with the malfunctioning intercom, checked the system, found the trouble and corrected it. When I was finished, instead of walking back to my tank along the road, I went up the railway bank to see what was going on. Before me was a sea of fire. The earth was ablaze with tracer shells and explosives, and I couldn't imagine how anybody could come out of such an onslaught alive.

That was my introduction to battle. After we supported the Lincoln and Wellands' withdrawal, we moved back to the bivouac area where we had spent the previous few days. The next morning the regiment returned to Caen for a short time until we made our next move. We spent our spare time prowling the rubble and snooping in the empty buildings.

Of course, any hint of barracks or billets was long gone. We were living in our tanks. We cooked our own food from the rations issued to us every day, and each member of the crew did his part in turn. There were no bathroom facilities. When nature called, you retired a few steps behind some shrubbery with a shovel to dig a hole. When we got up we would wash and shave, and that was it. Once we got into battle, we would go days without a wash or a shave, or much sleep, and we would get very wild and grubby-looking. We would look forward to coming out of action and going to a rest area, where we could get cleaned up at a mobile bath and laundry unit. The mobile bath unit had a boiler to heat water and a half dozen or so shower heads out in the open air; it was a very basic setup. You would have a shower and pick up clean underwear and shirts from the big pile provided, sorting through until you found something that would fit you, and throwing your dirty clothes in to be washed.

Rations were brought up each day, and we were well fed. We even had white bread. There was a lot of canned stuff: canned meat, canned stew, soup. I remember one ingenious device for heating soup. Down the centre of the can ran a tube with a fuse and a striking plate at the top. You took the top off the can, struck the fuse, let it burn for a minute or so, then opened up the can and enjoyed nice, hot soup. I always wondered why it was never adapted for the domestic market. One of the strangest concoctions in a ration pack was compo-tea, so named because of its composition of tea leaves and milk powder mixed together. Place two spoonfuls in a cup and add boiling water, and, presto, tea with milk. Not exactly like Mother brewed, but at least it was a hot drink. What those who preferred their tea without milk were supposed to drink obviously was of no concern to the inventor of this unpalatable mixture.

Cooking out in the field gave an opportunity for the Canadian soldier to demonstrate his ingenuity. The tanks were supplied with a small, pump-up gasoline stove, but it didn't cook fast enough. We soon learned to take a cut-down pail, fill it half full of sand, pour gasoline on the sand and light it. The gasoline fumes rising from the sand fuelled the flame and provided plenty of heat to cook with, although it wasn't entirely satisfactory because it blackened everything. Then someone invented what became known as the famous Western Front stove. They must have been inspired by the setup the squadron cooks had for outdoor use. This was a five foot long metal plate with a burner underneath to which white gasoline was pumped under pressure. The burner was similar to a blow torch, only much larger. When it was ignited, a hot, blue flame extended under the metal plate on which the cooking pots and pans sat.

Some bright lad adapted the idea for use at the tanks. You put about a half a gallon of gasoline in a five-gallon jerry can, just enough to produce fumes for the length of time you would need it for cooking. A jerry can was rectangular and had flat sides. You laid the can flat on one of the wider sides. In the middle of one of the narrow sides, about halfway up and halfway across, you punched a nailhole and plugged it with a wooden match. You raised the jerry can on a couple of stones or empty cans so there was a space beneath it. Then you sat a small can on a shovel, put a cup or so of gasoline in the small can and ignited it. You slid the can of burning gasoline under the jerry can. When the gasoline in the jerry can was heated enough that it was producing fumes under pressure, you pulled the match out of the nail hole and ignited the stream of vapour that ensued, creating a blowtorch effect. While the gasoline in the jerry can was heating you would have set up something to put your pots and cooking pans on, usually a scrounged grill of sorts, so you could do your cooking once the blowtorch was lit. If the flame was too strong, you withdrew the shovel with the can of burning gasoline until the jerry can cooled down. Once the flames started to get too low, you pushed the can of gasoline back underneath again.

Of course, the Western Front stove would never have been given any kind of approval. There were no safety valves or any other kind of safety device. Everybody knew the dangers of using it, and every so often somebody would say, "What if it blows up?" But the danger never seemed to worry us much; I guess it didn't seem particularly significant compared with the dangers we encountered every day. Fellows I knew didn't use it too often. We tried it a couple of times, but I think we found it was just too damned much effort. It was easier to dump some gas on a pail of sand or dirt and throw the dirt out when we were through.

The inventiveness and ingenuity shown by tank crews in their efforts to make life easier were amazing. It was a revelation to see what came out of the storage bins on a tank when bivouacs were set up. It was similarly remarkable to observe what was stowed on the back decks of a column of tanks, in addition to the pails and cooking pots and the laundry that hung, swinging, from the rear.

The night of August 7, 1944, we began our first major offensive as part of a plan to encircle and trap the German Seventh Army. The Fourth Division was part of an offensive drive attacking the German forces defending the road to Falaise. Daily attacks were mounted to capture towns and strong points along the road from the Germans. The Americans had been making a sweep around to the south and were making great gains, but it was necessary to break through the German armour. We were to attempt to penetrate the German lines at the point where their armour was concentrated. We were up against some of Germany's most ferocious and tenacious troops, led by Field Marshal von Kluge. The men of the 12th SS Panzer Division were fanatic young soldiers willing to die for their country. The Fourth Canadian Division met and fought against this crack German division in every campaign in France in 1944.

Our plan of attack was devised by General Simonds, our corps commander, and had never been tried before. On August 14 the whole Fourth Division lined up, led by the Governor General's Foot Guards and followed by the Fourth Armoured Brigade in lines of eight tanks abreast, fifteen feet apart. The SAR followed the Fourth Armoured Brigade. The formation leading the attack comprised some 250 tanks. The 10th Infantry Brigade followed, carried in armoured personnel carriers devised from Ram tanks with the turrets taken off, another of General Simonds's innovations. They were renamed "Priests." At midnight we began to move. Tracer shells were fired down the side of our route to show the way, and searchlights behind us shone into the sky to make artificial moonlight. A full division charge was the embodiment of the proverbial irresistible force, and we overran the enemy. I remember hearing reports coming in over the radio where somebody reported an anti-tank gun up front, and somebody else replied, "I know, I've just run over one."

And we broke through. I have no doubt there were tanks and men lost from the armoured units, although the 10th Infantry Brigade did not lose a single man, and there were instances when we were firing blindly, but we achieved our objective. We had broken through or bypassed the heavy concentration of German armour, opening the way for the eventual entrapment and destruction of the German Seventh Army. This action marked the beginning of the drive that culminated with the surrender of the German forces on May 8, 1945, in Oldenburg, Germany.

Come daylight, the scene I saw through my periscope was unbelievable. We had begun the charge with the division in orderly ranks, fighting units to the front, support units to the rear. What I now saw was chaos. Ahead of us were trucks carrying ammunition, infantry in carriers, cooks' trucks that should have been way at the back, fragments of this and fragments of that all mixed up in one great muddle and nobody knew who was where. I think it took about two days to get everybody back to their own units again. The comment was made that it seemed like the only people who knew what was going on were the Germans. A cartoon of the day showed some poor soldier who had been asked where his regiment was. He said, "Regiment, hell, I don't even know where my division is!" That we managed to muddle through illustrated one of the characteristics that distinguished the Canadian forces from the Germans. We were all trained so that if any of us, even a unit as small as a tank crew, became separated from the rest of the troop, someone could take command and the crew could carry on. If anything happened to a German officer, his men lost direction. There was nobody to take charge.

We had our answers now to the questions that had been in the backs of our minds as we approached the front line: What am I going to do in my first action? Am I going to be able to take it, am I going to be able to handle it? Will I be able to deal with my fear and carry out my duties without going to pieces? Am I going to be a coward? Am I going to be a hero? We had seen tanks hit, men wounded, killed, burned to death, and we found that we were able to handle it. You were always afraid, but you accepted what was happening and did what you had to do.

Shermans at a tank graveyard in Normandy. Our fitters sometimes found these repositories of disabled tanks to be the most expedient place to obtain spare parts for repairs. (SAR)

CHAPTER 11

France through a Periscope

Each day in action was pretty much the same as the one before. Being in a tank was something like being in a submarine. Every crew position was provided with a periscope that had a viewing slit one and a half by six inches (3.8 cm x 15.25 cm). The periscope rotated 360° so you could look in all directions. The gunner had a sight scope with crosshairs for sighting and aiming his gun. When we were not in battle, all hatches were open, and the driver and co-driver could raise their seats so that their heads were out. In action, only the troop commander rode with his head out of the top of the tank, just enough so he could see, and he directed the driver. Unless he was ordered otherwise, the driver drove straight ahead, observing what he could through his periscope. In extreme situations, when the crew commander closed his hatch because of snipers or air burst shells exploding overhead, the periscopes were the only visual contact with the outside, and all crew members kept a lookout in all directions.

I would never call a tank spacious, but it wasn't cramped, either. The use of space had been well planned, and each member of the crew had as much room as he needed to do his job without getting in anybody else's way. The driver and co-driver sat at the front of the tank, down in the hull, with the casing of the transmission in between them. The rest of us sat in the turret, which was something like a big metal basket set into the upper part of the tank. The whole turret could pivot 360° to traverse the gun. You had to be careful when you were in action that if you got into a situation where you had to "Abandon Tank!" the gun was pointed away from the driver's and co-driver's hatches so it didn't block them getting out. Inside there were openings in the turret to allow access to the hull and the sponson, as the storage area on the inside wall of the tank was called.

Ammunition was kept there, along with tools that weren't stored on the outside and the Homelite generator. I hated the damned thing. When we were stationary, I'd be stuck on wireless watch, alone in the tank, with the Homelite belching smoke and making a racket like an unmuffled motorcycle right beside my seat.

The inside of a tank on the move was a pretty noisy place anyway. You couldn't carry on a normal conversation. Most of the noise came from the engine fan, which sat right behind the turret in front of the radiator and engine, which were at the rear. The tank was well ventilated because the fan drew in air from the hatches at the front and blew it back over the radiator to cool the engine. Even in the dead of summer, it was never hot in a moving tank because of the air flow. Of course, in winter, it got too damn cold for the same reason! We didn't hear much over the fan; I don't remember hearing the tracks clanking, for example, and the hull was too thick for us to hear sounds from the outside unless they were very loud. In spite of the ventilation, a tank developed an odour all its own; part cordite and gun oil, part gasoline and engine oil, all mixed up with the tang of sweaty bodies and the smell of fear. Like the noise, most of the time you never thought about it. It was just part of being in a tank.

The other thing that interfered with conversation in a tank, and with hearing anything outside of the engine fan, was that we were all wearing radio headphones so that we could communicate with each other. Communications with other tanks or the squadron leader were carried on over the wireless, and through our headphones we could all hear the exchanges between all the tanks that were on net; but there was also an intercom system in the tank. If the crew commander wanted to direct the driver or the gunner, he turned the switch on his control box to intercom and spoke to him directly. Though most of the time I took a certain amount of comfort in the thought that I was protected inside that steel hull, the worst moments of apprehension I had were when we were getting close to where the fighting was going on, and the crew commander of a tank that was already in action opened his microphone to talk to another tank in the troop and his microphone picked up the sound of machine gun fire nearby. That was one of the worst sounds that I could ever hear, because now I knew what I was heading into.

Once we got into action, of course, there was all sorts of noise. If we were hit with small-arms fire, there would be a spatter of sound something like a hailstorm; though what struck me more, when we were close enough, was the sharp *crack!* you heard as the rifle or machine gun fired. When our own gun fired, there would be the loud explosion from the muzzle blast and then, almost simultaneously, the clank and clatter as the gun recoiled on the hydraulic mechanism and ejected the shell casing, which crashed against the shield that kept it from smashing into the radio set behind, then dropped with a sound like somebody beating on a brass pipe to the floor. There the casings would rattle around until somebody had time to discard them out the pistol port, a little opening in the side of the tank by the radio operator's seat. Empty casings were a handy toilet if somebody had to pee while we were on the move; they just got turfed out the pistol port after use.

When we were in action, there was no world outside the tank. As the wireless operator, although I had my own periscope, I saw almost nothing because it was my job to load the guns. I sat with the machine gun directly in front of me and the breech of the large gun beside me, on a seat that swivelled so that I was able to face either. I took the 75 mm shells from the rack and put them in the open breech of the gun each time it was fired, and loaded fresh belts of ammunition into the machine gun as they were needed. If the barrel burned out of the Browning, I was the one who pulled it out of its mounting, got a new barrel out of the rack and fastened it in place, set the headspace and did any other needed adjustments, threw it back in its mounting and told the crew commander and gunner it was ready to go. My days were filled with breathing cordite fumes, sticking belts into the Browning and throwing empty casings out through the pistol port. Everything I knew of what was happening outside came from the messages I received over the radio and the directions the crew commander gave to the driver and the gunner.

When we'd achieved our objective and the enemy had retired, my world expanded again. We'd stop the tank, and everybody but the radio operator would get out. There would be a load of gasoline coming up, and the driver and co-driver, with the gunner to help, would deal with that and check the oil and take care of anything else the tank needed. The crew commander would trot off to his debriefing at the squadron someplace. I had to stay with the radio until told to stand down, but at least I could climb up and sit on the rim of the hatch and breathe fresh air again.

At night, we would find a place where we were half safe, dig a hole and drive the tank over top of it, then crawl in with our bedrolls and sleep, taking turns standing watch on two-hour shifts all through the night. We soon learned to keep out of the big hedges that bordered some of the fields. They were thick, six or seven feet wide, and had up to four feet of soil at the bottom that had built up over the years. Occasionally there would be gaps cut in them. One of the tank crews from another squadron thought one of these gaps would be a nice place to park, because the tank would just blend into the hedge. When dark came, the Germans looked down and saw no hole in the hedge where they expected a hole to be, so they fired an 88 into the missing gap and that was the end of that sort of exercise. The Germans retreated, but they left behind one Sherman tank with a smashed transmission.

Our unit was unique. At the end of a day in battle, when it started to get dark and the position had been consolidated, most armoured regiments left maintaining the position to the infantry and moved back to service the tanks. It seems that our colonel decided we were there as infantry support, and we did not pull back at night. The infantry appreciated it, and we were well provided for. The regimental quartermaster came up each night with a column of supply trucks carrying gasoline, ammunition, clothing and rations, and the trucks always found us. I have great admiration for the truck drivers who kept us supplied. If anybody deserved a commendation, it was the truck drivers. They came through some terrible situations to bring us what we needed.

A lot of normal army protocol disappeared, along with our daily shave and polished boots. Rank badges were hidden because the enemy snipers would always try to pick off the officers and senior personnel. For the same reason, the troop officer never let his binoculars show, if possible, when he was on the ground. He kept them inside his tank suit or tunic. Relations between ranks were very relaxed. We called our troop officer Boss, and I think the same was true for most troops. Our troop officer was a very well-liked man, Lieutenant Jim Curley. I was in his tank. The gunner was Carl Wicke, who is still a very good friend, and the driver was Jimmy Mold. I don't remember the co-driver's name.

Jim Curley had a habit of stopping along the way, getting out of the tank and taking off on foot with the co-driver to look the situation over, leaving the rest of us sitting in the tank wondering what was going on. We weren't always able to see the other tanks. Once when Curley and the co-driver left to check out the situation with the sergeant's tank, which had been hit, I found my radio was not transmitting. I did my diagnostic tests and discovered I had a broken pigtail. A pigtail is a piece of light wire in the base of the antenna mount, which is a rubber cone on the outside of the tank at the top of the turret. The aerial, which was made of flexible copper rods that fit together like a telescope and could be pulled out to whatever length was needed, clipped into the antenna mount at the top and whipped back and forth as the tank drove along. The cone gave it flexibility. Inside the cone the pigtail, which was about two inches long, connected the aerial to the lead to the radio. If the aerial flexed too far, the pigtail broke, and that was what had happened. To repair it I had to go outside the tank, take the aerial out, undo six bolts and lift the cone off, unscrew the broken pieces, then fit the new pigtail in and put the aerial back up. We were out in the middle of a field with some houses and bushes about 100 yards away. We were in action, and I didn't relish the idea of climbing around the outside of the tank in such exposed circumstances. I said to the driver, "I've got to fix the pigtail."

"Well, fix it, then," he replied.

"All right, you going to move the tank?"

No, he was not going to move the tank. I had to climb out on top of the turret, nine feet off the ground. I got down on my knees beside the turret to reduce the size of target I presented, but I was sure I was not going to make it. I figured there was no way the Germans were going to let me stay up there like a sitting duck and get away with it. I sweated through the whole operation, absolutely certain I was going to meet my end at any moment; but I didn't. For some reason there were no snipers, nobody interested in taking potshots at radio operators fooling around on the top of tanks. I replaced the pigtail, Curley and the co-driver came back and got in, and we calmly went on our way.

A day or so later we got hit by an anti-tank gun. The shell hit the front of the tank with a crash like somebody had whacked it with a big sledge hammer, smashing the sprocket and breaking the track and bringing us to a sudden and unexpected halt. For a moment we wondered what we'd run into, but then the reality that we'd been hit sank in, and we bailed out of the tank and took cover beside it. There was an infantry section nearby, so Curley went over and asked them to take out the anti-tank gun for him. Off they went; they didn't mind attacking anti-tank guns. Then he told the co-driver to go back, find the recovery tank, and get him up there to fix our tank. The co-driver went down over the hill, and that was the last we saw of him. Curley took the sergeant's tank and left the sergeant to wait with us for the repairs. Later on that night the recovery tank arrived and the fitters replaced the sprocket and fixed the track and got us all ready to go for the next day. But they hadn't seen anything of the co-driver. Everybody figured he must have taken off.

It wasn't until a regimental reunion in 1993 that I found out what had happened to the co-driver. I didn't recognize him when we met, but after talking to him for a while I realized that he was the fellow who had gone missing. He explained that he hadn't really known just where to go when Jim Curley told him to go back and get us a recovery, but he knew which way to head, and figured he would be able to to find somebody and ask them for directions. He wanted to keep under cover as much as he could along the way, of course, and was creeping through a wheat field when the Lincoln and Wellands spotted him and thought he must be an enemy. They opened fire, and he was hit. The bullet went through the top of his helmet and creased his skull enough to knock him out. He was sent back to hospital, and when he recovered and was released, he went as a reinforcement to another unit.

To our sorrow, we didn't have Jim Curley very long. He was promoted to captain and left us. We were sorry to see him go; he was a good officer. His replacement, Ray Smith, was a fellow who had been with the regiment all along as a corporal and then a sergeant, then had gone off to officer's school and came back to us as a first lieutenant.

The attack on the German line continued, as did the routine of travelling and fighting during the day and settling into cover at night. One night the squadron was dispersed throughout a wooded area. Needles, the crazy rumrunner, was our troop's sentry on the ground. As we were in a forward position close to the enemy, the crews were still in place in their tanks. I climbed down and was chatting with Needles when we heard a jingling noise that sounded for all the world like harness on a horse. A few minutes later, out of the dark not thirty feet from where we were standing walked a white horse accompanied by a section of German infantry. I told Needles to fire, but Needles, being the well trained soldier he was and knowing that regulations required you to yell halt three times before you fired, said, "Halt!"

The reaction was exactly what I expected. The horse took off at the run, while the men disappeared into some bushes just out in front of the tank. Needles said, "What now?"

With the appearance of the enemy his sentry duty ended, and I told him he had better get back to his tank and join his crew. I climbed inside our tank to find the troop officer sitting in the operator's seat. I said, "We've got a German infantry section right in front of us some place."

He cocked the .30 calibre Browning machine gun. I told him not to fire because I didn't know whether the Germans knew what they had run into. I didn't want to reveal that we were just a tank with no ground support, rather than a large force of infantry, because I could imagine a *Panzerfaust* in the hands of a determined German creeping up on us. I went on the air and warned the other tank crews that there were German infantry in the area, then took four grenades from the grenade box, climbed out on the deck of the tank, and threw them off to the right, to the left, and to the front. Then I thought I should spray the bushes. I didn't want to open up with the tank's machine guns because that would identify us, so I picked up a Sten gun. I cocked it three times, and each time nothing happened. It didn't fire one shot. A few days earlier I had picked up a German Schmeisser submachine gun, so I went back to the blanket box on the back of the turret and pulled it out, then returned to the front of the turret and sprayed the bushes. The Schmeisser worked. I got back in the tank, and we stayed on the alert all night.

Next morning I had to stay in the tank to monitor the radio while the rest of the crew got out and cooked breakfast fifteen or twenty feet away.

I was sitting in the turret when out of the woods walked three Germans with their hands on their heads. I called to the other guys, who hadn't noticed our visitors. They looked around, then leapt to their feet, drawing their pistols. There was no need for the pistols; these men were surrendering. We searched them, and I took a little 7.65 mm pistol from the back pocket of one as a souvenir of the incident (it was stolen on the way home). The troop officer asked them where they came from. They pointed to the sky, and we supposed that they were reinforcements who had been dropped in by parachute. We were about to send them to our rear as prisoners, but they asked if they could bury their officer before they left, and I realized that I must have killed him, either with the grenades or with the Schmeisser. It's an indication of how callous a soldier becomes in combat that I felt not a moment's remorse.

They buried their officer and we pointed them in the right direction and sent them on their way. Most likely, the troop officer mentioned the prisoners when he reported the night's engagement to Squadron Headquarters. Theoretically they were supposed to have an escort, but we didn't have the personnel to provide one. It was quite common that small groups of prisoners would be sent off without an escort. As long as they kept their hands on their heads to show they had surrendered they were quite safe, and eventually they would reach Squadron Headquarters, where somebody would gather them up and turn them over to the military police to be taken to a prison camp. They were better off cooperating than trying to make it through our troops back to their own lines, and they knew it. There were very few who tried to sneak away.

We had a variety of engagements with the enemy until August 19, 1944, when we joined a coordinated effort to close the Falaise Gap, through which the Germans were trying to escape. By fate, the South Alberta Regiment, with the Poles fighting alongside, was in the forefront of the action and got a great deal of credit for the part it played. The regiment was ordered to attack down the Falaise Road. "C" Squadron, commanded by Major David Currie, led the attack. Currie moved in and managed to establish a position in the village of St. Lambert-sur-Dives, which he held against attack after attack with his own Headquarters tanks, part of another troop, and some infantry units he had gathered.

A "C" Squadron Sherman squeezes by a destroyed South Albertas tank in St. Lambert-sur-Dives, August 19, 1944. (National Archives of Canada PA-116522)

Major Currie was awarded the Victoria Cross for his actions, and was the only Armoured Corps officer to receive this medal.

"A" Squadron had been in reserve, but the fighting was very heavy and losses high, and the Germans were still infiltrating through the gap, so "A" Squadron was called into action. We went into a position between Regimental Headquarters and Currie's position at St. Lambert. In the middle of the afternoon, 4 Troop was ordered to break through and relieve some Americans who had been encircled and cut off from their own forces. We were forming up with the trucks that would carry the ammunition and rations for the Americans when word came that they had been relieved.

Instead, we were to move up to defend Headquarters. Headquarters seldom got into action, but they repulsed a couple of attacks during the battle for Falaise Gap. The Germans had cut off the road between "A" Squadron and Headquarters, and they were attacking. We were to throw them back. Our troop crossed an open field of forty or fifty acres on which grain had been cut with a binder and stooked, took up a defensive position and launched a counterattack. The Germans came across the field ducking from stook to stook, and the four tanks picked them off with the machine guns. It was just a slaughter.

In one of the best known photos of the war, Major Dave Currie of the South Alberta Regiment (centre left, holding a pistol) accepts the surrender of several Germans at St. Lambert-sur-Dives on August 19, 1944. Major Currie was awarded the Victoria Cross for his action in the defence of St. Lambert-sur-Dives, during which he spent three days without sleep, directing his small force of "C" squadron tanks and a badly understrength company of infantry in a successful effort to repulse attempts by much larger German forces to capture the village. (National Archives of Canada PA-111565)

I was loading the machine gun in my tank. All the crew commanders were keeping their heads down as far as possible, with only their eyes above the rims of their hatches – all except for Herb Roulston. I looked over through the periscope and saw him out of the turret on top of his tank, sitting with his feet across the opening of the hatch, having a turkey shoot with a captured German rifle, sniping at the Germans running from stook to stook through the field. I said to the troop officer, "Take a look at Roulston."

He took a look, then picked up the microphone and said over the radio, "Roulston, get down out of there. You're going to get shot."

Roulston picked up his own microphone and replied, "Haven't you heard? There's a war on," and stayed right where he was.

We repulsed the attack, and everything quieted down. We stayed in that position all through the night. It was harrowing. I was up quite a bit of the night on watch in the turret, and although it was dark, there was just enough light from the skyline that I could occasionally see columns of men going by. I knew they were Germans, but I never opened fire. I just mentioned to the troop officer, who was sitting in the operator's seat, that I could see them. If the machine gun company on the ground had started shooting we would have supported them, but we were very vulnerable in the dark, and it made more sense to let them go. The guys in some of the tanks told later about suddenly becoming aware of Germans right down beside their tanks. They would hear them feel the tank and whisper, "*Panzer! Panzer!*" then skitter off into the darkness. We were whispering into the radios, because we knew the Germans were infiltrating and didn't want them to overhear our communications. At one point we got a report that a hundred German tanks were coming toward our position. It turned out that ten or twenty German tanks carrying the commanding officers of the Seventh Army did make the break, but I don't remember tanks going through our position.

If the Germans had infiltrated through to Headquarters, they would have seen a strange sight: 500 German prisoners in an open unfenced area, guarded by a tank on each of the four sides with its spotlight trained on them. We were taking German prisoners by the score.

Morning came, and we could look out across the valley. It was just carnage. The previous day the Germans had been getting out any way they could, pushing their way through the resistance in columns, carrying their equipment in horse-drawn wagons as well as in whatever vehicles they had. Tanks had been picking off men, horses and equipment at both ends of the columns, while aircraft had been strafing the roads. The litter of abandoned German equipment and dead horses stretched for miles, and the roads were impassible. After the battle was all over, bulldozers were needed to go through and push all the bodies and debris off the roads before they could be used. As daylight strengthened, we became aware that down the valley were coming Germans by the thousands, in columns of regimental strength, led by men carrying white bedsheets tied between two poles to signal surrender. It was over. As they reached Allied positions, they were rounded up and briefly searched, and columns of anywhere from 100 to 500 men at a time were sent off, each group escorted by a tank, to the prison area where the military police took over.

I recall being out in the field searching German packs and personnel for weapons and whatever else they had. We took the money. They had loads of French money that they had apparently looted, and it wasn't going to do them any good where they were going. After I had been busily searching for some time, I happened to look up, and I realized that there was no one else who looked like a Canadian in sight. All I could see were Germans, and some of them were big Germans. It suddenly occurred to me that if these guys wanted to do away with me, I could just disappear and never be seen again. I made sure from then on that I always stayed in sight of a couple of other Canadians.

We spent most of the day searching Germans and sending them on their way. By the end of the day, there was French money all over that field. We'd kept nothing under a 100-franc note. A duffel bag full of French money lay on the back of our tank for months and months. We estimated that we had about $50,000 worth, but we didn't often go anywhere we could spend it. We used it at the cafés as long as we were in France, but finally the duffel bag got thrown out in a ditch. Some of the people who got wounded took francs back to England, imagining that they were going to be rich, but they found that the banks wouldn't accept them. It was wartime money, printed during the German occupation, and had no value outside France.

I quote here from Major R.A. Paterson's history of the 10th Canadian Infantry Brigade, in which he describes the aftermath of the battle for Falaise Gap the way I wish I could:

> *Orders came for a Brigade concentration* on the heights of Mount ORMEL. And so on the 23rd, in the afternoon, we climbed up the narrow road choked with dead horses, and men bloating, rotting, festering, in the summer sun. We climbed beyond the blackened tanks, the burnt out ammunition carts, the half tracks, the trucks. We climbed out of the valley of death, and we came to green fields, and clean air, and we thanked God for the ceasing of the guns, for the peace of the farm house, and for the quiet sleep under the apple trees.*

---

* The South Alberta Regiment and the three infantry regiments that we supported.

CHAPTER 12

Breakthrough to Belgium

We thought that we would now get a rest, but the Germans were re-treating. The Fourth Division, with the Polish Division alongside, was ordered in pursuit to keep the Germans running so they couldn't form another defensive line. We began a steady drive day and night, travelling down the road in columns. On night runs we used no headlights. The driver kept his position by watching the tail lights of the tank ahead. We were all dead tired, falling asleep in our seats. When we stopped, the co-driver would get out and lean on the tank ahead so that if the column started moving, he would wake up and go back to get his own tank going.

On the third day we reached the River Seine. We had a bit of a rest there because the Seine was not bridged and we had to wait to be ferried across. The infantry went over in storm boats – open boats about fifteen feet long with a square bow and stern, a fairly flat bottom and an outboard engine. Each could hold a half platoon of infantry. The tanks travelled on Class 9 rafts, which were large, flat scows, powered by an outboard motor. They could carry, if my memory is correct, four tanks at a time. On the far side of the Seine we were involved in a short fight. The Germans were mount-ing rearguard actions, trying to delay our advance, but they were break-ing and none of the battles lasted very long. In this case, the Germans were on top of the long slope out of the valley, but the infantry just went up the hill in line and took the position. There wasn't much resistance.

Shortly after we crossed the Seine, Herb Roulston distinguished him-self again. We were involved in a small action and one of the other troops lost a tank. It had gone forward between two buildings and been hit in the turret. One of the crew members was killed. The remainder bailed out and made their way back to safety, leaving the body in the tank and the

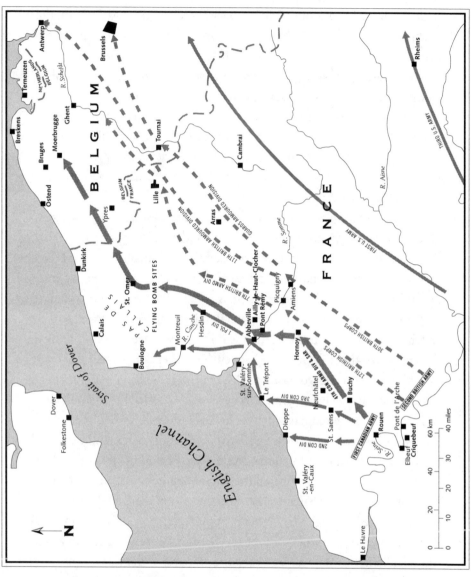

After crossing the River Seine at Elbeuf, we began the rapid advance across northern France and into the Low Countries. The Canadians were on the northern flank, responsible for clearing the Channel ports. We pushed forward day and night in an attempt to outrun the retreating German forces. At times, we passed – and ignored – columns of German vehicles on roads parallel to our line of travel, possibly carrying reinforcements for troops we had already overrun. The Germans sat in their trucks and watched as we drove by. (Map from *South Albertas: A Canadian Regiment at War*)

tank running. The indomitable Herb gathered up his co-driver, another Irishman, and the two of them walked up to the tank, backed it out and brought it in. He was awarded the Military Medal for his action.

We thought we were going to take Paris. We were the closest Allied troops, lined up in position seventy miles away, but politics prevailed, and they held us back and moved in the Free French, supported by American troops. Really, I guess it was right that the Free French should have been the ones to lead the way into Paris. Most likely, everything proceeded according to plan, but to us young men, the opportunity to achieve fame and glory by liberating Paris was our greatest desire.

The drive continued. Whenever we stopped somewhere long enough to get a bit of rest, the British or Americans would break through the German line again and we'd be off at a run. We had the odd small action, and there was one instance when, travelling down the road at top speed, we came around a corner and observed, on a road a quarter of a mile away, a column of German trucks with their drivers standing out by the front fenders watching us go by. We had overrun their line. By now we were beginning to liberate towns that the Germans had left. The reception we received made everything we'd been going through seem worthwhile. Passing through these villages was like being in a parade. People crowded the sidewalks and spilled out into the road; our drivers had to just creep through the mobs. We were showered with flowers and fruit, bottles of cognac and cider, and there were girls all over the tanks and trucks. I heard of one little village where every citizen, including all the school children, turned out early in the morning to line the main street, and they stood there all day as the infantry marched through. It was a very happy experience, and lifted our spirits so that we began to think maybe the Germans were going to run all the way back to Berlin and we would soon see the end of the war.

I remember one French town close to the Belgian border. We stopped at night and lined our tanks up on the roadway between the houses on either side. When I got up about six in the morning, a woman came out of the house next to us. I said, "*Bonjour.*"

Right away she answered in French, then asked me if I could speak the language. I knew a few simple phrases: "*Quelle heure est-il?*" (What time is it?), "*Comment vous appelez-vous?*" (What's your name?); so I said, "*Un petit peu*" (a little bit). She was happy and excited, and, chattering away in French, made signs by which I understood that she was inviting me into the house to have breakfast. The idea of a good, home-cooked breakfast appealed to me, so I followed her in and met her family.

As was common, there were no young men. The Germans had taken them all back to provide slave labour in the German factories. There were some older girls, and we communicated by sign language while the mother prepared the meal. Then they sat me down at the table and breakfast was delivered: two boiled eggs, some black bread, and, in the centre of the plate, a piece of meat. My appetite died. The meat looked as if it had been boiled, which I wasn't used to, it was very fat, and the fat didn't look well cooked; and my thought, as I contemplated it, was "Horsemeat." I knew they enjoyed their horsemeat in France, but the idea of eating it nauseated me. The thing was, though, that I knew these people had practically nothing, and it would have been a terrific insult to refuse it. They were doing their best to express their appreciation for me as their liberator. Ignoring my churning stomach, I ate the eggs, and I did manage to stuff down the majority of the piece of meat, but I felt terrible that I didn't really appreciate their kindness. I met them two or three times later in the day when we were wandering through the town, and they were happy to see me, so I guess I managed to hide my distaste. When I got back to the tank I dug out a gift for them: a couple of packages of the Woodbine cigarettes that we got in our ration packs and some cans of soup called Haricot Oxtail. Nobody liked the soup or the cigarettes, and we used them for trading to farmers for "*des oeufs.*"

We spent the afternoon prowling around the town. There was quite a bit going on. The Free French were busy rounding up all the collaborators, as they called the women who had had German boyfriends. They brought them into the town square, where they shaved off their hair. We had mixed feelings as we watched. We could understand, we thought, the antagonism the people felt toward those who had fraternized with their conquerors, but we questioned whether the humiliation and degradation we witnessed were really necessary.

Back at the tanks that evening, we discovered that Bobby Kerr, one of our drivers, was missing. Someone went to check, and word came back that Bobby had been arrested and charged with rape. This was a shock to everybody, because Bobby was a ladies' man. Whenever we went to a pub in England, it was never long before some girl would be indicating she would welcome his attention. He wasn't the type to resort to rape. The story that we eventually heard was that Bob and some fellow we didn't know from another squadron in the regiment had met a woman who invited them home and agreed to go to bed with them. Her story changed when her husband came in and caught them. He threatened to attack whoever was in bed with her at the time, upon which Bobby and his buddy pulled their pistols and held him off while they got dressed and left. When they were gone, the husband called the military police.

There was a short military trial resulting in a conviction, and the next morning I endured one of the most disturbing spectacles of my life. Bobby and his friend were drummed out of the regiment. For the drumming-out ceremony, the four squadrons of the regiment were formed into a square. The two convicted men were marched bare-headed into the centre of the square. The regimental sergeant major came out and unceremoniously ripped and cut off the Canada badge, their regimental badge, any rank insignia, until their uniforms were stripped of all insignia. Then they were marched off and sent to military jail.

I had a hard time believing that Bob was guilty. I tend to believe that the woman was a willing participant until the husband came along. I always wanted to find Bobby after the war and let him know that his Peewee buddies respected him, whatever had happened, and I wanted to get his version of the story. Unfortunately, by the time I finally learned where he was, he had been drowned on a fishing trip.

It was about seven o'clock on a fall night when we crossed the border into Belgium. As we drove through a village in the dark, I noticed tiny cracks of light showing through the doors on either side of the street as the occupants peeked out at us. On the spur of the moment, I yelled out, "*Vive la Belgique!*" And immediately every door on the street was opened wide and the people came pouring out. As it happened, the column stopped just then. I climbed down off the tank, and I was immediately swept up into the arms of a huge Belgian with a big, bushy beard and kissed on both cheeks, then handed around the crowd, where I received the same treatment from all and sundry. Everybody was happy and crying. The rest of the crew came down off the tank and we were marched into the nearest house, where the prize bottle of cognac was hauled out of the cupboard and drinks were had all round. Before long somebody came to tell us we were moving on, and we had to go back to the tank; but we were warmed by more than brandy as we lumbered off into the night.

We noticed immediately that Belgium was very different from France. Everything was so much cleaner. The French hadn't been fussy about their streets, which had been quite dirty. The Belgian streets were meticulous. As we drove by in the early mornings, the women would be out scrubbing the sidewalks in front of the houses. Belgium seemed to have a great many pretty girls who smiled at us as we passed. We found them very attractive.

As we moved deeper into Belgium, we started to run into more resistance. The Germans were beginning to build a defensive line, and our supply lines were starting to get very long and vulnerable to disruption. Supplies had been coming through all right, though we'd had to make the occasional day stop to allow the supply trucks to catch up with us.

I acquired a new duty. Each night when we halted, I was volunteered to go out and put up trip flares fifty or sixty yards in front of our lines. A trip flare was a flare that was triggered by a trip wire. The wire, which was about fifty feet long, would be strung where you thought someone who was creeping in on you would pass. The flare itself was about size of a tin of Campbell's soup and contained a substance that, when ignited, burned quite brightly, producing a light by which you could see whoever had triggered it. The flare was fastened to a quarter-inch rod about eighteen inches long which was forced into the earth. You pushed a similar rod into the ground some distance away, and ran the fine trip wire between the two. The firing device was a little flat metal lever, about three-eighths of an inch wide, that pivoted like a pendulum. When it was in its central position it was safe, but it would fire if moved from that position. Until the flare was armed, the lever was held in place by a pin inserted into a hole that had been drilled in the arm. Fastened to the arm were two small expansion springs. The outside spring, on the side opposite where the trip wire fastened, was attached to the frame. The inner spring was attached to the trip wire. You armed the flare by fastening the trip wire to the distant stake, bringing it over to the flare, then fastening it to the inside spring, using a wing nut and clamp to adjust the tension so it balanced the tension from the outside spring. If you adjusted it correctly, when you pulled the pin, the lever stayed in its central position. Once the flare was armed, it would fire if anything happened to upset the balance of tension. If somebody cut the trip wire, the tension would ease on the inside spring, causing the outside spring to pull the arm and fire the flare. If somebody ran into the wire with their foot, tension on the inside spring would be increased, and the flare would fire.

The nervewracking part of the job was that if you didn't get the tension just right when you were arming it, the flare would fire at the moment of truth when you had it all set up and pulled the pin. The fact that you were working largely by touch in total darkness didn't help matters, and the knowledge that if a flare went off you were in danger of being shot at by both sides did nothing to ease your anxiety. I never went out without assurance that the squadron had been notified that there was a party out putting up trip flares, but stumbling around in the dark, I could never quite get rid of the worry somebody might not have got the message. I held my breath every time I pulled a pin out, but I never fired a flare. Maybe that was why it became my job.

In the morning, we just left the trip flares behind. Even if they were accidentally triggered, they wouldn't hurt anybody.

The Allies had taken Antwerp on September 4, 1944, but the Scheldt River estuary, Walcheren Island in the estuary and many of the canals near the city were still held by the Germans. Those positions had to be cleared before the Allies could use the port of Antwerp, which is 80 kilometres from the mouth of the Scheldt River. The port of Antwerp of was of great importance to the Allies, as the supply lines from the coast of Normandy were becoming severely stretched. Before Antwerp could receive ships bringing supplies for the Allied offensive, the Scheldt had to be cleared of mines and obstructions, and the Germans driven from the estuary and Walcheren Island. In addition, the country to the north and west of Antwerp had to be captured from the Germans to remove the threat of shelling and ensure safe entry to the harbour.

General Montgomery handed the operation to the 1st Canadian Army.

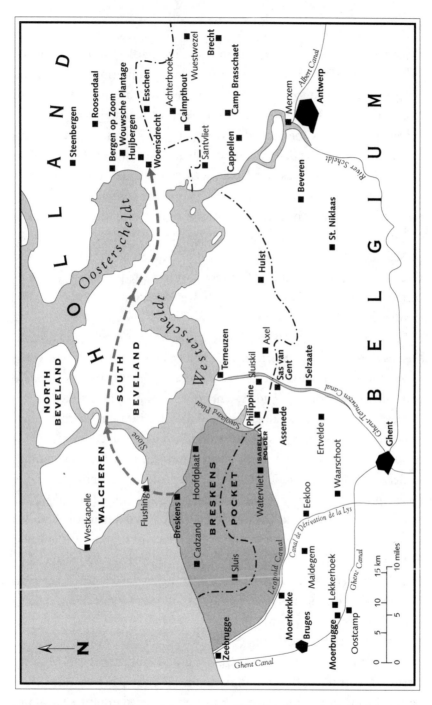

In September and October 1944 the Canadians fought to clear the Scheldt estuary to open the port of Antwerp. (Map from *South Albertas: A Canadian Regiment at War*)

What followed was a month or more of vicious battles, some of the worst the Canadians fought, and under the worst of conditions. The Second Division was tasked to clear the Germans off Walcheren Island and had to attack over land that was heavily flooded. The Fourth Division was involved in protecting the Second Division's right flank, clearing the mainland along the eastern bank of the Scheldt and pushing north to the Maas River. The offensive was mounted by three Canadian divisions, along with a Polish and a British division under Canadian command. My memories recall the actions fought by the SAR, "A" Squadron and 4 Troop. Since I did not keep a journal, although the names of the places through which we passed, including those of many towns and hamlets and the Leopold and Ghent Canals, come to mind, I cannot always relate particular battles or incidents to the specific locations where they occurred.

After fighting our way across the Ghent Canal, we were to take the village of Lekkerhoek. The night before the action, as we were digging in to defend the position, our troop officer, Lieutenant Ray Smith, said that he was going to win the Victoria Cross the next day. I recall saying to him, "Well, you're going to do it without me. I don't want no VC, or any sort of medal."

Next day we made our attack. A lot of the time I was in the troop officer's tank, but we sometimes moved around from crew to crew to cover for people who had gone on leave or been wounded. That day I was gunner in Sergeant Simon MacKenzie's tank. The leading troop attacked the enemy positions at the edge of the village and lost a couple of tanks. Four Troop, down to two tanks because of losses incurred during the fight for the Ghent Canal crossing, was ordered to attack in support of the troop in trouble. Our two tanks were some distance apart as we advanced to engage the enemy defences. The radio operator in the troop officer's tank came on air with the message, "Sunray* shot dead by sniper, am pulling back to take him out of our unit."

While that crew stayed back to take Ray Smith's body out of the tank, we moved in. We were attacking a building, and suddenly twenty or thirty Germans came out of the building with their hands up in surrender. I had been firing the Browning machine gun, and I lowered my aim so it would just cover them. And the Browning "cooked off." When the machine gun

---

* The code name for the person in command.

had been firing and was hot, occasionally a shell in the chamber would explode just from the heat of the barrel and chamber. The shell hit a prisoner in the middle of the group. I thought Mac was going to have a breakdown. I felt bad, too, because it was totally unintentional, and the poor guy had thought he was out of the war and safe.

We broke through the German defences on the edge of the town, moved on through and advanced up the roadway. Fighting was heavy, and we lost a number of tanks that day. You couldn't get off the road because the ground was too soft. The road was overhung by the branches of the large trees that lined it. They had been pruned to the height of about eight feet, which was adequate for ordinary traffic but meant that, although a tank driver could see down the road through his periscope, a troop commander in the turret could see nothing but trees.

We hit a mine that blew off a track and disabled the tank. Immediately afterwards we heard the crack of an anti-tank gun and a great *crash!* as an armour-piercing round hit the front of the tank, so we bailed out. I followed the sergeant over the top. The radio operator, Carl Wicke, followed me. The driver went out his hatch, but we were receiving fire from an enemy machine gun when the co-driver, who had snagged his headset and was delayed while he freed it, was about to go out his hatch, so he had to climb in through the turret and go out the escape hatch. It was a square metal plate at the bottom of the tank under the turret that dropped so you could clamber out. We all crawled into the ditch. There was more machine gun fire, but it stopped. The only weapon I had was my pistol, so when I saw a hand grenade, obviously from the Bren gun carrier that had been abandoned after hitting a mine just ahead of where we were hit, I picked it up and stuck it in the pocket of my pants.

We crawled down the ditch until we got far enough behind our own lines that it was safe to stand up, then we walked back to Headquarters Troop. There we joined two or three other tank crews whose tanks had also been hit. At Headquarters I fished the hand grenade out of my pocket and took a closer look. If I had ever had doubts about the existence of a Greater Being, they were dispelled at that moment. A hand grenade is armed when you pull a pin, but doesn't explode as long as you hold the firing lever down. When you throw the grenade and the firing lever is released, the firing pin strikes the detonator and the grenade explodes. One side of the metal boss that held the firing pin on the grenade I'd found had broken off, and the pin was sitting at an angle, barely holding the firing lever. And I'd crawled three quarters of a mile down the ditch with it in my pocket! I didn't know what to do with the thing, and finally took it out to an open field and got rid of it.

There were more people than normal in the Squadron Headquarters area. In addition to our crew, there were two other crews that had bailed out of disabled tanks, one from a tank that had burned. Two from that crew were wounded and had been evacuated for medical treatment. Sitting in a group on the roadway behind Headquarters was a group of around twenty German prisoners waiting to be escorted back to a prisoner of war compound. They had no guards and were being completely ignored by everyone. As they sat quietly talking to one another, they seemed quite satisfied that the war, for them, had ended.

The war was far from over for Sergeant MacKenzie. Lieutenant Smith's crew had taken care of his body and brought the tank up to Squadron Headquarters. The major directed MacKenzie to take command of it and go back into action. Half an hour later, he and the crew were back at HQ, without the tank. They had started out on the same route we had taken earlier. Before reaching our knocked-out tank, they made a side trip in an attempt to take out the anti-tank gun that had hit us. They thought they had outflanked it and were moving in to fire on it when they received a hit from a gun firing from a different location. So it was bail out and crawl back to Headquarters again. Mac barely had time for a smoke before he was ordered to take command of a tank whose crew commander, a sergeant, had been killed, and he was once again off to battle. I cannot recall how things went this third time, as I did not see him until he came back to his own troop next morning, but he took it all in his quiet Sergeant MacKenzie way.

In the meantime, I had been souvenir hunting in the German slit trenches we had captured. My greatest finds were six German pistols, which were to form part of the loot I was going to sell to finance my next leave. I never did sell them. As I recall, I gave them to the truck drivers who hauled our supplies and never had the opportunity to acquire such treasures.

That night our crew was taken back to "A" Echelon and, on the following morning, by truck back to the Ordnance Depot to be issued a new tank. Later we went downtown to find a café, as the bars were called in Belgium, to celebrate being alive, and just to let our hair down after all the weeks of chasing German forces without a break. We found a café with a generous supply of cognac and an old windup gramophone with plenty of good records, and we settled ourselves in to have a good time. We were loaded with cash we'd taken off the Germans and hadn't had a chance to spend, so we bought drinks for anybody who came in. The poor guys in the rear echelon, who had regular access to the cafés but not to the spoils of war, never had the funds to go on a tear like we did.

4 Troop of "A" Squadron at Putte, Belgium, October 1944. From left: Francis Tanner, Sergeant Robinson, Archie McLellan, Corporal John Galipeau, Bob Kerr (wearing the leather jerkin issued to him as driver), Nick Kateranchuk, Albert Broadbent, Ed Thorne. All except Robinson are Peewees. We are gathered around the troop officer's tank, where I served as wireless operator (the troop officer had gone to Headquarters for an Orders Group). The white patches on our berets would be our regimental badges, had they not been obliterated from the picture for security reasons. The tanks are the Sherman V with the 75 mm heavy gun. On the tank deck above Bob Kerr's head can be seen the duffel bag holding the fortune in French francs we gathered after the battle for the Falaise Gap. (National Archives of Canada PA-130219)

By closing time we were well into our cups. Everybody else had gone home, but we were having a wonderful time drinking with the owner and winding up the old gramophone so we could dance with his wife and daughter. The town policeman came in, since it was after hours, and told the owner to close up. We all said, "No! Not tonight! Tonight we drink and are merry, for tomorrow we may die." ("Eat, drink, and be merry, for tomorrow we die" was a popular saying in the First World War) The policeman looked at this bunch of wild men with loaded pistols hanging on their belts and decided that the best thing to do was to join the party, as we had invited him to do; and he did. Finally we decided we had better get some sleep, not that we really cared, so we said goodbye.

"You coming tomorrow?" asked the owner, who had no objection to our practice of doubling and tripling the price of a bottle of cognac.

"Oh, yeah, we'll be back tomorrow," we replied, but we didn't go back. The next day we were in our new tank and off to the front.

Our new tank was what we had been looking for all along. Ordnance had started to supply tanks equipped with a seventeen-pounder gun that was equal in firepower to the German 88. The new tanks carried only a four-man crew. The shells were so large that the co-driver's space was taken up by ammunition storage.

We were pretty pleased with our impressive new gun as we drove up to join the unit. We had the first seventeen-pounder in the squadron, maybe in the whole regiment. We caught up with the regiment just over the border in Holland. It was raining and soggy, and the Germans had flooded the area so that we had to travel the roads on top of the dikes. When we arrived, the major sent us up the dike to take out a blockhouse that was giving the infantry trouble. We parked on the dike about a thousand yards away from the blockhouse. I threw a shell into the seventeen-pounder, and the gunner sighted on the target and pressed the trigger. There was a click as the firing pin struck the cap of the detonator, but no boom. Following standard procedure for when a gun doesn't fire, I opened the breech and looked at the cap. The cap was struck, as I could see the indentation caused when the firing pin hit it. I closed the breech, the gunner fired again. Click, no boom; though the cap had been struck again.

With a second failure to fire I, as the loader, had to get rid of the shell; which meant I had to remove the shell from the breech, duck under the gun, climb out of the tank and onto the dike, and dump the shell in the water of the canal, in front of a large and interested audience of infantry. It was embarrassing. Three times we attempted to fire, and three times I had to make the trek from the tank to the dike to dump a shell. Finally Mac, the sergeant, decided there was something wrong with the gun and that we had better go back to get it fixed. There was still a shell in the breech of the gun, so we elevated the gun so the muzzle was pointing to the sky and drove back to the squadron. The gun fitter came up, but he couldn't find anything wrong.

At this time the Second Division was engaged in clearing the Scheldt River estuary. The Third Division, with the First Polish Armoured Division, was clearing the south side of the estuary in what was called the Breskens Pocket. The Fourth Division was still driving north to push the Germans back to the Maas River. Bit by bit, town by town and crossroad by crossroad we advanced, battling for every mile of territory we liberated.

"A" Squadron reached an open area called Philippine that was completely flooded, as was most of the territory we were travelling through, and moved into a farmyard that was on higher ground, providing a space to park the tanks. Four Troop was ordered to go forward and support the infantry regiment holding the line on our front. We slept in the tanks that night. I lay in the bottom of the tank with my feet shoved way back in an opening of the turret, and in the middle of the night I managed to kick the fire extinguishing system discharge lever and set it off. Immediately, two great, roaring nozzles of CO_2 set up a horrible racket, waking everybody in the vicinity. A strong suggestion that I watch my feet was the kindest of the many epithets directed my way.

In the morning, we again tried our seventeen-pounder on an enemy position. I was so sick and tired of the cursed gun that I didn't bother to slam the shell in. I just slid it forward without any excess energy, the breech closed, the gunner stepped on the firing button, and it fired. We were in a narrow street with houses on either side covered with nice, red tile roofs. When the gun fired, the concussion made all the tiles on the

The Low Countries. (Map: Robin Brass Studio)

houses nearest us come slithering down. We were very unpopular. The infantry had two or three men manning an observation post in each of the houses, and we had uncovered them. We were told to take our tank and our gun and go elsewhere.

However, we had learned our lesson. From then on we treated the shells gently, and the seventeen-pounder fired every time.

CHAPTER 13

Water, Water Everywhere

W e spent two or three days in our position in the Philippine. Each day, one tank would run up on the dike to fire a couple of rounds at the enemy positions, then pull back down behind the dike. Then "A" and "C" Squadrons were moved, leaving "B" Squadron behind. Regimental Headquarters and "C" Squadron established themselves in a town called Hulst with "A" Squadron five miles away. We settled in the area for a welcome two-week rest.

The two weeks in Hulst were a time of peacetime soldiering. Our best uniforms were unpacked and pressed, usually by some motherly local housewife in exchange for a few spare rations and cigarettes. As we were the first Canadian soldiers these good folks had seen, we cleaned up and dressed up so we would look smart. The cafés were open, movies were shown and the townspeople held dances for our benefit. We were far from idle while we waited to be called to battle. The tanks received much-needed cleaning and maintenance. Our only action against the enemy consisted of patrols along the shore of the liberated estuary to monitor the activities of the Germans in the occupied area, though we remained alert and ready to move if they made any attempt to break through the Allied lines. It was a most pleasant period.

On the 9th of October it all ended. We were ordered back to war. The regiment was moved to Fort Brasschaet and placed under the command of the Sixth Canadian Infantry Brigade, Second Division. "A" Squadron took over Brecht, a small town in the area. We were on one road with a row of houses along it, and a quarter of a mile over from our front was another road lined with houses, parallel to those we were in, held by the Germans. They occupied the houses on the opposite side of the road.

Every morning, our troop officer walked the quarter mile to the other road, entered one of the houses on the near side through the back door and went upstairs to see what the Germans were doing. He would come back and tell us that they were shaving or that they had eggs for breakfast. I understand that there was a henhouse nearby that used to get raided by both the Canadians and the Germans, until one day the Canadian boys arrived just as the Germans were leaving. A day or two later, the Canadians went out early with a patrol and gathered in the Germans.

The German forces in this area were not the elite troops we had fought in France. They were older fellows, and might have included some First World War veterans. Things were fairly quiet. The Germans made the occasional sortie over to our side of the village, but after a few bursts of the Browning they all ran back to where they were supposed to be.

We maintained the holding position in the village until October 20. We were covering a flank of the Third Division, which was engaged in a final drive to clear the south side of the Scheldt Estuary. Then the regiment moved out, reverting to Fourth Division Command, and was ordered to attack north in an action that would eventually see the SAR take the town of Bergen op Zoom. The morning of the move, the troop officer was ordered to report to Squadron Headquarters for an Orders Group, which is a meeting with the commanding officer to outline the day's orders, the points of attack, the operations and tactics for the day, and to distribute general information. His tank, which I was in, and Sergeant MacKenzie's set out for Squadron Headquarters about six in the morning.

I cannot recall why there were only two tanks in the troop. I can only surmise that, as often happened, we were severely under strength. As we drove along I kept track of where we were going through my periscope. Soon after we left I saw our infantry dug in, and it seemed to me they were facing the way we were going. Shortly after that I saw a trip flare fire, and I knew then we were not heading toward our rear lines. We were driving into enemy territory. I didn't say anything. The troop officer had a map, and I figured he must know what he was doing. We turned at a crossroad and went farther along, which, by my reckoning, had us circling back toward our own lines. Through my periscope I saw a farmhouse and farm buildings, around which were parked a number of German vehicles, and not just any old vehicles. One, obviously, was a wireless vehicle, because it had four antennas sticking out of it. Another with six wheels was quite an official looking van. It struck me that we were passing some sort of headquarters, but there was no challenge, and nobody seemed to pay any attention to us.

I could not understand why the troop officer did not seem to notice what was obviously an enemy headquarters; however, we passed by without incident, and it became obvious we were heading back into our own lines. The back country road we were following narrowed to pass between two huge oak trees. Just as we got between the trees, *ka-blam!* off went a mine, blowing off a track and disabling the tank. The sergeant, who had been in the lead, stopped his tank, and we all climbed out and looked at the damage, trying to decide what to do. We didn't have any spare track with us, so we were going to have to call Recovery and have them come and repair the tank. In the meantime, the troop officer decided that he had to get to his O Group, so he would take the sergeant's tank. Thinking of the building we had passed just a quarter of a mile back down the road, I said, "We're going with you," and went to the tank to get my small pack from where I kept it in the tool box on the back. In the time it took to open the tool box, the troop officer was up in the sergeant's tank and gone, leaving Mac and his own tank's crew standing beside the disabled tank feeling neglected and forlorn.

Before long one of our light Stuart reconnaissance tanks drove up at a good speed. We walked over and met him. He asked, "Where's the enemy?"

I pointed at the bushes behind our tank and said, "Right there." I thought he was going to give us a ride out, but he never even asked if we were all right. He made a U-turn, and he was gone as fast as his tank could go.

Back we walked to our disabled tank. It wasn't long before the question of what we were going to do next was decided for us. Somebody woke up, and the first mortar shell landed. We turned tail and ran. There must have been over seventy-five yards of open space to the barbed wire fence. I can't remember whether I went over that fence, through it or under it. All I cared about was getting into the woods on the other side. Once through the fence, we were under cover and ready to try to find our way out. The sergeant took the lead and started down a drainage ditch, crawling because the ditch was only two and a half or three feet deep and the Germans were dug in not too far away. If we stuck our heads up over the edge, we could see where they were and hear their rifles cracking as they fired over top of us. I remember cursing at poor old Mac for taking us down the ditch through the water. After a while we stopped and rested. I said, "Well, I don't care. If I'm going to die, I'm going to have a cigarette."

As soon as the first puff of smoke rose, four rifle shots zipped overhead. I can still recall the sharp crack of the rifles.

We spent most of the afternoon getting back to Regimental Headquarters. We must have crawled over a mile down the ditch before there was enough cover to creep out of it, and it was well on into the afternoon before we thought we were far enough behind our own lines that it was safe to get up and walk. The three of us walked through a grove of spruce trees and out onto a road, then picked a direction to go. Fifteen minutes later we met a carrier platoon from the Lincoln and Wellands and asked for directions. Somewhere farther along we picked up a ride. It was close to six in the evening when we finally arrived at Headquarters. The regimental sergeant major met us and said, "Well, we heard about you fellows," and told us our little morning jaunt had taken us about three miles back of the German lines. "Glad to see you're back," he said. "We'll let the squadron know you made it."

They had fixed up a little outbuilding like a chicken coop with some bunks, and the RSM kicked out the four recruits who had been bunking there, settled us in and handed us a bottle of rum. We got something to eat, then found some hot water to mix with the rum. We had two or three belts each and went to bed.

I should say something about our rum ration. We were entitled to the same ration as the navy, an ounce and a half a day of thick, heavy, rich Navy rum. It wasn't something you drank straight; at least, I wasn't man enough to. It was meant to be put in a cup with hot water and drunk as a toddy. It wasn't always possible to give us our ration each day, so the rum came up periodically with other supplies. We would get a week's supply at once and fill all the water bottles with it so we had it when we wanted it. There were always two or three water bottles full of rum around. If somebody got wounded, we would put a shell dressing on the wound, give the guy a cigarette and tuck a water bottle of rum in the stretcher beside him: "There you go, buddy." We used to picture him arriving at the first aid station singing "Lili Marlene" and offering drinks to the orderlies, and never gave a thought to the possibility that they might want to operate on him at the first field hospital he came to. When I studied first aid later on, I realized that giving the guy a bottle of rum was about the worst thing we could have done for him.

We were given a good deal of training in first aid, but when a buddy was hit, our first thought was to ease his suffering. We each carried a morphine syrette, which was a hypodermic needle attached to what resembled a small toothpaste tube containing morphine. When someone was wounded, the needle was uncovered and pushed into an arm or leg and the morphine injected. I feel the rum was merely to show our buddy we cared and wished him well.

The next morning we picked up a new tank at Ordnance, then moved on to catch up with the regiment. We arrived just in time for the last little scrap in the capture of Bergen op Zoom. "B" and "C" Squadrons had done most of the work. "A" Squadron moved in last and we went with them. Luckily, the Germans had pulled back so we didn't have to fight our way in.

We were two or three days in Bergen op Zoom, which gave us a chance to hear about what we had missed while we were making our way back from behind enemy lines. The regiment had had a terrible battle to take the town. A lot of tanks were lost, including the troop officer's tank, and he lost a leg. It was a bad area, through a forest where Germans had not only placed anti-tank mines, but had planted 500-pound aerial bombs beneath them. When that combination blew, it didn't just damage a tank or take off a track, it turned the tank over. I heard terrible stories from some of the fellows, and I didn't know how I felt about missing the action. I blamed the troop officer for the fact that we weren't there to do our part, but at the same time I was glad we hadn't had to face what the rest of the squadron did on the fight through to Bergen op Zoom.

Then there was the story about the brewery the infantry found the night they attacked. An infantry unit had managed to get across the canal and had established a defensive position in this brewery. It was filled with vats of spirits, but it had been shelled and some of the tanks had been broken. Somebody said there was gin an inch or two deep all over the floor. Of course, the guys lost no time quenching their thirst, and they were soon challenging the Germans to come and get them. All night long the Germans attacked that building, but they couldn't chase our guys out. You put a Canadian in a brewery and you can bet he's not going to budge. There was a rumour that the infantry defended the brewery against a force as big as a German brigade, but I think that was probably a slight exaggeration. In the morning when the Germans retreated, the infantry fellows were relieved by another company of their regiment. The officer in charge of the relief company asked the lieutenant, an American, what kind of a night they had had. He was so far into his cups that he was weaving as he slurred, "It was terrific!"

I don't know how authentic this story is, but I do know there was no shortage of booze in Bergen op Zoom during the time I spent there. There were stories of army trucks arriving at the brewery and loading up. Liberated liquor aside, our three days in Bergen op Zoom were three days of celebration. We moved into the hotels and had a few parties, some of them with the citizens of the town. One was held at the Town Hall. The town had a band come in, and everybody, military and townspeople alike, joined in the festivities. There was lots to drink, and everybody got more than a little bit drunk.

Before we left Bergen op Zoom, we also found out what happened to the tank we had abandoned. Later that day, the fitters went in with a recovery tank to bring it back. Nobody bothered them as they drove up to it and hooked on the tow bar. The tow bar was an A-frame with the apex attached to the recovery tank and two brackets at the bottom that hooked onto the damaged tank. Why they didn't take a closer look at the tank I don't know, because when they started to pull it, the bogies (the wheels the tank ran on) came off the track and sank into the dirt, stopping the tank dead and causing the recovery tank to stall. That was when the Germans decided that the fun was over and opened up on them. Somebody had to crawl down through the escape hatch, sneak along the ground back to the Sherman, and disconnect the tow bar so they could leave. After that, the major sent in one of our tanks to destroy the damaged tank so the Germans couldn't use it. They put nine shells in it before it caught fire, which interested me because so often in action a tank would burn when the first shell hit.

When the time came to leave Bergen op Zoom and resume our attack north, we moved on without Mac. The major had called in Sergeant MacKenzie when we came in from behind the enemy lines and relieved him from active duty. Mac was thirty-five years old, and I guess the major figured he'd gone through enough. Mac remained with the SAR but was sent to the Ordnance Corps, where he was put in charge of preparing recovered tanks for issue to the regiments.

With Mac gone, I became a tank commander, the second of the two corporals in the troop that commanded a tank. A new sergeant, Sergeant Sands, had been detailed to take over the troop, but he didn't leave Bergen op Zoom with us. Sands had spent the afternoon drinking, and when it came time to move off, the major noticed his condition and, relieving him of his duty and his pistol, placed him under open arrest.

I took command of the sergeant's tank with the seventeen-pounder, and off we went. After travelling two or three hours with little opposition, we arrived at a village where the infantry was attacking and meeting stiff opposition. Sergeant Gove, who was taking charge of the troop temporarily, caught up to us in a tank mounted with a 75 mm gun. He came up to my tank on foot, called me out onto the ground and told me there was a report that a Tiger tank was concealed behind a barn we could see a quarter of a mile out, sitting by itself in an open field. He wanted me to take it out with the seventeen-pounder on my tank. I wasn't happy. I figured that if there was a Tiger sitting behind that barn, he could see me sooner than I could see him, and any kind of frontal attack was going to be suicide.

As Sergeant Gove and I discussed the best way to handle the alleged Tiger, the decision was taken away from us. There was a double explosion as two rounds of high explosive shells from an 88 landed nearby moments apart. We were standing beside a building with a heavy dirt roof, well constructed, but only five or six feet high. It looked like it might have been built as a bomb shelter. The only entrance to the building was an opening about two and a half feet square, and the two of us went through that opening at once.

We forgot about going after the Tiger.

Sergeant Gove was the sergeant that the Peewees had rebelled against when we were at Niagara-on-the-Lake. When he wanted to send me across a quarter mile of clear space after a Tiger tank, I couldn't help but wonder if he was getting his pound of flesh.

Sergeant Sands was delivered to our position in the major's scout car, having sobered up enough to resume his duties. There was no more action that night. The infantry was putting in an attack, and we were on the flank and weren't involved. The crew went into the house beside the tank and lit the little gas stove so we could cook a bit of food. The rest of the troop stayed outside. The village was receiving heavy shelling, targeted at the houses, and they preferred the dirt-roofed structure we had sheltered in earlier. The wireless operator stood wireless watch in the tank, and, after we'd eaten, Sergeant Sands and I lay on the floor in the house. I remember the conversation we had while the shells were coming down. I told Sands, "I got a letter from Ivy today. I understand her brother-in-law," who was in Canada with the Service Corps, "has been posted to Australia."

"That'd be a hell of a place to get posted," Sands replied, as the shells crashed and boomed all around us.

The room we were in had sliding doors to another room. They were closed, but I heard something scrabbling on the other side. Imagining some German trying to sneak in, I got up and walked over, drew my pistol, cocked and aimed it, and pulled the door wide open. Standing there was Lieutenant Barford, the officer who had been with Sergeant Gove during the Peewee rebellion. He was also the officer who would sneak up on sentries when we were on guard on the canals at Niagara and almost got himself shot the night he surprised Pete Winters. I greeted him with, "Sir, you do love to live dangerously."

The following day the infantry had taken their objective, and on November 4, 1944, we pushed through to the village of Steenbergen, where we stayed for several days doing maintenance and fitting. On November 9 we moved to positions along the Maas River, where we took over from the British Seventh Armoured Division. The Germans held the north side of the river and the Allies held the south side. The SAR was given 1,000 yards of front along the river to patrol. This was to be our winter area, a static position with no fighting to speak of. When occasionally the Germans shelled us, we took compass bearings on the direction the shelling came from and reported them to the artillery. When the artillery had sufficient information to establish the location of the guns, they shelled back, but that was the extent of the fighting.

We did quite a lot of patrolling, which was miserable. It was winter, raining and wet and cold. One of our duties was to go out at night on a road that ran to the river and spend a three-hour shift at a listening post. It was nervewracking. You lay on the road in the wet and the cold, keeping watch for German patrols. It was so dark you couldn't see anyone coming, so you had to listen for any movement. You couldn't speak above a whisper, and then only if you had to, and your nerves were on edge because you never knew when a patrol might come by. Still, we were better off than the infantry. Some of them spent their duty time in slit trenches that were half filled with water.

The villagers along the river were all still in their homes, and most of us were billeted with them. Many of the villagers had an empty room where we would put two or three men. We paid for the billets in coke for fuel and shared our rations. The billets were arranged by an officer from Brigade or Division Headquarters. He surveyed the home owners, recording how many soldiers each could accommodate, then prepared a list and distributed it to the regiments manning the positions on the river. In many places, we were living and sleeping in the hay lofts of barns. For the most part, we prepared our own meals beside our tanks from the ration packs brought to us, same as when we were in action. In some cases, the housewife with a small family would cook some meals, and the fellows would share the food with them. We only went inside the houses at night to sleep, but usually we were invited to join the family in the living room to play cards or chat, and the crews became quite friendly with their hosts. At all times, there was at least one man on guard at the tank overnight. Guard duty was rotated based on a schedule drawn up by the troop sergeant. Since both the Germans and the Allies frequently sent patrols across the river into each other's territory, we had to be constantly alert and prepared for attack.

When we weren't on the river, we were quartered in a former German SS barracks in the Dutch village of Vught, a few miles south of the river.

Servicing SAR tanks in Bergen op Zoom. Wherever we went we attracted a crowd of children. Hanging off the back of the nearest tank is a pan that was used as wash basin, bath tub, stewpot or anything else as the need arose. On the ground behind the tank is a jerry can holding water (identifiable by the size and shape of the spout and cap). Hanging from the end of the storage box are the helmets issued to armoured corps personnel, which were seldom worn. The legend "B20" identifies this as the tank of the troop commander for 2 Troop, "B" Squadron. The troop sergeant's tank was designated "B22," the corporal's "B23." (National Archives of Canada PA-140896)

Originally it had been a monastery. There would be two squadrons up on the river and one back in the monastery, and we relieved in rotation much as we had when we were on canal guard duty in Niagara.

As we were in the area for an extended period, we became well acquainted with the local people. Children were always hanging around, and we spoiled them with candy, gum and chocolate. Having them around reminded us that civilization still existed. We picked up quite a bit of the language from them.

We could see first hand what the villagers were suffering. They had absolutely nothing: no meat, no food, no clothing. They scavenged what they could and lived on potatoes, tulip bulbs and beets. We saw little children with their bellies distended from malnutrition. It was heartrending, but there was little we could do. Interim military governments were set up to help restore the essentials of living, but the combat troops had to concentrate on liberating the country.

Late in December the German General von Rundstedt attacked the American forces in the Ardennes region with a great deal of success in the now-famous Battle of the Bulge, so-named because of the bulge that the Germans forced into the American line of defence. With the success the Germans were having in their attack, it was expected that they would stage an assault across the Maas on the Canadian positions. To counter this possibility, the Fourth Division was relieved by the Poles on December 24 and concentrated in the Vught-Boxtel area as a mobile reserve for the First British Corps. Prior to this move, the South Albertas were on extensive reconnaissance patrols throughout the region, planning, as we were told, routes for troop movement should an attack come. The reconnaissance drives took us to many towns and villages where we would stay for a day or so.

During one of our stops in a small town, our cooks took over a kitchen in an empty café and cooked hot meals for us. Because of the inadequacies of the field kitchen equipment and the conditions under which the cooks had to work, the meals were pretty crude. We might have quite fatty roast beef and potatoes in their skins, along with carrots or peas. We ate out of two mess tins that fit into one another and drank from a tin cup. At meal time you went into the café and the cooks would dish out a mess of pottage into one tin and dessert, some kind of cake or pudding or tinned fruit, into the other, and you had your tea in your enamel mug. The food was not great, and there would be leftovers. The facilities for washing dishes were not very good. They set out three large pots of water: one was soapy, one contained disinfectant, one was clear water. To make washing your dishes easier, when you finished eating, you threw whatever hot tea you had left into the half eaten potatoes and bits of greasy meat in your mess tin and you dumped it into the slop pit that had been dug behind the kitchen. When you got to the slop heap, there would be anywhere from six to ten children, six, seven, eight, nine years old, reaching into your tin to try and pull out a bit of food before you threw it all away.

I don't know what the others thought, but I felt ashamed at having to push these children away so I could throw my leftover scraps in the slop pit. We knew that we couldn't feed them all. There were so many of them and so few of us, and the little extra food we had wasn't going to make any real difference. We realized, too, that if we didn't eat and keep ourselves in condition, they would never be free of German domination. I was trying to leave the children with a little dignity when I pushed them away, but underneath I was hurting. To me, it isn't the people who were bombed and shot and killed, the healthy young men trying to destroy one another, that embody the ravages and horrors of war. It's these children standing around the slop pit trying to snatch our leftovers before we threw them out. That image will be with me till the day I die.

Field graves of Canadian soldiers killed liberating Bergen op Zoom, covered with flowers by the Dutch townspeople. When the war was over, the remains were moved to a Commonwealth War Graves cemetery near the town. (Photo courtesy Leon Rosenboom)

CHAPTER 14

Farewell to Friendly, Smiling Faces

O n December 16, 1944, the Germans tried to break out of the Ardennes, giving the American army a rough time. They almost made it. During that time, we were driving hither and yon all over the area on patrol, in case the German troops across the river from us mounted an attack. In particular, we were on the lookout for paratroopers. The German offensive failed, and we went back to our winter routine.

We celebrated Christmas in the monastery. We had a good dinner, and, as was traditional, the officers and senior NCOs served the meal. We also put on a Christmas party for the children in the village. We were happy to be able to do something for them, however little it was.

Quite a few new officers had come in as reinforcements and several troopers had been promoted to NCO status, so in January 1945 a divisional battle school to upgrade their technical skills and knowledge was set up in a town called Loon op Zand. I was sent to it, and I don't know why, because it was just a repeat of training I had had in the infantry: close order drill, firing weapons, attack and defence under fire, and drill instruction methods. With us were two fellows from an English regiment, part of the Fourth British Division attached to the Second Canadian Corps, and to amuse ourselves we decided make them honorary Canadians. We wrangled with the quartermaster stores and got them Canadian uniforms with Canadian patches on the shoulders, the good Canadian Armoured Corps black beret and Canadian boots. They were happy as larks.

They were two good fellows. Both had fine voices and sang very well. Most of their songs were barroom ballads, which were quite coarse. I still remember the words, but I will not repeat them. We would be sitting in a lecture and all of a sudden they would break into one of these goofy songs. We had a great time with them.

The town of Tilburg was close by, and in the evening we would wander down to see we if could find anything to drink. Somebody was bootlegging something that was supposed to be drinkable liquor, but the first time I tried it I realized that it contained a good percentage of ether. I remember it being a red colour. It didn't kill any of us, but, according to rumour, there were some guys who drank too much and died or went blind. The Englishmen got quite a kick out of the hijinks we rowdy Canadians would get into when we'd had a few. They said that if they tried anything of the sort with the fellows of their their own unit, they would be told to shut up and act proper.

While I was away at battle school, the High Command decided it was time to kick the Germans off an island in the Maas River. The island, called the Kapelsche Veer, was about one and a half miles long and 800 yards wide, and an infantry brigade was to attack and take it. As I understand now, the attack on the island was a diversion for Operation Vertibo, which was an attack from Nijmegen into the Reichswald Forest in Germany. The Polish Division and the Royal Marine Commandos had already made unsuccessful attempts to take the island before the 10th Brigade Infantry, supported by the armour of the Fourth Division, succeeded. The fighting was fierce and the conditions terrible, and there was a great loss of life. The temperature was well below freezing; many of the troops suffered frozen feet.

The tanks went in to support the infantry. After one of them bogged crossways on the road, nothing else could move past it on the soggy ground. The Germans had tunnelled the island, so they could attack in one place and then, when they had drawn Allied fire, they could disappear and pop up somewhere else. In spite of the difficulties, the attack was successful and the island taken. It was turned over to the Poles to occupy after the battle. We didn't even try to recover the tanks, not even the ones that were operational. Some were shot up, some were bogged down, and the rest couldn't move because the roads were blocked. We just left them there for the Poles.

Two of our fellows distinguished themselves in the action: Troopers Broadbent and Tillsley. Broadbent was one of the Peewees. To look at him, he was the last man you would expect to achieve what he did. He was a quiet fellow who more or less stayed in the background, but he was also the most rumpled-looking soldier you could ever find. No matter what he did to himself he looked untidy. He never even had his beret on properly. During the battle the troop officer got killed and all the NCOs were wounded or killed, and it was Broadbent who stepped into the breech, took charge and directed the operations of "A" Troop, particularly the firing of the guns.

One of the gunners Broadbent directed was Slim Tillsley, who was in my tank and an excellent gunner. Slim was sort of a strange character. He was six feet tall and certainly outgoing, but he was artistic as well. There were white walls inside the tank, and when he wasn't busy while we were riding along, he covered them with cartoons. I can still picture him sitting in the tank with his partial plate hanging out of his mouth, drawing on the wall with a crayon.

After the battle, when the island was cleared, a senior German warrant officer who had been taken prisoner said that what lost the Germans the battle was Broadbent's skill in directing the tank operations and Slim's accuracy as a sniper with the 75 mm. Broadbent was awarded the Distinguished Conduct Medal by General Montgomery on February 23, 1945. Slim was not decorated, because he was just doing his job as a gunner, but it was acknowledged that his skill in doing his job had been an important factor in the victory.

I almost left battle school when news of the action on the island reached me. I wanted to be with my troop, and I always regretted that I wasn't with them. It just didn't feel right. I visited the island in 1992, but it didn't mean much to me because I hadn't been in the action there.

We went back to Tilburg early in February 1945 to prepare for the spring offensive into Germany. We spent time cleaning up the tanks and getting them in shape, stocking them with ammunition, and doing some training. On February 21, we were off and away to join the rest of the Canadian army in the attack on Germany. As soon as we crossed the border we became aware of a new and sombre atmosphere. The rainy weather and dark, low clouds were reflected in the attitudes of the people. We were no longer the liberators, we were the invaders. Where we had been greeted by townspeople cheering and throwing flowers and handing out bottles of liquor, now we encountered townspeople throwing rocks. It was a strange feeling. Our attitude changed, too. No longer were we the nice guys. We were ruthless. If we had any action in a town, we destroyed it. Because of the horrors I'd seen committed by the German troops on the people of countries they had occupied, I had no feelings for the people of Germany.

Our objective at the time was the Hochwald Forest. It was part of the north end of the Siegfried Line and was well defended. Since the Reichswald Forest had been cleared, the Hochwald was one of the last barriers to the crossing of the Rhine by the Canadians. The SAR was to push on to the town of Uedem,* on the edge of the Hochwald Forest. Once we reached Uedem, where the Fourth Brigade with the Lincoln and Wellands and the Argylls under command had taken some high ground, we were to cross a valley and attack an opening in the forest where the railroad went through, called the Hochwald Gap. We were to capture the Gap and hold it as a starting position for the drive down and across the Rhine. The Second Division was to clear the rest of the Hochwald Forest and the Third Division was to clear the town of Uedem.

Herb Roulston, who had been away in hospital for a couple of weeks, caught up to us in a small Dutch town on the German border as we were on our way to the Hochwald. By this time Herb had been promoted to sergeant, which meant he was entitled to a monthly issue of liquor, and he came back with three bottles of good Canadian booze. We all gathered in what had been a café where it was warm and the lights were on, and we did quite well with Herb's booze. I had drunk enough that I was feeling quite good when it came time to move out around midnight. It was a nice, bright moonlight night, and I remember looking at the moon as we loaded into the tanks.

As tank commander, I was standing up in the turret as we started off. Everything was fine until the glow from the booze started to disappear.

---

* Most journals and regimental histories spell the name of the town "Udem." I discovered the correct spelling on a visit to the area in 1995. I asked how to get to the town of "oodem," and was directed to Udem in Holland. When we finally reached the place we were seeking, I learned that the correct spelling was Uedem, pronounced "eedem" by the inhabitants.

We were sailing along through the dark, and all I could see ahead were the taillights of the tank in front. As the hours went by I started to get sleepy, and then sick. Finally I had had enough. It was all I could do to keep my eyes open, and the crew didn't need me. I crawled behind the turret, out on the back deck, pulled loose the tarp we kept there with the bedrolls tied up beneath it, slipped under the tarp and went to sleep. There I rode in solid comfort until daylight arrived and we stopped to have a break and cook some breakfast. The crew all got out of the tank, and then I pulled myself out from under the tarp and climbed down to join them.

"Where did you come from?" they asked.

"I've been up on the back deck."

"We had a stop, and we looked around and couldn't find you. We thought you'd fallen off."

Naturally, I regretted the whole evening's episode, because I had a terrible head. I don't know how Herb was, but knowing his capacity for drink, I don't imagine it fazed him one bit.

Conditions were terrible as we made our approach to Uedem. The area is predominantly farmland. It was late February, raining, and the ground had thawed. We were travelling cross-country and the fields were a morass of mud. By the time we reached our destination, we had left twelve tanks bogged. There was a road the Third and Fourth Division transports were trying to use, and by the time they got through, the road was ploughed into ruts. To add to the atmosphere, our movements were being screened by huge generators that had been set to spew out smoke all along our route. As we made our way past banks of roiling smoke, the whole ordeal resembled something out of a science fiction or horror movie.

We reached Uedem late in the afternoon of February 26, topped up our fuel tanks and loaded more ammunition. The area we were going into was well defended, and the Germans were making their last stand. They had concentrated their power and brought in some of their top troops. We weren't going to have an easy time of it. We knew we wouldn't be able to restock ammunition once we got into action, so we loaded every shell rack on the tank and then stacked more shells on the floor. All the tanks in 4 Troop had extra supplies of smoke shells, because we were to be the reserve troop and would use the smoke to shield our actions from the enemy. I didn't know what we were going to do if we met a Tiger tank. I figured we were going to have to smother him, because we would have had to dig through all the smoke shells to get at the heavy explosive and armour-piercing shells.

We moved off at midnight. We were to execute a right hook, which meant we would drive down along the edge of the town, across the railroad tracks, and then parallel the tracks to cross back over right at the bottom of the hill below the Gap. We were travelling in column, accompanied by a carrier platoon from one of the infantry units. As we came to the edge of Uedem we were stopped by a tank ditch, a moat eight or ten feet deep that surrounded the town. While we waited for the engineers to find us a crossing, I noticed movement ahead of me and realized that there were Germans walking up and down the ditch. I reported that I had enemy movement and was ordered not to open fire. The same order was given to somebody else who spotted what they thought was a tank. We were to conserve ammunition.

After an hour or so a crossing was found and we started off again. The plan had been for us to cross the valley in the dark, but we were behind schedule and it was breaking daylight as we went down the edge of the town. The troop officer ordered Sergeant Sands and me to place our tanks in a holding position on either side of the road while the rest of the squadron, including him, went on. Sands and I were maybe fifty yards apart and could see each other. There was not much on the radio until suddenly the lead tank reported that he could see something on the road in front of him. He got permission from the squadron commander to open fire. I heard him report that the shot had ricocheted off and he was engaging again. Then somebody else reported that he was being fired on, and the squadron commander himself came on the air and reported he was receiving fire. Immediately afterwards, I heard him directing his gunner: "Gunner, traverse right." And again, "Gunner, traverse right!"

I realized that the squadron commander had forgotten to switch to the intercom and was broadcasting his order over the air, which meant the gunner couldn't hear him. I flipped my microphone switch and said, "You're on the A set." And that was it. That was the last transmission from the squadron, or from anybody else up there. As I learned later, the squadron had been ambushed when they reached the railway, and within moments they were wiped out. We lost eight of our tanks and a number of the men were taken prisoner. The Germans had hit the front and back tanks first so that nobody else could move. The ground was so swampy the tanks couldn't leave the road, so the crews bailed out and left them. Those who could worked their way across to the anti-tank ditch and escaped.

Meanwhile, Sergeant Sands and I were sitting in our holding position without any idea what was going on. I picked up the mike and said to Sands, "What do you think, Duke?"

"I don't know," he replied. "Sounds like everything's gone."

As we waited, I looked behind me to see two Germans walking up behind my tank with their hands on their heads to indicate their intention to surrender. I went for my pistol so fast that one of the boys in the tank said, "That's the quickest draw I ever saw." I told them, "Hands on *kopf.* Throw away your weapons." Then I pointed to where "C" Squadron, which was in reserve that day, was harboured with the Lake Superior Regiment and said, "March." They dutifully took off with their hands on their heads.

It was close to half an hour later that some fellows from the knocked-out tanks who had managed to get to the tank ditch and work their way back appeared over a rise in front of us. Among them was the "A" Squadron commander, who walked up to my tank and told me about the ambush. I asked him what they were going to do about Sergeant Sands and me. He said he thought we would be pulled out eventually, but I didn't have the radio frequency of Headquarters and so couldn't call to report what had happened. Duke and I stayed in position until close to supper time, when somebody arrived and said we were to harbour in "C" Squadron. I imagine the squadron commander had told them about us when he reported to Regimental Headquarters. Two or three other "A" Squadron tanks that had been pulled out of the mud showed up and joined us, and we ended up with a ragtag group of maybe a troop and a half from "A" Squadron.

I've never been happy about what happened that day. Our regular squadron leader, Major Lavoie, was away on leave, and I think it would have been a much different operation had he been there. Major Lavoie would never have led the column going in. Under normal circumstances, the squadron leader would have remained where Duke Sands and I were left, where he would get reports from the troops and be able to direct the action and call for help if needed. When the squadron commander is in the lead, as was the case that day, he has to fight his own tank and his own troop, while the squadron as a whole loses all direction. I feel somebody made an error in judgment.

"C" Squadron made its attack in the morning, directly across the valley to the Gap. Who did they put out front to lead the way but what was left of "A" Squadron. We were all on net (all radios tuned to the same frequency) and were doing fine as we went down across the valley – until we got into the cursed mud again. We ploughed along as best we could, but my tank bogged. We churned away for ten or fifteen minutes, but the tracks just dug in deeper. Off to my right Sergeant Robinson was also bogged, but Sergeant Sands had managed to go on. As I found out later, he made a drive all the way through up to the Gap.

We weren't going to sit out there in the mud and we were right beside a farm, so the ten of us, Robby's crew and mine, got out of the tanks and moved into the farmyard. The farm was a large, fairly efficient operation, by the look of it. It had a lot of land and two houses. The main house was a big brick building with some six bedrooms, and there was also a little two-room house occupied by an old couple in their sixties, apparently the parents of the family who owned the farm. We thought we would take over the small house, but when I saw the old couple I looked at Robby and he looked at me and we agreed we couldn't do them out of their home.

Through the rest of the day we stayed outside, the way we always did, to cook our meals and pass the time. When night came, most of the fellows bedded down in the barn, but I decided I was going to go into the house and sleep in a bed. Nobody would join me, so I went in on my own, found a bedroom, crawled into bed, and went to sleep. Sometime during the night somebody came in and looked at me, but nobody bothered me.

About six in the morning I was awakened by a party of engineers who had no reservations about moving into the house. They came storming in without even looking to see who was occupying it. It was time for me to get up and get going anyway, and I went out and joined the fellows in the barnyard for breakfast.

Hochwald Forest. Knocked out tanks, theirs and ours: a German mobile anti-tank gun on the left, and a Canadian Sherman on the right. (SAR)

Destruction in the German town of Uedem, near the Hochwald. Uedem was not damaged as severely as many of the other towns we went through; in fact, some neighbourhoods were completely untouched. This picture was taken after the war, when cleanup was in progress. (SAR)

We had no hesitation in using whatever facilities we needed that were available. As we drove the German forces back, those parts of Germany we had conquered were considered occupied. If we needed shelter, we took over a barn or a house and didn't think twice about it. We left the inhabitants alone as much as possible, but if they argued, they would find themselves looking for somewhere to sleep.

It wasn't until evening of the second day that the recovery tank came through and pulled Robinson's and my tanks out and we made it back to the regiment. It took so long because the recovery tanks, which were lighter and less likely to get bogged, were being used to haul supplies up to the infantry who had made it up to the Gap. We missed out on the action. By the time our tanks were mobile again, the battle for the Hochwald Gap was winding down. We harboured with a group of "A" Squadron tanks, and I temporarily lost my tank and crew. Our commanding officer, Colonel Wotherspoon, was covering for the brigadier, who was on leave. Major Coffin had command of the regiment. He had gone through four tanks that had all been bogged, so he took my tank and my crew went with him. I took over a tank with a reinforcement crew for the first part of the next action, and then my crew came back. I thought they would be mad about losing their nice, soft spot in Regimental Headquarters, but they said, "No, we're happy even to see you. All we do at Headquarters is cook meals and run errands for the colonel."

The Hochwald Gap was taken, and we continued the drive to the Rhine River. Our next objective was a town called Veen. We had a few little actions along the way. I recall one where we were supporting the Argyll and Sutherlands. They had artillery support as they went into the attack. Either the artillery barrage came down short or the Argylls were ahead of schedule, because they took an awful pounding and lost a lot of men to their own artillery.

A Peewee again distinguished himself on the drive to Veen, although he was no longer with the Peewees. Trooper Forbes was another unlikely type, a mousy sort of fellow, very slim, quiet, not at all aggressive. He was gunner in a tank that was hit by an 88. The rest of the crew bailed out, but Forbes stayed with the tank and fired his gun at the enemy positions until he ran out of ammunition. He was awarded the Military Medal for his actions.

On March 3, 1945, we began our attack to capture the town of Veen. The Germans were in an entrenched area, and their positions were so well fortified that what started out to be a show by "C" Squadron finally took a whole brigade to accomplish.

"B" and "C" Squadrons began the attack with infantry support, with "A" Squadron in reserve. After they attacked three or four times without making much headway, "A" Squadron was sent in on the outskirts of town from a different direction, supporting a company of the Argyll and Sutherland Highlanders. On the final drive of the day, my troop and the few remaining members of an infantry platoon were to establish a defensive position at a crossroad on the edge of town. One of the roads led into town, but the houses ended at the crossroad, on one corner of which were the three stone houses that were our objective. As was often the case, we only had three tanks in the troop because one that had been lost hadn't yet been replaced, due to the loss of men in the Hochwald Battle.

We had to cross an opening of about half a mile to reach the houses. I was in the lead, with Sergeant Sands and the troop officer behind me. As we drove across to the three houses I told my driver, "Take wing, Nick";

The Hochwald. This was once a Sherman, destroyed when the ammunition exploded – an illustration of why the Germans nicknamed the tanks "Ronsons" after the cigarette lighter. It always amazed me how something made of steel could burn so readily. (SAR)

An SAR Sherman and Stuart (the smaller tank in the rear) advancing near Veen. This shot clearly shows extra tank tracks welded to the armour on the Sherman to give added protection. The crews of both tanks fastened evergreen branches to the sides to help camouflage the tanks' shapes. The main job of the light Stuart VI in our Recce Troop was to search out and report the location of the enemy. (DND Photo)

whenever we crossed an open area, I wanted us moving as fast as we could move, making ourselves a more difficult target for the enemy. Sands and I got across without incident, and I parked my tank on one side of the house on the corner while Duke took the other side. Then we discovered that the troop officer wasn't following. Sergeant Sands called his tank on the radio and reported: "Have reached a position at the crossroads, what now?"

The troop officer's wireless operator came on the air to say that Sunray, the troop officer, had been injured and they were taking him back to Squadron Headquarters for medical treatment. He'd been riding with the hatch open but hadn't latched it, and the hatch had come down on his hand and broken it. I knew that when a tank was hit the crew walked out to safety and that a radio call would have brought a Jeep ambulance for him, and I felt like saying, "Well, why not just drop him off and let him walk back? Come on up here, we need you," but it wasn't my place to make such a comment.

We held our position for two days, waiting for orders to attack or withdraw. There were snipers everywhere, and we didn't get out of the tanks during the day the whole time. Sergeant Sands and his crew were on the side opposite the enemy positions, and so were safe to dismount and move around to heat up some food. My tank faced the enemy positions. We ate hard tack and bully beef and drank cold water from our water bottles. With us was a small group of infantry, an officer and ten or a dozen men. Two or three were lost to snipers, and one when he went down into the basement of the house and lay down on a bed. It was boobytrapped and blew up. I knew there were German infantry in the second house, about fifty feet away, but they didn't bother us and we didn't bother them. I guess they didn't want to show themselves.

We made an assault on the third house, but it was useless. The houses had been built in about the 1400s, and they were made to last with stone walls three feet thick. That position should have had forty or fifty infantry for house clearing and a full troop of tanks instead of the ten or so men and two tanks we had.

We were pretty much cut off from the rest of the squadron. The tank radios were the only means of communication with our regiments and headquarters for both the infantry and ourselves. One night a message came through to tell the infantry officer that they had ten green reinforcements for him. His immediate answer was that he didn't want them. Where we were was no place for men who had no battle experience.

The second night I knew it was all over. I woke up about three in the morning to hear what I had come to recognize as the signal the Germans gave when they were pulling back: three quick bursts on the Schmeisser machine gun. Later that day, a tank arrived with a new troop officer and the news that we were to move into the town. The officer's name in the regiment was synonymous with derring-do, and he had a reputation as a real tank killer. He got us out of our tanks to tell us the plan: I would lead, he would go second and Sergeant Sands was to follow. We climbed back in our tanks and waited for his signal to move out. The troop officer came on the air and said, "4 Baker Charlie," which was the call sign for my tank, "follow me."

"Oh," I thought, "he's going to lead the way." I stood in the turret, waiting for him to move out, but he looked over at me and waved for me to go ahead, in contradiction to what everybody would have heard over the radio. I felt I'd had a telling insight into how he had acquired his reputation.

I moved off and encountered a bit of machine gun fire, which we took care of with a burst from the .30 calibre Browning coax, then moved into cover. No sooner did I reach cover than the troop officer came on the air again, "4 Baker, move on."

It was standard procedure that when you didn't know what opposition you were going to meet you moved from one position where buildings or trees protected you from the enemy's view to another position with cover, then paused to survey what lay ahead before moving on; but each time, as soon as I reached a new position, the troop officer was on the radio, "4 Baker, move on." At one point we had to make a left turn at an intersection to go straight into town, again across a quarter mile of open space. I didn't know whether there might be somebody waiting to snipe at us while we were exposed, so I told Nick, my driver, "OK, let's go. Full speed. Sprout wings," and away we tore across the open space. This continued until we hit the edge of the town, which was just the type of spot I would expect the enemy to put mines, and I thought our troop officer might exercise a little more caution, but what came over the air every time I stopped to look for evidence of mines? "4 Baker, move on."

We moved into the town, pulled up the driveway of a house and turned into the yard, prepared to search the house to make sure it was clear of German troops. We were occupying the town and had to make sure the enemy had left. As we got down from the tank the family came out and lined up along the side of the house. There were eight or nine of them. I noticed first a young fellow around eighteen and a boy in his early teens. There were a couple of teenage girls, a middle aged woman and man, and, at the end, one little old lady in her seventies. They all looked apprehensive, but her knees were shaking as she held her arms up in the air as high as she could get them. She was terrified! I went to her and said, "*Nein, nein.* Put your hands down." Then I took her hands and brought her arms down to her side. I felt badly that this little, harmless grandmother should be frightened of me.

Leaving the family outside, I went in to search the house. The only thing of interest I found was a Walther P-38 pistol lying on the table. You were always suspicious when you saw a prize like that lying in plain sight. You wondered whether it might be hooked to a wire so it would blow up if you moved it. I took a chance and picked it up and cocked it. Everything was fine. I decided that some German soldier had given his pistol to one of the young fellows to fight us off. Instead, it had become a trophy for me.

The battle had ground down, and the town of Veen was taken. The British Second Army had moved across the Rhine River at Wesel and Rees, and the Americans had taken the bridge at Remagen and crossed there. We settled in the town for a couple of days and kept ourselves busy looting. Veen had been so badly shelled and hammered that very few civilians had stayed. I recall coming out of a shoe store with a nice pair of new dress shoes and meeting a young woman who said, "*Ah, comme ci, comme ça.*" We went into the basements of the houses and were shocked by the amount of food we found. There was bottled fruit, pickles, hams, bacon, sugar; every cellar was full.

We helped ourselves to what we could, and when we moved out on March 12, the column looked like a gypsy caravan. The back of every tank was loaded with bicycles, radios, sacks of sugar, everything you could think of. In one night's drive, we moved all the way back to the training area at Tilburg in Holland, where we settled down for about a week to service the tanks, do some retraining and have a bit of a break. We got rid of our loot to the Dutch. The food we gave them; everything else we sold for what we could get. I remember a bicycle in good shape brought 400 guilders.

From Major Paterson's *History*:

Coming back to Holland, to people who would look you in the eye and smile, seemed like "Paradise Regained". And so it was, for winter turned to spring, and the branches of the new budded trees lifted and sighed to an almost summer breeze, and the sun shone all during that late March.

CHAPTER 15

Sergeant Galipeau

We had a lot of work to do at Tilburg. In addition to the maintenance and restocking of supplies on the tanks, the guns had to be sighted; the sights had a tendency to drift, which meant we couldn't fire accurately. We received new tanks to replace the ones that had been lost, and quite a few reinforcements who needed training. I don't know what our personnel losses had been, but the SAR records show a loss of 42 tanks, 18 of them to enemy action in Operation "Blockbuster" to clear the Hochwald Gap. The toll of enemy personnel and equipment claimed by the SAR amounted to 350 casualties, 3 ground-mounted 88 mm anti-tank guns, 4 Mark IV tanks and two 75 mm SP (self propelled) guns. These statistics are among the reasons those of us who served with the regiment are proud of our service and of having contributed to the excellent reputation the SAR had among the other units of the 10th Brigade.

It was one of the reinforcements we received who, accidentally, sent Herb Roulston home. About two days after we arrived in Tilburg, we were out servicing the tanks. I was on top of mine, taking orders from my crew for new socks, pants, shirts, whatever they needed. Suddenly there was an explosion from the tank two away from ours. I heard shouting and rushed down to find three or four people gathered around Herb. A grenade had gone off in his hand, and his hand was gone and his thighs were full of shrapnel. The other fellows wrapped a shell dressing around his hand, pulled his pants down to give first aid to the shrapnel wounds as best they could and sent him off to hospital.

It wasn't until I met Herb after the war that I learned the whole story. He and his crew were restocking the tank with ammunition, which included having to clean and arm grenades. New hand grenades came unarmed and covered in beeswax. The wax had to be cleaned off, and then a detonator had to be put in the bottom. To install a detonator, you pulled the pin and took the firing lever off, which would allow the firing pin to strike the base plug where the detonator would be when the grenade was armed. This was not a prescribed procedure, but as was so often the case, this shortcut was used by experienced soldiers. Then you unscrewed the base plug, took it out and cleaned everything up, put the detonator in, then replaced the firing pin and affixed the firing pin lever, inserted the safety pin to secure the lever, replaced the base plug and returned everything to its original position.

One of the reinforcements in Herb's crew was sitting on the tarp beside the turret doing this job. Herb was standing in the turret next to him. Suddenly the new guy said, "Sarge, this grenade is smoking."

Herb looked down and realized that the fellow, in error, had picked up and pulled the pin on one of the grenades that was already primed, and it was about to explode. The kid dropped it, and it rolled down by the tarpaulin. Herb scrambled to undo the tarp strings so he could get it. Finally he had the grenade in his hand, and he had to decide what to do with it. He didn't know whether to drop it in the tank or on the street or to throw it. If he were to throw it, he couldn't see where it was going to land, and there were children all over the place. Before he could make a decision the grenade exploded, and that was the end of the war for Herb. He was sent back to Canada.

A couple of days after we arrived in Tilburg, our squadron second in command told me that I was being considered for promotion to sergeant. Due to the losses incurred in battle, promotions in action were a matter of course, and as a result of our recent actions in Germany, there was a sergeant's position open in "A" Squadron. The 2 I/C told me that I and two or three others were being considered, and that he was pushing for me to be chosen. The others were being strongly presented by their troop officers. However, I had seniority, so he was taking my case to the major. He asked that I not let him be proven wrong in his choice. Soon afterward, I received my third stripe and became a lance sergeant. A month later I was named acting sergeant, and just before the war ended, I was confirmed in the rank of full sergeant.

I suppose I was happy to have been chosen for promotion and to feel that I had been recognized, but the most important differences to me were the increase in pay and the fact that, as a sergeant, I was entitled to purchase a 40 ounce bottle of liquor once a month. There were other privileges that went along with the rank, but they didn't mean much in the field. If we went back into garrison, the sergeants had their own mess and their own quarters. You didn't sleep in barracks with the noise and commotion that went on until lights out at 10 p.m. At the end of the day you walked away and left everything to the corporals for the night, while you could relax in the privacy of your own room without fear of disruption.

A couple of times we were in rest areas where the sergeants had their own cook, and I took advantage of the opportunity. I figured that if you accept the responsibility, you might as well enjoy the privileges. Herb Roulston had been just the opposite. He took his third stripe, but would have nothing to do with segregated facilities. At times I felt that Herb protested a bit too much, just for effect. In reality I believed he would have been happy to accept the privileges. In the field, though, you were just part of the crew. You had additional authority, but it didn't mean much as far as privileges went.

There was quite a change in responsibilities. The sergeant was second in command of the troop, and was the troop commander's right-hand man. Instead of just being concerned about your own crew, you were concerned about the troop as a whole. The troop officer was the general administrator, but the sergeant was the one who saw that the decisions the troop commander made were carried out. The troop officer directed the troop and was the one who knew the tactics and objectives for the day, but the sergeant was the one who really knew the men who would be carrying out the orders, and often had more battle experience. It seemed as though new troop officers who came to us directly from Officer Training School without NCO experience in battle often became early casualties. Troop officers who were not killed were promoted and moved to more senior positions with the squadron or at Regimental Headquarters, but the sergeant was there day after day. The officers relied a lot on the sergeants. I can remember the colonel making a speech at Christmas time and saying, "I have to state that the gains made by and the success of this regiment to this point have depended mostly on the sergeants. I have to thank them."

With our tanks serviced and supplied and our reinforcements placed in their new crews, we were off to carry the war to the Germans. We left Tilburg and went to a position where we bivouacked for the night, ready to head for Germany the next day.

During the day, a brand new troop officer with four green recruits came up to 4 Troop. As troop sergeant, I decided I'd better make the acquaintance of the troop officer and have a little talk with the recruits. I wanted to find out what they had in the way of experience and training. I learned that none of them, including the officer, had any battle experience whatsoever. The crew had been to the Canadian Armoured Corps School in Camp Borden, going through the same training as we'd had in Debert, and then had been sent overseas, been assigned to this tank and this lieutenant, and then had come straight to the regiment as reinforcements.

I didn't say too much to the troop officer, but he stood and listened while I talked to the crew. I explained to them what they were getting into,

Signs at the border reminded us we were entering enemy territory, where we were not regarded as liberators. The "No fraternising" order (which meant that we were to make no contact whatever with the German people, except as directed by our officers) was a terrible burden to inflict on healthy young soldiers, especially when a lovely German *Fräulein* sent

clear signals that she would definitely like to fraternise. The fact that being caught fraternising would cost us every benefit we were entitled to helped us to resist the siren's appeal; as did the fact that the order came directly from Field Marshal B.L. Montgomery. There is no official record of any member of the SAR disobeying this order. (SAR) told them what to be prepared for, passed on the kinds of things you learn through experience, such as to close the hatches when they were in action and bail out when a tank is hit, but to stay with it unless they were told to get out. We can always replace tanks, I told them, but men are harder to replace. I tried to point out the small errors that, in battle, can cost you your life.

The next day we moved out. Our role as part of the Allied offensive was to enter Germany, cross the Rhine River and defeat the Germans completely. The Second and Third Divisions were advancing northward, with the Second Division veering slightly west while the Third went slightly east, so that the space between them gradually widened. The Fourth Division was to cover the space between. The SAR was handed the task of protecting their flanks and filling in the gaps that occurred.

The Third Division had crossed the Rhine and was attacking the city of Emmerich. They were meeting stiff opposition. The Germans we fought were either riffraff or quality troops, and Emmerich was well defended by the latter. Since a tank is actually a mobile piece of artillery, the decision was made to line up the 180 tanks of the Fourth Division and use them alongside the artillery of the Third and Fourth Divisions, firing on the city to support the attack. Each tank was going to be firing 1,200 rounds of ammunition a day. The tanks were placed in position as if they were artillery guns, then direction and elevation to fix the guns on target were established. To achieve this, one gun was fired, and the spot where the shell landed was observed. The gun was then redirected and fired again until it was on target. Then it was locked in that position, and the other tanks aimed and locked their guns in the same position, according to the readings on the azimuth indicator and directional quadrant of the test gun.

On March 28, 1945, we started to shoot. We continued to shoot for three days, twenty-four hours a day. Most days, the regiment fired 16,000 rounds. In total, we fired over 38,000 rounds on Emmerich. Everybody spent time in the turret firing the gun or loading while the rest of the crew on the ground unloaded truckloads of ammunition and unpacked boxes of shells. Each shell was wrapped in a cylinder of heavy cardboard with caps on the end which had to be taken off and thrown away before the

Rhine shoot: the intensive shelling of the city of Emmerich. Here, "C" Squadron is busy unpacking ammunition and loading and firing the tank guns to augment the artillery of the Third and Fourth Divisions. Each crew member took his turn loading or firing the gun. Orderly stacks of shells can be seen behind the tanks and on the tank decks, while piles of empty shell casings and cardboard packing sleeves lie where they were dropped on the ground. In the bottom left corner of the picture are a tarpaulin crew shelter, a couple of jerry cans, a box of rations and some mess tins. (SAR)

ammunition could be stacked outside ready to be passed into the turret. The *Maple Leaf*, the newspaper of the Canadian Forces overseas, reported that the Third Division was advancing on Emmerich behind a curtain of steel. When it was over, the town was annihilated, and the Third Div commander sent a note to the Fourth Div commander thanking us for our assistance.

Not surprisingly, it wasn't only the town of Emmerich that suffered the effects of seventy-two hours of continuous bombardment. I was one of many people who suffered a hearing loss and ended up with a small pension as a result.

On the first of April 1945, we crossed the Rhine on a pontoon bridge and drove north along the German-Dutch border. The border curved back and forth, and we wove our way along so that we were sometimes in Holland and other times in Germany. The Second and Third Divisions had some rough going, but we met little resistance. Often what we did meet came from positions held by youngsters. Somebody, usually the troop officer, would dismount, take a white flag, walk up to them, find somebody who spoke or understood English, and ask them what they were doing there and suggest they surrender. As you would expect from a teenager, the reply would usually be, "We were ordered to fight to the last man and the last bullet."

The lieutenant would shrug and walk back to the tank, get in and give the order to advance. By the time we got to the position, the kids would have left.

From my point of view, it was just as well we were having an easy time, because I had enough troubles with my new troop officer and his new crew. My talk had not sunk in one bit. The officer had neither the experience nor the natural ability to understand what was required, and the young guys in his crew were no better. I felt sorry for the officer. He was misemployed, thrown into a situation he was not prepared for. I had the impression he had been taken off a desk job somewhere and moved to the front, and was not comfortable with it. When young men fresh out of officers' training school came up there was no telling them anything, but this fellow was an older man, and he was just the opposite. He never really took command; instead, he deferred to everything I suggested. I wanted to do the best I could to keep him alive, and that was all I was concerned about.

His crew didn't seem to have an ounce of survival instinct. We ran across a small airfield out in the countryside, and our troop attacked it while the rest of the squadron was engaged elsewhere in the vicinity. I fired on the airport, then led a dash across an open area. I looked back to see the troop officer's tank sailing along behind like they were on a Sunday drive in Camp Borden. The driver and co-driver had opened their hatches and raised their seats, and were enjoying the ride – and making themselves perfect targets for any snipers in the area. I got on the radio and shouted at them to get those hatches closed, but it didn't happen. Luckily for them, the Germans only put up a little fight and then ran. I used to wish that we would run into a real fire fight that would scare some sense into these guys, but we had no such luck.

A little while later we took a village and went into a holding position there while advances were being made elsewhere. It was the middle of the afternoon, so, while remaining ready to repulse an attack or move off whenever the word came, we took the time to have a meal. My green crew and troop officer had parked their tank by a house, and I decided to go and see how they were doing.

It was a sight to behold. At any of the tanks with experienced crews, all that had been unloaded was the cooking gear. Give them two minutes, and they would be back in the tank and rolling. This lot had their tank completely unloaded. They had laid out their bedrolls and taken off their pistols and hung them on the tank, and they were busy washing and shaving. The officer had hauled a chair out of the house and was sitting in the sun with his tunic off. I didn't know what to say, but I had to say something. "What's going on here?" I asked the troop officer. "What are you going to do when we get orders to move? When those orders come, we have to be gone five minutes ago; and you've got this tank all torn apart! What are you going to do if we're attacked?"

"What do you mean?" he said, confused.

"This isn't a cease fire," I told him. "There's no stand down. We're in Germany, and those guys out there in those funny uniforms are out to blow our heads off. I'm not fooling. I left a lot of good friends behind on the way up here. Just because things are quiet now doesn't mean they're going to stay that way. I'll tell you this, if we have to move out, you're going to have to leave this stuff behind and do without; and you won't be answering to me, Sir, you will be answering to Major Lavoie."

I blathered on for a while, and then I gave up and went back to my tank. I told my crew what I'd found and said, "Jesus, guys, I don't know what we've got here. You'd think they were out on a weekend camping trip!"

Now, after all these years, an explanation for these men's incomprehensible behaviour has occurred to me. During their short military life in a reinforcement depot, sergeants and corporals had always been smartly dressed with everything shining and clean and their rank badges very much in evidence, the very picture of military authority. When they got to the front, they encountered a grubby little man in a torn and filthy tank suit, wearing boots that had not seen a decent polish in weeks, his beret shoved to the back of his head and not a rank badge in sight, acting like he had some authority. I suspect they saw no need to listen to me. They had been trained at the Armoured Corps School in Camp Borden and knew it already.

For my part, I was not the stern, order-barking sergeant they probably expected. The men I had supervised from the day I became a corporal had not needed orders. They did their jobs without question, accepting my seniority in rank much as the players accept the captain of a sports team. When a job needed doing, I mentioned it and it was done. Should there be a major decision to make, I consulted with my men before making it, and in all cases I found their input most helpful. I believe this policy led to decisions that kept us alive in many instances. I now realize that when I went to speak to that new, inexperienced crew, it might have been more effective to have them stand at attention while I questioned them individually as to their training, stand them at ease while I gave them my spiel, then bring them to attention again before breaking them off, all very military and proper. Then, they probably would have understood.

The next day we made an attack on another village. The corporal's tank was in the lead, followed by the officer's, while mine held back and covered them. The troop sergeant always had the tank equipped with the seventeen-pounder, and it was routine to have a tank with a 75 mm gun, which was capable of more rapid fire when engaging infantry, lead the way. The seventeen pounder would lead against enemy tanks. We always tried to keep one tank back covering the others because a stationary tank could fire more accurately than a moving one. The officer reached his position, then came on the air and said, "I've just been fired at. There was an explosion and a little while later another explosion. What would it be?"

It sounded to me like a gun had fired a high-explosive shell. I told him, "Well, sounds like somebody's potting at you with a long-barrelled 75. If you're not hit, just stay there, and I'll see what I can find."

He was sitting on the roadway just outside the front yard of a house. Suddenly the house started to smoke, and I realized what had happened.

Whoever was in the house had got hold of a *Panzer-faust* and fired the bazooka at the officer's tank. Instead of destroying the tank, the shell had hit the hedge and exploded. In the meantime, the flame from the bazooka had set the house on fire.

Just then I noticed some German infantry creeping through the low bushes on the edge of the village. Since the officer was ahead of me, I said, "I've spotted enemy infantry on the edge of the village. Can you open fire?"

He said, "My gun's jammed."

I told him to stay where he was, and asked Risdale, the corporal, to cover me while I went after the Germans. The ground was all soggy and boggy, so I went down the road as far as I could, but I couldn't leave the road. By the time I got near, they had disappeared into the brush. The corporal and I left the troop officer and his crew sitting by the house and went on into the village. Since we had gone ahead and had no infantry with us we didn't check the houses. As we got to the far outskirts, out of the woods came some of the wild and crazy British Special Air Service troops. These were special forces troops who drove armoured jeeps with machine guns mounted through the armour plate placed where the windshield should be. They were tough customers. I told them about the German soldiers in the bush and left them to clear the village while I went back and got the troop officer going again. I explained what had happened with the *Panzerfaust* and my gunner, Slim Tillsley, gave some instruction on clearing a jammed gun, and we moved on to our next objective.

Shortly after that we harboured overnight alongside a concentration camp occupied by women from the Polish army who had been captured when the Germans overran Poland. The camp had been liberated a day or two before, not by the Canadians, as was reported back in Canada, but by the Polish Division that was fighting with us. It was a poignant story, as I learned some time later. The Allies were advancing, driving the Germans farther and farther into Germany. These Polish women could hear the battle getting closer, and one day the German commandant and guards left and the women could hear armoured vehicles coming up the road. They all went out to the gate and stood watching anxiously as four tanks appeared. The lead tank came driving up and stopped. One of the women looked up at the tank commander and asked, "Are you English?"

He shook his head, no.

"Are you French?"

Shake of the head, no.

"Are you American?"

Shake of the head, no. Finally the fellow on the tank said, "We're Polish."

Of course, there was a great reunion, and a party to end all parties. The Polish Division had been intent on getting to Warsaw, and to unexpectedly be able to liberate a group of their countrywomen was a moving experience for them.

We carried on northward into Germany. We continued to meet opposition, sometimes from a fairly well trained group who would put up a bit of a battle, in other cases from a band of young people, maybe no more than fifteen years old. Quite often we ended up taking prisoners. I mentioned earlier how we became ruthless when we entered Germany, not hesitating to destroy a town or wipe out any opposition we encountered, but our hostility was moderated once men surrendered.

Early in the campaign, so the history books say, there were instances where Canadian prisoners were shot because they wouldn't give the Germans the information they wanted. A General Kurt Meyer in the German army was charged with such action. According to the grapevine, some German prisoners were shot in retaliation. Such incidents were not the norm. Certainly prisoners were treated as prisoners. They were disarmed, anything they were carrying that we thought they shouldn't have, or that we could use, was confiscated, they were confined and kept under guard. But, for the most part, they were not abused. There's a rapport that develops between fighting men, between soldiers who shoot at each other on the front line. There are times you hate your enemy, times you don't; but you have an understanding of what the other fellow is going through.

Once during our drive through Germany we'd had a couple of little scuffles and taken five or six prisoners. We were in a defensive position waiting to advance, so we'd given the prisoners cigarettes and sat them down to await transport back to a prisoner of war camp. The regimental quartermaster brought up rations and supplies. He couldn't get his trucks in to where we were with the tanks, about a quarter of a mile from the road, so he mounted a fatigue party to haul up the supplies. Then he saw the prisoners and decided to use them to carry the boxes. That was standard procedure. The Germans did the same with our fellows, put them to work while they were waiting to be shipped off to a camp. It may have been a violation of the Geneva Convention – I don't know – but it was a common practice, and the prisoners didn't make any complaints. They weren't in a position to.

So the quartermaster lined the prisoners up and marched them to where he was taking the stuff off the trucks. Each loaded a ration pack or a jerry can of gasoline onto his shoulder and started back to the tanks. The quartermaster decided he wasn't happy with them walking, so he ordered them to run. He ran them in, ran them back out to the trucks, put a second load on them and began running them back in again. We decided enough was enough. Two or three of us went out and told him to knock it off. I was standing by the radio and couldn't go out, but I yelled at him to leave the guys be. He wasn't too happy and made comments about how were were a bunch of German-lovers and so forth, but we told him we didn't care what he thought about it. He was not going to treat them like that in front of us. The guys were tired and beaten, and we were not going to see them abused needlessly. It just wasn't the Canadian way to kick a fellow when he was down.

I don't think it was in the nature of the Canadian to hate. That wasn't true for all the Allies; but then, those who came from German-occupied countries, the Poles, the French, the Czechoslovakians, all had much more reason to hate than did we.

Sometime in the middle of April I temporarily lost my crew. When the clutch started to slip so badly the driver could not change gears and the tank had to go back to the Light Aid Detachment for repairs, the major said the crew had to go with it. I took over a tank that had come up with a reinforcement crew and began one of the worst periods of my life. They were a surly, unfriendly bunch. Slim, Nick, Henning and I had been through so much together that we had become very close. I had no rapport at all with this new crew. It was like being with strangers. As if that weren't enough, they weren't very good at their jobs. The driver was all right, he was an experienced fellow, but the operator couldn't keep the radio on net. I had to net the radio in anytime I wanted to talk to some-body. As for the gunner, he was slow to respond and didn't seem to be able to hit anything anyway.

Our last real battle of the war took place in the town of Garrel, which was quite heavily fortified. The colonel had given an ultimatum: either the town surrendered or we would flatten it. We began our assault in the morning, with part of the squadron executing a frontal attack while the rest of us, including my troop, bypassed the town and came in from the other side. My troop officer got bogged down. His tank sank into the mud on one side so that the gun could only traverse up in the air and down on the ground and he couldn't fight. We began to get shelled, so we took cover in some anti-aircraft gun emplacements. Then a section of enemy infantry came down the road out of town, so I called for the gunner to fire at them with the Browning. With Slim, all I had to do was give him a short order and he would respond immediately. By the time the rein-forcement gunner got around to it, the Germans had all disappeared into the woods. We sprayed the woods anyway and managed to set a couple of buildings on fire.

We were still getting mortared and shelled, so I decided there had to be an observer someplace directing the fire. They were just too accurate. I spotted a church with a steeple, which was the kind of place they loved to put observers, and told the gunner to knock off the steeple. He fired a heavy explosive shell. I could see no sign of where the shell went. I put him on it again. Same story. After twenty minutes we had fired off every-thing we had, including the armour piercing shells. There wasn't a shell left in the tank, and he hadn't hit a thing. Not one thing! I couldn't believe it. I asked myself again and again, "Where did these guys come from?"

Since we had none left, I called Squadron Headquarters and asked per-mission to pull out and get loaded with ammunition. We made our way to a field where the trucks could reach us when they came up with the ammunition. I couldn't believe what happened next. So far as these guys were concerned, the war was over. They started to unload all their stuff from the tank, preparing to clean up and shave. I was boiling, and I really laid into them: "What're you guys doing?! First of all, if we didn't hit that steeple because the gun sights are off, we've got to sight that damn seventeen pounder. You're going to have ammunition to load, and all the guns have got to be cleaned. What are you doing messing around getting ready to shave when there's guys up there depending on us?"

They stood there with their mouths hanging open, but I must have got through to them, because they got busy cleaning the guns. By the time the truck came up with the ammunition, everything had been taken care of and as soon as we loaded we were on our way.

I've wondered since whether the gunner managed not to take out that steeple because he was a devout Christian. Bunch of heathens that we were, all through France, whenever we saw a church steeple, we blew it down. A church steeple made an ideal observation point or sniper post for the Germans.

After Garrel, we had rather a leisurely war. On other fronts there was some stiff resistance and heavy fighting, but not in our area. We would get up and on our way at nine in the morning, meeting a bit of resistance here and there, but nothing very demanding. We began finding a lot of German uniforms and became very suspicious of any young man in civvies we saw. We realized that they were deciding that their war was over and shedding their uniforms to escape capture by our forces. They were fairly safe. Given the position their country, and their army, was in, they wouldn't be charged with desertion, and as civilians they weren't going to be taken prisoner; but we didn't trust them.

We may have been having a relatively easy time, but what we accomplished was important nonetheless. From Major Paterson's *History:*

All this while, the Poles were swinging nearer to the division from the west, and the 2nd Division was advancing slowly north to Oldenburg. The South Albertas were busy writing an Odyssey of their own. They had been given the task of working north toward Oldenburg on the west of the 2nd Division, but not in contact with it. Their front was 20 kilometres. They had one company of Lincolns, and some wild British SAS with them for a while, but their magnificent effort was mostly their own – just one regiment of tanks, and no artillery support except what they could wangle from the blue patch* friends to the east. The roads were terribly

---

* Second Division

cratered. They did their own filling. There were many small bridges blown and a large one across the Lethe River. They built their own. There were hostile populated towns such as Garrel. They did their own negotiating and held the peace. They were infantry rearguards. They captured and killed scores. There was a well defended airport, they captured it and knocked out two SP's and a Tiger tank in the doing. They lost over 40 tanks, and but few men. Had it not been for the broad Kustin Canal and a lack of heavy bridging material, they might well have been in Oldenburg before the 2nd Division. They did a job unparalleled for initiative, and did it in true Albertan style – well.

I got my own crew back and the corporal got stuck with the other crew. My frustration eased, though I remained pretty disgusted with the calibre of people Canada was sending us. It seemed to me that the ones I had to deal with had not had even basic training. If I'd had time to work with these reinforcement crews, I might have been able to do something with them, but not when we were in combat; that just was not a training situation. I think the stress must have started to show, because one night around the end of April Sergeant Sands from Squadron Headquarters came to my tank and had a chat with me. I was a month overdue for leave. I hadn't gone earlier because we had so many new NCOs and reinforcements that the squadron commander was reluctant to let a sergeant go until there was a lull in the fighting. Now, with the war winding down, Duke encouraged me to take my leave. I wasn't sure that I wanted to be away just then, and thought about it for quite a while before I decided I would go. On April 29 Headquarters sent up a sergeant on temporary duty from a reinforcement depot to take over the troop, and I left for London.

I spent my leave doing the rounds of the pubs and feeling guilty because I wasn't with my troop. I was in bed at a service club on the early morning of May 8, 1945, when all the bells in the city started to ring, and I knew it was over. I went out to find the streets of London packed with people celebrating the victory, and in the midst of all those thousands, I had never been so lonely in my life. I wanted to be with the troop.

CHAPTER 16

Can It Really Be Over?

Major Paterson gave a very effective description of the feelings of the troops in the field when the war ended. He said that when the message announcing the end of hostilities arrived:

…we were silent in wonder. How many had listened for those words before, and had always said to themselves – "to-morrow".

And now to-morrow had come – a to-morrow called peace. But to us it didn't seem like the end of anything as yet. The skies were overcast, the rain dripped slowly from the thatched roof of the farmhouse, the lake looked grey and cold and a cutting wind shook steel-like raindrops from the new green leaves. All was very quiet. The men at Brigade had been gambling by the stove when they heard the broadcast. They rushed outside and called wildly to one another. Five minutes later, they were back by the fire and their cards. The quiet returned. No it was not apathy – it was something there are no words for, a feeling too large to express, to know, yes, even to exist. One kept saying to oneself – "it's over," "it's over," all the time half expecting to see a rainbow in the sky, to hear the shouts of millions in Trafalgar or Times Square, to experience some outward manifestation of joy, praise, thankfulness, or of great emotion flooding through the gates of restraint. But nothing happened. There were no bells in Germany, there were no happy people, and the conquerors were dumb in the greatness of their relief.

Perhaps in the months to come will that fabulous "to-morrow" really be to-day – a day when all the bells and voices of our great memory shall ring out, cry out, peal, and shout, in one wild, tumultuous song of thanksgiving. Sometime, while dreaming over a sun drenched lake, while paus-

ing in the fields to watch the summer clouds pile one upon the other, or in
the quiet half hour before sleep, we shall each hear that symphony we once
listened for, and it shall swell and reverberate through our beings in un-
forgettable strength and beauty so that we shall know that to-day has
come, and that those black yesterdays are forever left behind.

After my leave I went back to Oldenburg, Germany, where the regiment had taken an airfield and established a barracks in a former insane
asylum that had been used as a barracks by the Germans. There was a
prison camp for Polish women in the same area, which resulted in some
strange goings-on. Fellows showed up for breakfast with four mess tins.
Nothing was ever said and nothing done, but everybody knew they were
sharing with the women. Not too often, but on the odd occasion, somebody would come in for breakfast after being missing all night.

Since we were now in garrison, I had duty as Sergeant of the Guard. As
much as anything else, this brought it home to me that peace had indeed
come. I could not recall the regiment mounting a formal guard since leaving Maresfield Camp in England. Of course, peace also brought back all
the uniform pressing, boot and button shining and polishing, and drill of
days past. Only now, I did not do sentry duty myself. As Sergeant of the
Guard, I marched the new guard to the guard house and led the ceremony
through which the new guard took over from the old. When the old guard
marched off, the corporal posted the sentries for the first two-hour shift,
while the rest of the guard were "broken off" and retired to the guard
house to await their turn in the two hours on, four hours off rotation.
Guard duty was for a twenty-four hour period, from 1800 hrs. one day
until 1800 hrs. the next. I remained in the guard house unless a situation
required my attention. Ah, boring, beautiful, *boring* peace time!

A non-fraternising order came from Field Marshal Montgomery,
Commander in Chief of the 21st Army Group, by letter to all officers and
men of the 21st Army Group. The military police were on the alert for any
possible fraternisation. The fellows would get plenty of come-on from the
local cuties when they went for a walk in town, but there was too much at
stake. No one in the regiment would have turned in a buddy, but had any
of the senior officers become aware of any infraction, it would have been

Deventer, Holland, June 21, 1945. "A" Squadron transport sergeant Cecil Fick and troop sergeant John Galipeau pose with the 5 cwt. truck that served as their personal recreation vehicle. The truck was discovered, broken-down and abandoned, in Italy by Sergeant Fick's brother, a sergeant in the transport section of the Loyal Edmonton Regiment. Repaired and re-painted by the Edmonton Regiment mechanics, with tactical identification markings in place and a serial number

taken from a map reference painted on the cab doors, the truck joined the regimental fleet as the sergeant's personal vehicle. When Cecil's brother was repatriated to Canada, the truck changed hands as the result of the purchase of a keg of beer for the Edmonton Regiment's sergeant's mess. It was given SAR identification and used by Cecil and me until we, too, went home.

dealt with severely. Anyone who was caught ran the risk of losing all rights and privileges as well as any leave they had coming to them.

While we were in Oldenburg we had to clean up the tanks, strip off all the extra armour, and unload all the ammunition in preparation for turning them over to Ordnance. We moved back to Holland, where "A" Squadron settled in the little village of Heeten and did the final cleanup. They were shining like new the sad day we said goodbye to our tanks before the drivers, with somebody along in the turrets as a guide, drove off to turn them in.

Now we were at loose ends. Many volunteered to go over to the Pacific to fight the Japanese, while the rest of us waited to be sent home. We went home according to a point system. You were credited with points according to the length of time you had served, how long you had been overseas, whether or not you were married and had children. We still had reinforcements coming in to replace the men who were being repatriated. The regiment needed the reinforcements to maintain the unit at full strength, as there was a possibility that it would become part of a German Occupation Force. After I had left for home, the regiment moved to an area near Amsterdam. They stayed there until late in the year, then sailed for Canada and disbandment.

I found myself in the position Sergeant Gove and Lieutenant Barford had been at Niagara-on-the-Lake. I had a few old hands in my troop, but most of the men were reinforcements. There wasn't much for them to do, so I'd be out in the morning putting them through foot drill and close order drill. My enthusiasm wasn't any greater than theirs, but it had to be done. At that stage I wasn't about to put up with very much from anybody, and so I adopted the no-nonsense attitude of Sergeant Gove's successor, but as often as not I'd march the men around until we found a haystack some place, and then I'd say, "That's it. Hang out here till it's time to go back for dinner."

We wiled away the summer until finally on August 7, 1945, I was notified that I was on the draft to go home. I packed up everything, happy as a lark, said goodbye to the few of the old fellows who were left, climbed into a truck and headed off to the Nijmegen Staging Area en route to London. I spent a week on leave in London with very little money because I knew I was going to need everything I had when I got back to Canada and didn't want to spend anything or draw extra from my pay. On August 29

Tanks of "A" Squadron, South Alberta Regiment, cleaned and stripped of extras for return to Ordnance at the end of hostilities. When the tanks were taken away, I felt a sense of loss. Their presence had been an essential part of our identity as an armoured regiment; their care and maintenance had structured our daily routine. I couldn't see any point in training without our tanks, and the rest of the troop seemed to feel the same. (SAR)

I boarded the *Scythia*, bound for Quebec. The *Scythia* was a troop ship that had been used in the Pacific, and it smelled twice as high as the old *Strathmore* had. Conditions were no better than they had been on the trip over, and it was stormy and the crossing was even rougher, but we didn't want to spend much time on deck. The upper deck was reserved for members of the Canadian Women's Army Corps. When they got sick and went to the rail, we didn't want to be on the rail down below them.

We landed in Quebec on September 10, 1945, and immediately boarded the good old Canadian train that would take us home. It was hard to believe that such a thing still existed, after what we'd been through. On the train everybody had a berth, white sheets, a porter, just like regular travellers. We hadn't seen white sheets in so long that they were a novelty. At mealtimes we went into the dining room, and there was fruit juice and roast beef and steak with mashed potatoes, things we'd practically forgotten about, except in our dreams. It was a five-day trip from Quebec to Calgary, where I had a two-hour stopover before I caught the train to Edmonton. At every train stop we were greeted by the Ladies' Auxiliary to the Legion and people from other organizations. They handed out cards to tell us "Welcome Home," soft drinks, oranges, apples, candy bars – just little things, but they made us feel like returning heroes. When we saw that the country was just the same as we'd left it, and that the people seemed to appreciate what we'd done, we got the feeling that maybe the whole thing had been worthwhile.

Ivy had come out from Nanaimo and was in Edmonton to meet me when I arrived. I had thirty days' homecoming leave, and we needed that to get reacquainted. After three years apart and all we'd been through, I was a different person, and so was she. That first month must have been very hard on Ivy. I didn't realize until some time later how much I'd changed.

On October 24 I went to the Military District Headquarters in Calgary to be discharged. I convinced Ivy to let me buy a car. Cars of any kind were in short supply, but I found a 1930 six cylinder Whippet that became my very first automobile. I drove down to Calgary, arriving late at night. Now, the last time I had been in a regular garrison, I had still been a private. Although I had been a sergeant for several months, I had never served as a sergeant in a situation where formal procedures were followed. What I should have done was to contact the orderly sergeant on duty, who would have given me a room. Instead, I did the much same thing I would have done when we were in action or on leave in Europe. I parked my car, wandered into the first barracks I could find, found an empty bunk by the light coming from the washroom door, took off my uniform and lay down on the mattress, pulling my greatcoat over me, and went to sleep.

Morning came, and the troops started to stir. They were all young privates; my tunic with three stripes on the sleeve was hanging on the end of the bed. I woke up and said good morning to two or three of them, and they looked strangely at me and mumbled good morning in return. I went into the washroom to shave. There was a row of twelve or more basins, but on each side of me there were two basins empty while men waited in line for the others. I began to wonder what was wrong with these guys. They acted like I had the plague. When I was shaved and cleaned up, I went over to the mess hall to get breakfast. I didn't need mess tins, there were real plates. I picked up my food, took it to a table, sat down and started to eat. I was halfway through my breakfast when the orderly officer came along and asked me what I was doing there.

"I'm having breakfast."

"You're not supposed to be in here," he said.

"Well, I'm happy here," I replied. "It's all right, the food's OK."

He insisted that I leave. I insisted that I was going to finish my breakfast. He finally said I could finish eating, "But then," he said, "you go to the sergeant's mess."

That was when it dawned at me that there was protocol I was supposed to follow. That was why those kids were looking at me so strangely. They didn't expect to wake up in the morning and find a sergeant sleeping in their barracks, especially one with ribbons on his tunic. However, I certainly wasn't any happier in the sergeant's mess. No one acknowledged me, and I felt very much out of place. Most of the fellows were quite a bit younger than me, and their conversation seemed very juvenile. There was no one else with battle ribbons up. I missed my old gang.

I had my dinner in the sergeant's mess, then was given my medical exam and went through the rest of the discharge process. Then I walked out the door, no longer Sergeant Galipeau. I was civilian Mr. Galipeau once more. I wended my way back to Edmonton and began a new life as a family man.

Return to Places Remembered

I had often wanted to return to see the places we where had served and suffered in battle. My first opportunity came at the end of a trip Ivy and I took to Wales in the late 1950s to visit her birthplace and relatives. On the spur of the moment we made our way from London to Amsterdam. There we obtained lodging in a bed and breakfast establishment and set out by train each day so I could show Ivy some of the locations where the South Alberta Regiment had been. Not having a vehicle, we were unable to travel to the rural regions and had to be satisfied with visits to towns and cities.

The larger places had not changed since the day we first entered them in 1944. Some, such as Bergen op Zoom, have the same city centre as they did in the fifteenth century, so I had very little difficulty finding the spots I wanted to visit. On the other hand, the town of Tilburg and the surrounding area where we had spent the winter of 1944 had undergone a great deal of reconstruction, and I could not locate the streets and buildings I had known during that time. I was somewhat disappointed that I was unable to find the place where we had parked our tanks on our return from the battle for the Hochwald Gap. I feel the same disappointment when I am in London and try to track down the Orange Tree Pub where Herb, Danny and I spent so much time on leave. Euston Square, where it was located, is still there, but our pub has disappeared. Danny has also looked, with the same results. When we meet at a regimental reunion we always have a discussion about what could have happened to our favourite watering hole.

Major General George Kitching was the featured speaker at a reunion of the South Alberta Regiment Veteran's Association in 1989. In his talk he pointed out that the SAR Veterans had never returned to Europe to the places where we had distinguished ourselves in battle, thereby earning the regiment honourable mention in history, and said that the historians were waiting for our return. General Kitching's words prompted a decision to initiate a fundraising campaign to pay the cost of having monuments, cairns and plaques constructed and placed in the towns and areas where we had been victorious in major battles.

In May of 1992 the SAR Veterans embarked on a pilgrimage through Normandy, Belgium, Holland and Uedem, Germany, to dedicate the cairns and conduct memorial services at the cemeteries where our comrades who had made the supreme sacrifice were laid to rest. The ceremonies at the cemeteries evoked many emotions: anger at the waste of young lives, sadness at the loss of friends, wonder as to why they were taken and we were not, and some guilt at feeling thankful we were spared the bullets that would have ended our lives. Cairns were placed at Saint Lambert-sur-Dives in Normandy where Major Dave Currie held the Germans at bay to close the Falaise Gap, and in the town hall at Bergen op Zoom. At Eekloo, Belgium, a Sherman tank bearing South Alberta Regiment tactical insignia serves as a monument to the regiment's action in the battle of the Leopold Canal. We visited the Normandy beach where we landed in 1944 and toured the war museum in Bayeux, where we discovered one whole room that detailed the action of the South Alberta Regiment at the Battle of the Falaise Gap, the only regiment to be thus singled out for recognition in the museum displays.

In May of 1995, Ivy and I joined the thousands of Canadians that travelled to Europe for the celebrations of the fiftieth anniversary of Liberation. We were amazed at the enthusiastic welcome and hospitality shown us by the population of the countries we visited. I have never felt so accepted and acknowledged. Everywhere we went the people expressed gratitude for the actions that gave them back their freedom in 1945. Canadian flags flew everywhere, and the streets of every town and village were decorated with the maple leaf, far exceeding any display of those symbols you will find in Canada on the First of July.

The first parade we took part in was in the small city of Katswi (pronounced Cats-wee) in Holland. The Canadian veterans assembled in a large military garage. Those who were fit were to march in formation; those who felt the walk would be too far for their seventy-year-old legs were given seats in the backs of Dutch army trucks. Outside the garage a regiment of young men of the Dutch army were formed up. As the Canadian veterans emerged, these young men cheered and clapped hands throughout the time it took the column to pass by. The people lining the parade route reacted in the same manner. We were deluged with applause and words of thanks.

A day or so later, one thousand five hundred Canadians assembled in a park on the edge of the city of Apeldoorn to take part in a major celebration and parade. Again, some rode in trucks, while the remainder marched in column; and again, as we emerged from the park we were greeted with enthusiastic cheers and applause. The crowd on either side pressed in until the marching column of three became a straggling line of veterans making their way through the throng. All along the two-kilometre parade route there was unbroken applause, singing and constant calls of "Thank you, Canada!" Youngsters held signs that said, "The third generation thanks you!!" The Canadian veterans were handed flowers, drinks and fruit and had their hands shaken. It was Liberation Day once more as three hundred thousand participants jammed the city of Apeldoorn for the party. We, in turn, shook hands, hugged and kissed the women within reach, and gave Canadian flag lapel pins to the youngsters in true party spirit.

Meeting such an outpouring of gratitude from the people, I felt a great many mixed emotions. There was so much warmth and affection from the *Hollanders* that I felt humble. Receiving their accolades I felt pride, not so much for myself as for my country, and in being Canadian. All the while, I knew the tribute was not for me alone, nor just for the military, but for all the people of Canada who by their sacrifices and efforts provided their soldiers with the means to finish the job. And I was pleased that I had been a soldier in our army when it liberated Holland, and had been able to do my part.

After observing so much admiration for Canada, I feel a great sense of sadness and frustration on July 1st. I fail to understand the disinterest and apathy shown by the citizens of this great country on Canada Day. It would seem to me that Canada is loved more by the people of Holland than by its own. I can only ask why Canadians refrain from demonstrating pride in Canada. Why?

The Battle's O'er

I return to the fields of glory where the green and
    flowers grow
And the wind softly sings the story of the brave lads of
    long ago.

March no more, my soldier laddie, there is peace now
    where once was war,
Sleep in peace, my soldier laddie, sleep in peace now the
    battle's o'er.

In the great glen they lie a-sleeping, where the cool
    waters gently flow,
And the grey mist is sadly weeping for the brave lads of
    long ago.

See the tall grass is there a-waving, as their flags were so
    long ago,
With their heads high were forward braving, marching
    onwards to meet the foe.

Some returned from the fields of glory to their loved
    ones who held them dear
But some fell in their hour of glory, and were left to their
    resting here.

AUTHOR UNKNOWN

*The above words are from a war song of either the
First or Second World War.*

Major Arnold James Lavoie

I would not be satisfied should I end my story without paying tribute to a man who I feel contributed to my survival in the many battles "A" Squadron fought. I realize that good fortune played a part in keeping me alive through those nine months in combat, but I cannot help but feel that the man who directed the squadron in its encounters against a determined and experienced enemy deserves recognition. His tactical skills, knowledge and wisdom kept the casualty count below what it might otherwise have been.

In addition to his skills, Major Arnold Lavoie demonstrated a deep concern for the men he sent out to battle. I firmly believe he felt grief and a sense of personal loss each time one of his men died.

Early in my army career, I regarded commissioned officers as some form of deity, lacking the mundane feelings common to the mere mortals in the lower ranks. I wondered how I would ever be able to hold a conversation with such an astute and honourable personage.

I discovered the human being behind the King's Commission one night when the regiment was in a static position in Belgium. I had been detailed to a period of wireless watch in the bombed-out house we had taken as Squadron Headquarters, with the responsibility for maintaining radio contact with and receiving messages from Regimental Headquarters. Around 9 p.m. the Squadron Commander, Major Lavoie, came in, sat down at the table that served as his desk and busied himself with paperwork. When he was finished he sat back and said to me, "How's it going, Corporal?"

The conversation that began then lasted until my shift came to an end. The rank badges disappeared, and we became nothing more than two tired, anxious soldiers having a talk. He told me of his family, his vocation before joining the service, the concern he felt when the squadron went into battle. I told him of my wife and family, and of my hopes for the future at war's end.

That was the only conversation I ever had with him as a comrade-in-arms. All our subsequent meetings for the duration of my military service were conducted with normal military formality.

Major Lavoie toasting "A" Squadron at the squadron reunion Christmas dinner, 1974. From left: Major Wright, Mrs. Wright, Major Lavoie, Mrs. Jean Lavoie.

I again saw the man behind the commission at regimental reunions after the war. I recall that on the Sunday morning at the end of a three-day reunion Major Lavoie would arrive wearing the look of a man with a king-size hangover. In his jacket pockets he would have at least two bottles of beer. After taking his seat, he would remove one, take off the top, and proceed to quench the internal fires ignited the previous evening.

When he died, I attended the funeral service at the church and at the graveside. As we left to drive to the family reception, I looked back. The casket containing the body of my comrade stood above the open grave, unadorned and alone, appearing abandoned in an expanse of snow-covered ground and leafless trees; and I was overwhelmed with sadness and remorse. I wanted to return and stand guard, to keep him company until his body was lowered into the grave and covered and I knew he was at rest.

I did not return, it was not possible at the time; but the image of that lonely casket returns to my mind, and I feel again an echo of the sadness I felt that day.

So, Major Arnold James Lavoie, I shall remember you as a man I admired, and I will always try to live by your favourite saying, "Be Charitable." I write these pages at the end of my story in your memory.

ARNOLD JAMES LAVOIE, MAJOR, "A" SQUADRON, SAR
Born September 21, 1908, New Liskeard, Ontario, Canada
Died January 24, 1979, Edmonton, Alberta, Canada
Interment in Holy Cross Cemetery, Edmonton

"You led us to the green fields of victory, Major."

Index

About the authors

Born in Edmonton in 1921, **John A. Galipeau**, son of a logging camp cook, spent his early years travelling around the western provinces. His haphazard education ended at Grade 8 in a country school. With jobs for uneducated backwoods boys few and far between, he enlisted in the South Alberta Regiment in 1940 and was assigned to a platoon of short fellows, setting the stage for the events chronicled in *Peewees on Parade*. He met and married Ivy Davies while on training in Nanaimo, B.C. The regiment was converted to armour, and John saw service overseas from the turret of a Sherman tank. He was discharged from the army with the rank of sergeant in October 1945. John worked as a licensed mechanic until the mid-1950s, when he was hired as a civilian firefighter by the Department of National Defence in Wainwright, Alberta. After his retirement in 1984, John and Ivy moved to Brentwood, near Victoria. Their son, Brian, was born in 1947, and they now have four grandchildren. John enjoys a variety of activities, including curling, golf, fishing and birdwatching. He indulges his passion for music by playing the electric organ, and has recently taken on development of a rural retreat on Salt Spring Island. A member of the Royal Canadian Legion, John attends regimental reunions as often as he can to reminisce with his buddies from the Peewees.

Pattie Whitehouse and John A. Galipeau.
(Photo by Robert Irvine)

A native of Vancouver Island's Saanich Peninsula, **Pattie Whitehouse** has worked as a professional personal historian since 1992. While most of her personal histories are intended primarily as family keepsakes, *Peewees on Parade* is the second such project to be published. *Mr. Chemainus*, Joy Lang Anderson's tribute to her station agent father, was published in 1995 by Fir Grove Publishing.

Fighting for Canada: Seven Battles, 1758–1945

Edited by Donald E. Graves

A fascinating detailed study of seven battles fought either to defend Canada or by Canadians overseas on behalf of their nation:

- *Ticonderoga, 1758,* by Ian M. McCulloch
- *Queenston Heights, 1812,* by Robert Malcomson
- *Ridgeway, 1866,* by Brian A. Reid
- *Leliefontein, 1900,* by Brian A. Reid
- *Moreuil Wood, 1918,* by John R. Grodzinski & Michael R. McNorgan
- *Le Mesnil-Patry, 1944,* by Michael R. McNorgan
- *Kapelsche Veer, 1945,* by Donald E. Graves.

446 pages • 6.75 x 9.75 inches • about 160 pictures, maps • hardcover $44.95 • paperback $25.95

South Albertas: A Canadian Regiment at War

Donald E. Graves

The gripping account of a Canadian World War II regiment, born on the Prairies, that forged a splendid record at the Battle of the Falaise Gap and in the Allied advance across northwest Europe.

"Without a doubt *South Albertas* is one of the finest unit histories ever published and in fact transcends that genre to rate as a truly great history of Canada at war." Christopher Evans, *Canadian Military History*

408 pages • 8.5 x 11 inches • about 300 pictures • 19 maps • 8 pages of colour photos • hardcover $59.95 (NOTE: At the time of writing, this book is out of stock pending a reprint decision. Please enquire.)

The Royal Canadian Armoured Corps: An Illustrated History

John Marteinson & Michael R. McNorgan

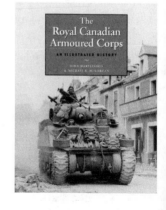

Lavishly illustrated with photos, war art, maps and diagrams, the book traces the history of the RCAC from its cavalry ancestors through World War I and the interwar period that saw the advent of the tank and other new forms of armour. Most of the book deals with World War II as Canadian armoured units played important roles in the defeat of the Third Reich.

"It transcends visual flash with solid and informative text ... that provides a fine history of an important element of the Allied victory in western Europe during World War II. Recommended." *Stone & Stone Second World War Books*

448 pages • 8.5 x 11 inches • 300+ photographs, illustrations, maps, diagrams • hardcover $69.95

Prices shown are Canadian prices at the time of publication. Different prices may apply in other markets.